The Heart of the Hero

YOUR INNER GUIDE TO PERSONAL TRANSFORMATION

Stephen Linsteadt

Natural Healing House Press

LA QUINTA, CALIFORNIA

Stephen Linsteadt/Natural Healing House Press
PO Box 562
La Quinta, CA 92253
www.NaturalHealingHousePress.com

Ordering Information:
Quantity sales. Special discounts are available on quantity purchases by corporations, associations, and others. For details, contact the "Special Sales Department" at the address above.

Editor, Susan M. Waterman
Cover Image, djgis (Shutterstock)

The information contained in this book is intended for research and educational purposes only. The author does not present any part of this work, directly or indirectly, for the diagnoses or prescription of any disease or condition. People who use the information from this book are advised to take responsibility for consulting the health professional of their choice regarding all matters pertaining to their physical, emotional or mental health.

The Heart of the Hero / Stephen Linsteadt. —1st ed.
ISBN 978-0-9741123-3-6
Library of Congress Control Number: 2015913632

Natural Healing House Press
La Quinta, California

Contents

*Dedicated to
my children and grandchildren
and to the hearts of the next seven generations.*

"Knowing our own darkness is the best method for dealing with the darkness of other people."

~ *Carl Jung*

Introduction

Many of the great stories from antiquity delve into the notion that human beings suffer one sacred wound or another during their lives. These wounds, in mythology—and as we face them in real life—Joseph Campbell suggested prefigure a turning point in the life of a mortal being. That turning point is the "Call to Adventure." The "Call" provides the motivation for an individual or society to change.

Answering the Call requires some bravery as the ultimate destination is usually unclear and often presents challenges befitting the courage of a hero. Joseph Campbell was so convinced that this Hero's Journey, told through the world's myths and legends going back as far as the first stories ever told, lies at the foundation of what it is to be human that he termed it the *Monomyth*.[1] The hero is a *Monohero*, a kind of composite hero, who undertakes a journey of re-discovery to what was within the Heart of the Hero the whole time.[2] In order to discover what lies within, the Hero must leave the outside world and the comforts of his or her "normal" world. Ironically, the universal tragedies of humanity often serve to help us release the hold the world has on our heart. It is through the agitations of the outside world that we are called on the Journey of the heart. If your heart has called you to read this book, then most likely you are about to embark upon the Hero's Journey. The purpose of this book is to help you, the reader, answer the Call.

This book will provide you with a tool, like a roadmap or compass, to help you navigate through the darkest of times. The tool is a process whereby we can access the wisdom of our own heart and obtain guidance on how to best respond to our problems and troubles from a place of compassion, as opposed to simply reacting from habituated patterns assimilated from our parents and societal conditioning. The process is called *Scalar Heart Connection*; how to utilize this tool will be revealed within the remaining pages of this book. Through the Scalar Heart Connection process you will tap into the wisdom of the heart. Your heart becomes your guide for facing life's challenges with courage and equanimity.

To resist change is the inclination of human nature. We resist change because we are afraid of the unknown. We often behave like unborn chicks refusing to leave the protection of the shell. Nature, however, has a way of shaking us out of our comfort zone. Either we suffocate from the pressure of our shell on our lungs, collapsing against the boundaries of what lies beyond, or we shatter our limiting beliefs and step into a world of new possibilities. Our limiting beliefs are those we have acquired through a lifetime of social conditioning: what we are taught in school, exposed to in the media, or mimic from the behavior of friends and family. Social conditioning, for some, holds us back from expressing the creativity of our authentic self. The need to fit in and to please others comes with a price. The price is often one of constraining our individuation. It also arrests our journey of self-discovery. It is a journey we finally give ourselves permission to embark upon when we recognize that everyone else is also afraid.

Fear holds us in limitation. It prevents us from realizing we are powerful and ultimately without limitations. When we remain in a state of perceived limitation, we assume the behavior patterns of those around us, the people we want to fit in with. In doing so, we become a reflection of their hopes and dreams, not ours. Our thoughts and emotions are vibrations, and therefore our mental and emotional states create a resonance pattern that attracts what is similar. According to the principle of resonance, like attracts like. Moreover, how we treat the planet and other people is a reflection of how we treat ourselves. Consequently, if our external conditions are less than ideal, it is possible that they are reflecting the nature of our inner state. In the bigger picture, the implication is that our current environmental crises, as well as the social, political, and economic issues, are manifestations of who we are as a collective consciousness. This suggests that changes to our external conditions will only happen when we change ourselves. When we give up our fear of the unknown and bravely continue on our journey, we have the potential to become the change we want to see in others, and in so doing contribute to the changes our planet desperately needs.

Our current environmental crisis is the Call to Adventure for the global community. Individually, we are being called to attend to our relationship with Earth and with ourselves. Are the events of the outer world causing us to experience inner turmoil? Are we stuck experiencing limiting beliefs or feelings of anxiety or depression? Is this our *natural* way of being? Asking these questions and listening to the guidance of the heart will lead us into the Hero's calling. Our limitations, areas where we need to do our work, become our gifts. Our attention to these areas will lead us back into the heart that beats in rhythm with the planet's heart—the Heart of the Hero.

Our mental conditioning perpetuates our isolation through the belief system that our self-worth depends on what we possess, what we know, what job we have, how many television sets we own. This creates more consumerism, more competition, more envy, greed, deeper isolation, self-loathing, anger, resentment, and even hatred. Changing our beliefs means learning to control our mind's endless list of wants, the things it falsely believes will make it happy. It means releasing thoughts about perfection: what we think we should be or should have done with our lives. It takes courage to break out of the comfort zone of our familiar, yet restrictive, shell. The challenges of climate change may be Nature's way, as a self-regulating system, of helping us in the same way She motivates the hatching chick. Hurricanes, earthquakes, and drought are only a few of the tools Nature has at her disposal to drive us to re-evaluate what is truly important. We have reached a critical threshold where our future may depend on how well we break free of our perceived limitations, our habituated patterns, and change our worldview. Since what we see on the outside, in the environment and political/economic landscape, is a reflection of who we are on the inside, the chaos we are experiencing globally becomes our Call to Adventure to change, grow, and transform.

Change is not possible without action. Action was the hallmark of Martin Luther King Jr. and Mahatma Gandhi. It is the action taken by the sacred warrior—the person dedicated to self-awareness, non-violence, and service to others. The instrument of change (re-evolution) is heart-consciousness. Reconnecting to heart-consciousness starts by first learning to care for ourselves so we can connect with others. We care for ourselves when we silence the mind's chatter of negative beliefs. The mind's chatter is the repetition of our conditioned reactions, those that insist we are safer when we fit in. By silencing this worn-out recording and replacing it with the life-affirming "knowing" of our heart, we are able to develop an inner sensitivity to the subtle vibrations of the heart. Tapping into the intuition of the heart can give us the strength to overcome our fears and limitations.

Individually and collectively we are at a turning point. Every human being has the opportunity to create more caring relationships with others and the planet and to access intuition and higher levels of awareness. By maintaining optimism we make room for positive change. Our every thought and emotion ripples across the fabric of spacetime. Nothing we do or think is wasted or unseen or unheard. We are all contributing something, even if on the outside we don't appear to be doing much. By traveling on our journey with our heart as the guide, we come to realize the influence we are always having on the world.

But when we are in pain or experiencing depression, the last thing we want to do is take a journey. A journey sounds far too exhausting and, honestly, hardly worth the trouble. Most find it better to numb or escape. The paradox, however, is that the longer we ignore the call of our heart, the louder it becomes, manifesting outwardly until we are forced into action. Carl Jung said that until the unconscious becomes conscious, it will direct our life and we will call it fate. It is the Hero's Journey that takes us through the labyrinth of our unconscious, working to make our fate conscious. When we reconnect to the knowing of the heart and to those unconscious parts of ourselves, we may find we are being led by our heart back into the rhythm of the universal heartbeat. Therefore, it is appropriate to refer to this transformative adventure of self-discovery and self-development as the Hero's Journey of the Heart.

The heart, while the portal of love, is also the cause of much suffering. Psychologists point out that almost all of their clients come to them with issues of love.[3] We are born needing to bond with our mother, our father, family, later with friends, and eventually with a partner or spouse. The death of a loved one, or a break-up with one we love, has taught us how painful love can be. Eventually, even in the closest of relationships, we discover something intangible is missing from what we were expecting to receive or gain from that relationship.

The saints and prophets have offered an expanded perspective on the subject of love: a view that encompasses more than just our immediate family, our community, or nation. This is the message of Christ, who asked, "Who is my mother and who are my brethren?" to illustrate our tendency of restricting love to our close relations while neglecting a broader scope of love's possibilities. Likewise, Guru Nanak, the first of the Ten Sikh Gurus (starting from 1469), said that all relationships of the world are false. Our limited perception of these relationships is what makes them temporary and, therefore, illusory or false. When we are disconnected or out of sync with our heart, we experience the illusion of separation and therefore unconsciously seek relationships in order to feel whole; we thus discover the elusiveness of romantic satisfaction.

In Dante's *Inferno* it was said, "In the middle of the journey of this life I awoke to find myself in a dark wood, for I had wandered off from the straight path." Jean Houston, in *The Search for the Beloved*, related Dante's "dark wood" to the Sacred Wound, which represents our journey through life, where pain and suffering can sometimes feel unrelenting and unbearable.[4] These wounds are primarily of the heart: our jealousies, passions, attachments, narcissism, our perceived failures, and our loneliness. When we are able to detach from the cause of our suffering long enough to realize that it is not as personal as our ego would like to think, we begin to experience this journey—life—from the Hero's perspective. The Journey of the Hero is similar to nature, with seasons and cycles: life and death, and then, to our fresh springtime delight, life again. By accepting the cycle of wounding, the natural rhythm of life's experiences no longer creates impassable mountains in the middle of our path. The wounds become sacred when we realize how they provided the needed motivation to let go of our limited perspective and inspired us to stretch our hearts wide enough to embrace all of creation, including devastating and inconvenient mountains and chasms.

If Keats was correct that the purpose of the world is that of Soulmaking,[5] then we should be able to see the transformative process of the Hero's Journey working at many levels in the world. Indeed, as this book will explain, the Heart of the Hero will remain agitated until the transformative process is recognized and honored.

Collectively, we are being called to an unprecedented adventure. Many of us can relate to this agitation and wonder what we can do to ameliorate the environmental crisis we face and to "save the planet." The first step is to acknowledge this agitation and listen to its message. By doing so, Nature will be honored and the Hero will begin to see that there is no real boundary or distinction between the self and the planet. Indeed, the Journey serves to teach the Hero that we are one singular consciousness. The only difference between one person and another is the way consciousness flows over their respective nervous systems. We are like the characters in a dream all playing our individual parts, but we are all the product of the same Dreamer. When the Hero crosses the threshold of this understanding, the veil of false relationships is lifted and the connection among all hearts reveals that Nature's heart and the heart of Earth is our own.

As you read this book you will journey through what lies within the Heart of the Hero. It will also provide ways, through the process of Scalar Heart Connection, in which we can ask our heart for guidance about what is troubling us or holding us in limitation. The method allows us to bypass the mind's reactivity, so we can hear the heart's loving messages to us and identify what is holding us back from realizing our full potential and unique gifts. What would your life look like if you were guided by heart-consciousness?

The process of Scalar Heart Connection got its name partly from a term found in quantum physics—*scalar.* Scalar refers to a unit of measurement related to the amplitude of the quantum waveform, which is the probability function where all possibilities exist. The *Heart Connection* part of the name relates to the heart as the bridge or connection between matter and psyche. The name implies that matter and psyche are connected to the same scalar field of unlimited consciousness where all possibilities can be actualized. Through the "observer effect" in quantum physics we gain a better understanding of the building blocks of our physical universe, which scientists and sages say is a conscious Universe.

The process of Scalar Heart Connection also utilizes the scientific understanding that all particles and subatomic particles are in motion. Everything is vibrating. Everything is vibrating in synch with the movement of the primordial ocean from which creation arose. The New Testament informs us that "In the beginning was the Word" (John 1:1). The vibration of the Word, in other traditions, is called the Cosmic Song, Music of the Spheres, Logos, Tao, among many other depictions. Scalar Heart Connection understands this vibration to be Universal Consciousness, and that ultimately we are one with Universal Consciousness. Our physical and beating heart is, by its nature, in synch with the heartbeat of the Universe. This is why the heart is known as the organ of intuition—it knows what the Universe knows.

The heart's resonance with the vibration of the Cosmic Song is related to number. Number informs us of vibration. It also informs us when we are in tune or out of tune with the number of heartbeats of the Cosmic Song. This is how the heart informs us when something doesn't feel right. It knows when our thoughts and actions are not aligned with the resonance of Universal Intelligence. The heart's connection to number and to a higher and wiser intelligence is the foundation of Scalar Heart Connection.

In order for us to tap into the knowing of our heart, we need a matrix or menu from which we can ask our heart for guidance, as well as receive its response. In the following chapters you will discover the matrix as a way of accessing the answers you need according to a corresponding system of numbers. The numbers shown to you intuitively by the heart at each step of the Scalar Heart Connection process reference statements that provide heart-centered guidance into a problem or situation for which you are seeking clarity. The statements come from the various emotions and attitudes found in the chakras and organ meridians, and the archetypal personality traits found in the various houses of the zodiac. The statements are then organized within a matrix derived from the geometry of Metatron's Cube, a specific sacred geometric figure comprised of thirteen equal circles connected by lines between their centers and the centers of the other twelve circles. Assigning numbers to the angles found Metatron's Cube allows us to organize questions and answers into broad categories and makes the whole process extremely user friendly.

In subsequent chapters we will also see how the various categories of questions and answers fall within certain personality behavior patterns. These patterns can be characterized as archetypal patterns and have roots in astrology as well as the twelve stages of the Hero's Journey. In other words, human beings tend to share the same problems. It always feels like our problems are unique, but we only have to peek into mythology to find that we are suffering the same love story as was suffered thousands of years ago. The actors have all changed, but the drama and tragedies have remained fundamentally the same. The archetypal nature of our problems provides an added dimension to the framework and matrix of the Scalar Heart Connection process.

When we connect to the innate knowing of our heart, we are connecting to a larger field of Intelligence. Our mind cannot grasp the nature of that Intelligence or its Source. However, one might imagine that the field of Universal Intelligence is the source of synchronicity. Synchronicity can be seen as the guiding force that seems to arrange events in our lives in meaningful ways, as if serving to provide guidance to the earnest Hero. What lies behind the meaning is the guiding hand of Universal Intelligence, one that has our best interest at heart. When we allow synchronicity to become our mentor, our heart becomes the guide, the traveler lost in the dark wood, and the ultimate reward, all in One.

NOTES:

1. Joseph Campbell, *The Hero with a Thousand Faces*, (Novato, CA: New World Library, 2008), p. 1.
2. Ibid, p. 29.
3. Thomas Moore, *Care of the Soul.* (New York: Harper Collins Publishers, 1998), p. 18.
4. Jean Houston, *The Search for the Beloved* (New York: Jeremy P. Tarcher/Putnam, 1987), p. 105.
5. John Keats, letter to George and Georgiana Keats, April 1819.

CHAPTER 1

Synchronicity

Synchronicity reveals the meaningful connections
between the subjective and objective world.
~ C. G. Jung

Have you ever thought of a friend and suddenly they call or send a text? Many years ago, I had the thought to call my best friend. It was during the days of push-button phones, not a Blackberry, but the version one step above the rotary. I picked up the receiver to make the call, but there was no dial tone. I could hear someone breathing on the other end. I said, "Hello?" It was my friend. He had just dialed my number and I picked up the receiver just as the line connected and a split second before the ringer activated. Over the years, we have made it a game to see who can make the other call by "thinking" about them.

My wife is the great-granddaughter of a Mapuche shaman, La Machi. Her mother, my mother-in-law, also inherited certain metaphysical gifts. For example, she tells the story of looking up at her kitchen clock one day and seeing the second hand stop and then take a few clicks counter-clockwise before continuing as normal. She noted the time and discovered at the end of the day that a good friend of hers had died at that exact time.

Life with my wife affords me an opportunity to participate in many synchronistic events. Ravens have a tendency to follow us, I mean her, when we go to town. Hummingbirds hover inches from her face when she is sad or upset by something. Unusual and unexpected things happen when we travel overseas and are in need of assistance or guidance. It almost feels like the spirit of La Machi is always with us.

While these events can be attributed to mere coincidence, something in the circumstances communicates information. It generally happens that when we are open to receiving that flash of insight, we find ourselves assisted in some way as though it were our guardian angel impelling us towards right or safe action.

I recently had one of those coincidences. I had just watched a movie one evening that contained a scene with a blind man. It made me want to paint a blind man, although I thought a blind woman would be more intriguing and ripe with allegory. Blindness was a theme explored by Rembrandt and Picasso. Morris Graves painted blind birds. It can be a challenge—intimidating—to embark on a painting when famous artists have mastered the subject. It is the nature of my mind to miss out on the joy of exploration by judging the merit of the expedition by what others have already excavated.

I awoke the next morning with the slumber of self-doubt still lingering in my intention of painting blindness. After clearing my head with a morning yerba maté, I checked my emails and found a message from a poet friend. She was responding to a message I had sent her about a dream I had with her in it: something to do with poetry, but in that strange dream kind of way where she was telling me something important as I struggled to grasp the meaning. She responded in her email that my dream occurred around the time she was reviewing dates for a poetry reading I was scheduled to attend. Something had come up and the event needed to be postponed.

She suspected the coincidence was deeper than that and attached an essay on blindness written by Jorge Luis Borges, one of my favorite poets and authors.[1] In the essay Borges wrote about his age-related onset blindness and paraphrased Rudolf Steiner: "We only know what we have lost, not what we will gain." This is where the coincidence turned synchronistic. Yes, I was thinking about blindness just before I opened the email. However, I was also preoccupied with a downturn in my business. I had become anxious and fearful about my future. I was asking the Universe for guidance and direction. Borges provided the solace I needed to maintain my equilibrium. In his essay he wrote: "For the task of an artist, blindness is not a total misfortune. It may be an instrument."[2] He said that everything that happens to us has been given for a purpose. "Everything that happens, including humiliations, embarrassments, misfortunes, all have been given like clay, like material for one's art." He said humiliation, unhappiness, and discord are the "ancient food of heroes." "Those things are given to us to transform, so that we may make from the miserable circumstances of our lives things that are eternal, or aspire to be so." [3]

Life's experiences can drag us to the depths of depression and despair. When bad things happen to us it is hard not to take it personally. We may find some comfort in Borges's idea that the aim of such hardships is to force us to reinvent ourselves. The point isn't to pretend a traumatic event never happened. When they do happen, as is often the case with being human, their effects stay with us for life. However, if we can trust in the Divine guidance of these events, we can use them to gain deeper insight into our true nature. If our experiences are precisely orchestrated by an invisible intelligence, then perhaps our best course of action through life is one of surrender.

This invisible intelligence has a sense of humor, as I discovered at a recent family reunion. Once a year, my extended family gathers at a beach house on the Mendocino coast. It is our custom to play games after the main mid-day meal. This year, we played bingo and set out thirty-nine gift bags for the winners of each round. No one knew the contents of the bags until someone got a bingo. The winner of each round selected a bag and then revealed its contents to the others. We liked to add some tension to the family dynamics by allowing the next person to get bingo to have the choice of choosing a bag with an unknown gift or steal a gift from someone who has already opened their bag. We play until everyone has a gift. Choosing a gift is arbitrary. Stealing a gift adds a component of free will, which is voided when someone steals what someone else has already stolen. For the most part, what people end up with is not within their control.

At some point during the bingo game, I noticed that people were receiving gifts appropriate to them. The whole group laughed when eighty-four-year-old Uncle Fred opened his bag and found a Nat King Cole CD, his favorite. My brother Ken received a Bill Cosby CD, his favorite childhood comedian and the one album he didn't have in his collection. His wife Jean, the garden designer, got a packet of fairy seeds. My sister-in-law Laura received earrings, which we later discovered my brother Dan originally bought for her birthday, but later decided to donate to the gift bags. My mother, who stays up late every night working crossword puzzles, received—you guessed it—a crossword puzzle book. The last person to open a gift was five-year-old Noah, whose twin brother is Mason. Noah pulled out of his bag two plastic water guns. Without hesitation, he handed Mason one of the guns and they both ran outside to squirt each other. The coincidences of the bingo game were all so uncanny that we all commented on how amazing it was that the gifts almost had a mind of their own.

There was only one apparent flaw in the gift giving that prevented people from thinking it was "miraculous," and that was my gift. I ended up with a pinecone. It was a last minute thing my brother picked up from his backyard to complete the gift bags—it was for bag number thirty-nine. It's good to be the subject of a great laugh once in a while. We all seem to take our turn at the reunions. People who love you the most feel free to laugh at you. Laughter tickles the heart because it is the one thing the heart and brain can agree to. And funny is just funny. I didn't want to ruin the laugh so I kept quiet about the research I had done the week before about the pinecone being an ancient symbol for the pineal gland and the expanded levels of consciousness that entails. Besides, not everyone at the reunion would have enjoyed a lecture from me on the pinecone being a symbol for Osiris. My nephew Simon said he had done a math paper in high school about the pinecone, and how the spiral it contains relates to the Fibonacci number series: 3, 6, 9, 15, 24, 39... I couldn't help but notice that the number 39 was the same number of gift bags set out for the bingo game.

Some of my students have questioned whether synchronicity exists if no one is there to observe it. I wondered if the family members who were noticing the coincidence of the gifts were also searching for meaning behind the coincidence. Is a synchronistic event still synchronistic if we don't see the meaning? This question made me take another look at the Fibonacci series. I had to know if there was a message for me in the pinecone. I later discovered the meaning in the story of Osiris, which I will share in another chapter. First, I wanted to know that if such magical and synchronistic circumstances are given to us for our betterment or to impel us towards the transcendental, then who is the Giver? If there is meaning in synchronistic events, then there must be a Formulator of such meaning. And how do we decipher the meaning?

Synchronicity sometimes taps us on the shoulder to make sure we are paying attention to the magic. The magic is like a spell or an invisible "attractor" that causes events to play out purposefully, as though each moment evolves toward a predestined result. In chaos theory, the term "attractor" is applied to a set of physical properties towards which a system evolves regardless of the starting conditions. Terrence McKenna believed that our universe is being pulled towards a unifying and connecting Attractor that exists ahead of us in time.[4] Rupert Sheldrake, author of *Science Set Free,* used the term "attractor" to describe the energetic blueprint of morphic resonance fields that draw matter into form.[5] When synchronicity makes itself known, one can't help but sense the Attractor—that self-organizing element that pulls or attracts events in space-time in some meaningful way.

Psychologist Carl G. Jung used the term "archetype" to describe common themes or patterns of meaning that lie at the root of synchronistic events.[6] The idea of archetypes is an old one, going back to Plato and most likely to a time before him. Plato described these messengers as "Forms" or essences that transcend the physical world, yet give the world its form and meaning.

Attempts to define the concept of archetype are elusive by the very transcendent nature of these forms. In the *Symposium,* for example, Plato said of the Form of Beauty: "It will be neither words, nor knowledge, nor a something that exists in something else, such as a living creature, or the earth, or the heavens, or anything that is—but subsisting of itself and by itself in an eternal oneness. . ."[7] We may sense the presence of an archetype through synchronistic events, dream symbols, or common cultural/religious structures and impulses. The presence of an archetype, as Plato suggested, is like a shadowy form hazily visible from the other side of a drapery. The outline of some unknown form or essence leaves our imagination to fill in the rest. At best, we see a two-dimensional symbol that requires interpretation. Jung, who dedicated his life to the interpretation and cataloging of archetypal symbols, came to understand that we are surrounded by a living matrix of meaning, like an ocean of super-consciousness pregnant with synchronistic potential. Our every-day events are ripe with meaning and ready for our consumption if we could only "see" with transcendent eyes.

Native peoples are known for their affinity of "seeing" meaning in the workings of Nature. When a bolt of lightning strikes in the middle of a heated argument, they take notice. A gust of wind is seen as a warning of danger. A bird crashing into a hut is an announcement of an imminent visitor. Animals appearing in one's path always bring with them a message. Our modern society calls this superstitious and naive. We have lost our connection to Nature and Her guiding messages. Hopefully, Nature, and the unseen intelligence behind Her, hasn't given up on us. We are in a time of great unrest and uncertainty. We have taken Nature to the limit of sustainability under our current ways of interacting with Her. In our darkest moments, a lightning bolt might be a welcomed sign that a power larger than us is listening. Hummingbirds on my patio tell me I don't have anything to worry about—if I would just surrender and follow the messages.

Our mind wants us to believe it is in charge. This is the age of empiricism and technology—the crowning achievement of the mind. But something has been lost in the process. That "something" is now impelling us towards itself. Outer circumstances are forcing us to re-examine our purpose as we seek meaning in our lives at this great turning point in our history. Joseph Campbell referred to this turning point as the "Call to Adventure" where the global community, as well as each individual, is forced to change.[8] Resisting change is what human beings do best because our mind-brains are afraid of the unknown.

The story of *Philomena* is a good example of a mother seeking a lost part of herself, seeking closure and wholeness. It is the story of an elderly Irish woman, whose Call to Adventure was the search for the son she was forced to give up for adoption fifty years earlier. At the end of the film version, and after the journey has brought her back to where she started (with a deeper understanding), her travelling companion quoted T. S. Elliot:

We shall not cease from exploration
And at the end of all our exploring
Will be to arrive where we started
And know the place for the first time.

The morning after I saw *Philomena,* I sat down to finish the book *Cosmos and Psyche* by Richard Tarnas. [9] I only had a couple pages of the epilogue left to read. The book finished with a quote:

We shall not cease from exploration
And at the end of all our exploring
Will be to arrive where we started
And know the place for the first time.

NOTES:

1. Jorge Luis Borges, *Selected Non-Fictions,* (New York: Viking, 1999), p. 473.

2. Ibid, p. 482.

3. Ibid, p. 483.

4. Terrence Mckenna, https://www.youtube.com/watch?t=52&v=Cget6JxSpfQ. See also, Terrence Mckenna and Dennis Mckenna, *The Invisible Landscape: Mind, Hallucinogens, and The I Ching,* (New York: HarperOne, 1993), p. 40.

5. Rupert Sheldrake, *Science Set Free,* (New York: Deepak Chopra Books, 2013).

6. Carl Jung, *The Structure and Dynamics of the Psyche,* Bolllingen Series XX, (New York: Pantheon Books, 1960), p. 518.

7. Plato, *Symposium* (211b)

8. Joseph Campbell, *The Hero with a Thousand Faces,* (Novato, CA: New World Library, 2008), p. 43.

9. Richard Tarnas, *Cosmos and Psyche* (New York: Plume, 2007), p. 492.

CHAPTER 2

We are Story

In the bosom of such as these
the spirit dwells in rhythmic silence.
~Kahlil Gibran

Have you ever heard the saying, "You are what you think"? Well, we spend much of our lives unwittingly believing and acting out the stories we tell ourselves. Story is how we make sense of our environment and the nature of the self. We have been passing down stories since the beginning of time. A myth is not a fictitious idea or false belief, but a story told over and over because it holds an essential and ultimate truth for our understanding of life's experiences. The inhale of a story is exhaled into a myth. Through the ancient, sacred art of storytelling we continue to understand medicinal uses for certain plants, appropriate societal behaviors, and the comforting reminders of "that which doesn't kill you makes you stronger." We tell ourselves the stories of "I think I can, I think I can" and "when one door closes, another opens." But we also remind ourselves of past pains and traumas until we eventually become so identified with a story that we lose the ability to differentiate between the past and the present.

We all have a story, a series of events that when put together reflects who we are and why we are who we are—who we appear to be. Our personal story is a series of causes and effects that influences our beliefs, behaviors, and thought patterns. Most can relate to living in fear when the mind is the primary storyteller. This is because the mind serves as the overbearing parent who wants to protect us from the present because "there was this one time..." The story of safety and protection begins to override our heart's desire for connection and new experiences, thus creating stagnation and discomfort. We are actively creating our reality with every story we tell ourselves, whether our story is "I'm not good enough" or "it's safe for me to stay small." Each thought has a vibration.

Scientists and mystics, along with mythology, agree that everything is vibration; everything is in motion. Quantum string theorists claim that tiny strings are dancing to the vibration of the quantum field and come together on the cosmic dance floor until they reach a critical mass that gives rise to the fundamental building blocks of matter. This concept agrees with stories told for centuries from all parts of the world. For example, Celtic mythology told the story that the song of Oran Mór created the Universe. The Hopi Indians told how Spider Woman sang a song over clumps of clay, giving birth to human beings. The Orphic mysteries described Venus as rising from ocean foam, dancing to a melody before giving birth to the Cosmic Egg. Islam, Judaism, and Christianity all share the idea that creation is the result of the Word, or vibration.

Mythology also taught that the human heart is the grand concert hall where the inaudible Great Melody becomes audible, not through the five senses, but through the sense of heart-consciousness, where every beat, syncopation, and staccato are felt and known. The heart's connection to the Universal Intelligence of the Song prompted mythology to refer to the heart as the gateway between the seen world and the unseen world. It is through the power of the Song that Orpheus could divert the course of rivers and allure the trees, the wild beasts, and rocks into dance.

We all have our own personal story. It may not be fair or accurate to label it as a myth. It is said that the legacy of thousands of years creates a myth; I'm not sure that's true. But as a society, we have not yet created our own collective story, a contemporary mythology of our time. Therefore, we rely on the stories earlier civilizations told their children, who asked how they got here. Children generally follow this question with another: "Now what?" Stories don't become myths if the stories are never told and so it is important to tell our story, but it is more important to tell our true story, the one that vibrates in rhythm with the Great Melody.

The story of our life, the attempt at meaning-making in telling who we are, opens in a similar fashion to our dreams—without a clear beginning. We build upon stories told to us by others, faint memories created from photographs, or our own fleeting remembrances. When we are born, no one is there to reconnect us to the Song so immediately we begin to cry. We seek the lost Song in the bosom of our mother, whose beating heart faintly echoes with the melody of the Song. Losing connection to the Cosmic Song is only the beginning of our problems. Even before birth, the voices of our parents imprint their anxieties and fears onto us while in the womb, causing us to create our own apprehension of the journey into life. After hours of struggle through the birth canal, we are delivered into the hands of a nurse who turns us upside down and gives us a good whack. The nurse lays us on a stainless steel counter top, measures us, puts acid in our eyes, and probes around like a government scientist in an Area 51 examination room. Indeed, we are in an alien land, without a logbook to tell us our mission or give us the directions back to our home base. We are not even out of the delivery room and already our first imprint is, "life is painful and dangerous."

Mythology describes the human being as the special child or the star-born child, abandoned by its parents and left exposed to fate and the conditions of time and space. This exposure to the elements allows the child to grow and mature into someone powerful and aware. These myths also tell of the child's journey back to its original home, where after its odysseys it learns of its true and royal heritage.

The journey of the child involves the unlearning of those paradigms that screen us from perceiving and knowing the profound truth. We essentially have to learn to unlearn. We have to learn to think and feel with the Heart of the Hero. The Hero is the human being who leaves the comforts and ideologies of what is secure, familiar (including emotional patterns), and culturally indoctrinated. The Hero follows their inner voice of wisdom and ventures into the unknown world of the heart.

Telling our own personal story shouldn't be that difficult. George Lucas, in his *Star Wars* epic, borrowed the concept of the Hero's Journey from Joseph Campbell and provided us with a formula for writing myths about heroes and their adventures. Literary students and screenplay writers learn the essential plot-points of this blockbuster formula. As moviegoers, we automatically recognize, even if only on a visceral or genetic/ancestral level, the archetypal pattern of the Hero's Journey. The success of this formula explains the resurgence of myth and fairytale remakes: "Prometheus," "The Titans," and "Snow White" with a huntsman twist. And although we recognize the Hero's Journey and can relate to it, we have become so disconnected from the archetypal message that we leave the movie feeling simultaneously inspired and disillusioned. This is why, at the end of these myth-based movies, we struggle with the take-home message. I resort to Aesop explanations when talking to my kids: "Don't eat apples from strangers"; "Don't date women who have snakes for hair"; and "Whatever you do, don't open the box."

So much has been written about the Journey of the Hero that some people's eyes begin to roll when you mention it to them. My hope is that the Journey of the Heart of the Hero will help bring the mythological to life. Perhaps what we need is a new story or at least a fresh perspective for the 21st century about the deeper meaning of the Journey. When we view the Journey as a roadmap for conscious evolution, there is a part of our inner self that bends an ear. Indeed, Joseph Campbell outlined the plot of the archetypal story in twelve stages of progress along the Journey towards higher levels of conscious awareness:[1]

Stage One: Home in Society / Ordinary World

Stage Two: Call to Adventure

Stage Three: Refusal of the Call

Stage Four: Meeting the Mentor

Stage Five: Accept the Challenge / Crossing the Threshold

Stage Six: Road of Trials / Tests, Allies, and Enemies

Stage Seven: Approach the Inmost Cave

Stage Eight: Belly of the Whale / Supreme Ordeal

Stage Nine: Reward

Stage Ten: Road Home

Stage Eleven: Transformation

Stage Twelve: Return with the Elixir

In the following chapters, we will discover how these twelve stages align with the twelve signs and houses of the zodiac and how they provide a roadmap for our evolutionary journey. Most of what I knew about the zodiac came from my daily newspaper horoscope. The root of the word zodiac, *zo,* always reminded me of *zoo,* and it just felt like a bunch of farm animals tied to a big wheel in the sky. The term *zodiac* comes from the Greek *zōdiakos kyklos,* meaning "circle of animals," derived from the diminutive of *zōon*—"animal." However, there are also human figures in the zodiac signs so perhaps there is another meaning. Guttman and Johnson in their book *Mythic Astrology* viewed the Greek *zōon* as referring to all biological life as in the "science of organisms." [2] From this perspective, the zodiac becomes *The Circle of Life* and the prototype of Joseph Campbell's myth of the Hero. The zodiac signifies the process of conscious development and the essential story of the human soul.[3]

Human beings are explorers by nature and by cosmic design. We all have a Hero within us. We are all called to explore this evolutionary journey at one point or another. The Call to Adventure comes to us from the archetypes, as the following story of one person's guided exploration with the Scalar Heart Connection process illustrates.

Janet received a Call to Adventure after her fourteenth car accident. She wanted to know if her heart could help her get to the bottom of why she continued to have car accidents.

Using the process of Scalar Heart Connection, which will be described in detail further into this book, Janet's heart directed her to the Pelvis Chakra and the **Emotion**, "Cravings." She immediately identified the feeling of craving with wanting to feel nurtured by her father. She related that when she was four years old she was in a car accident in front of her house. She remembered her father climbing over a four-foot fence and running to see if her mother was okay. Her mom was pregnant and had already lost a baby to a miscarriage. Her father, concerned with the well-being of the unborn baby, inadvertently gave his four-year-old daughter, shaken up in the back seat, the impression that she was not important. Janet said, "It made me feel that I was not valued."

Janet's heart then directed her to the number corresponding to **the Negative Mind-brain Conditioned Response or Belief** she needed to become aware of with the statement, "I suppress and anesthetize my feelings." Janet could relate to how she had not found the root of the feeling that she was somehow not enough. She wondered out loud if all her subsequent car accidents were connected to a subconscious desire to see her father run to her.

The **Positive Heart Message** she chose was, "I celebrate my uniqueness." This statement felt to Janet like an echo of a session she had the day before in a Scalar Heart Connection workshop, where she became aware of her mind-talk that said her feelings are dangerous and she could never live up to the hope of the family. She then had the insight that her earlier experience at age four had created a pattern of not being willing to receive love from others.

Next in the process, Janet's heart directed her to a number for the **Unmet Heart Need**, which was the statement, "Faith." The resonance pattern of not being able to receive love from others shouted over the vibration of faith. She had lost faith in God and that she was protected. She felt life was dangerous and at any moment the carpet could be pulled out from under her—that she could be in a car accident any day.

Next in the series of inquiries, Janet's heart directed her to the **Archetypal Hero Pattern** 9-5-3, identifying the **Issue**, **Obstacle**, and **Action**, which will be described in more detail later. This pattern revealed that the Issue of wanting to feel nurtured was really a call to finding meaning and purpose in the ninth stage of the Hero's Journey, where the Hero obtains the Reward. The Reward is the joy we experience when we realize we are already enough. The 9-5-3 pattern informs us that the archetypal Obstacle the Hero is facing is in the fifth stage of the Hero's Journey. This is the point where the Hero steps into her personal power and Accepts the Call to Adventure. This was Janet's Obstacle, as her mind had convinced her it was safer not to express her feelings—her craving for acceptance. This subconscious belief prevented her from fully expressing herself and her creativity. The Action she needed to take was found in the third stage of the Hero's Journey, the Refusal of the Call. Janet was being called to overcome her mind's judgment of herself based on her perception of how she thinks others accept her.

The Action was to push through her fears and to be what she could really be without all of her limiting beliefs.

From everything that came up in Janet's session, she created the **Positive Statement**, "I am nurtured from within and I share my light with all." She was then asked to pick a number related to her **Mind Resistance** to her Positive Statement. She chose the number related to, "If I change I will abandon those I love." Lurking in Janet's subconscious was a fear that her friends and family would run away from her if she embodied self-power. Janet could now see and consciously integrate what had been holding her back all these years.

To help bring the resonance of Janet's Positive Statement into a new behavioral pattern, she needed to listen to the sound or vibration of the Heart Chakra along with the tone of the Throat Chakra, the center of personal expression. These vibrations have been recorded on a CD titled "Quantum Healing Codes" and will be explored in more detail. This combination of frequencies helped Janet bring her new connection to her heart into creative expression. After listening to the codes, Janet could see herself embodying the positive elements of the Fifth House (Leo), which is the Hero's Acceptance of the Challenge, and related to the Heart Chakra. She could see herself as the bold lion. With this new conscious awareness, she decided to ignore her mind's fears and to drive her car with confidence—like a lion. More importantly, she gave herself permission to drive her life like a lion.

Janet's story is a good example of how our problems (car accidents in her case) create the wound that forces us into action as the Hero's Call to Adventure. From this perspective we also begin to see how external circumstances can be synchronistic. Clearly there were underlying messages in her car accidents, messages held in Janet's subconscious and accessible through the wisdom of her heart.

NOTES:

1. Joseph Campbell, *The Hero with a Thousand Faces*, (Novato, CA: New World Library, 2008).

2. Arielle Guttman and K. Johnson, *Mythic Astrology: Archetypal Powers in the Horoscope*, (St. Paul, MN: Llewellyn Publications, 1993), p. 182.

3. Ibid, p. 183.

CHAPTER 3

Archetypal Patterns within Sacred Geometry

> The whole thing is a number.
> ~ Pythagoras

Archetypes call us to adventure; they put us in harm's way, provide guidance, and pull us out of the fray in the nick of time. Their ultimate mission is to lead us back to ourselves—not to our limited "thinking" self, but to our Higher Self. Jung suggested that it was his Higher Self that was dreaming him into existence. If so, then it may be that the archetypes are the messengers sent by our Higher Self to help guide us out of our slumber to return to our Self, where we will truly know that place for the first time.

When an archetype places a challenge in our life's path, we don't need to wait for a car accident, a bird to fly into our kitchen window, or a snake to slither across our path to tell us we are about to embark on yet another journey of Self-discovery and transformation. We generally already feel something is in the air. The early warning signals come from our feelings and emotions. When we become emotionally uncomfortable, it might be a good time to seek guidance. Jung found *The I Ching* or *Book of Changes* to be helpful in providing guidance. Others are drawn to animal medicine cards, runes, oracle cards, astrology, dreams, and other tools for advice and direction. Prayer, meditation, depth psychology, and transpersonal psychology can also be helpful in interpreting the messages of the archetypes that have activated along our path. Not everyone, however, is convinced that these tools actually work. Our minds want proof, and science has been slow to provide proof. And so we somehow manage to maintain a state of denial.

Rupert Sheldrake, who introduced us to the unseen guiding hand of the Attractor, has attempted to convince our minds that we "know" certain things before our thinking brain realizes what we already suspected. In his book *The Sense of Being Stared At,* he shared his research and that of independent research teams investigating unexplained human abilities, such as the sense of being stared at, phone telepathy, remote viewing, precognition, and animal premonitions.[1] He revealed that these abilities were actually normal and depended largely on social bonding—i.e., heart-connection.

Researchers in 2012 performed a meta-analysis of experiments from seven independent laboratories and found that the human body unconsciously reacts to events up to ten seconds before they happen.[2] The phenomenon has been labeled "feeling the future" or "predictive anticipatory activity" (PAA), also called "presentiment," and involve changes in the cardiopulmonary (heart), skin, and nervous systems.[3] One particular study conducted by Rollin McCraty found that the heart perceived stimulus from the future and then communicated the pre-stimulus information to the brain.[4] This study validated an example of precognition shared by Marie-Louise von Franz, a colleague of Jung. She cited the example of an experiment where a medium in New York was able to accurately "guess" what playing cards a card-dealing machine would deal out two days later in Budapest.[5]

When I think of the word "presentiment," I am reminded of "sentimental" and then picture myself receiving a Hallmark card from the heart with a "pre-sentimental" message like, "You will feel sad in two more days when your cat dies." Presentiment challenges the very foundation of our brain's concept of time. But this was precisely the point of the research conducted by Sheldrake, McCraty, and others. Our heart's connection to the beat of the Universe explains why animals react *before* an earthquake, and why elephants are known for running to high ground *before* a tsunami arrives.

I was particularly interested in the work of Dean Radin, who designed experiments to elicit an emotional response in test subjects by displaying calm or emotionally arousing (disturbing) images on a computer monitor. It was discovered that when randomly selected emotional images were about to appear, test subjects displayed changes in heart rate, blood volume, and electrodermal activity approximately five seconds *before* the picture appeared on the monitor.[6]

Radin's experiments gave me an idea. During several of my Scalar Heart Connection presentations I attempted to duplicate a modified version of his experiments by asking people to "think" about an image I was about to project onto a screen. I'm not a researcher, so I can get away with leading my subjects with subliminal instructions like "*think* about the next image." I was confident that if I said "think" their brains would rely solely on the outside information to form a guess of the next image. I was certain that if they guessed, the result would be that 50% of the audience would guess correctly and the other 50% would guess wrong. I made it less complicated by having people choose between a blue screen and an orange screen, both of which are emotionally neutral. The result was 50/50 between blue and orange. Then I asked people to "feel" whether the next image was a happy picture or a sad one. Again, I subtly prompted people with the word "feel." People guessed the correct image by almost 70%. Every time I have repeated this experiment I have gotten the same results—50/50 for guessing (*thinking*) between blue and orange, and 70/30 for *feeling* if the image was happy or sad.

The research of McCraty and Radin made me feel that if the heart knows what is about to come up on a monitor, then I should be able to replace images with written statements. I wrote ten different statements pertaining to the probable cause of someone's emotional distress on ten different cards, and the person could pick a card by asking their heart which card contained the statement they needed to hear. All I needed was a way to structure the statements in a numeric, geometric pattern that would serve to link mind-brain consciousness and heart-consciousness, the field of unlimited Consciousness. This matrix would allow us to communicate directly with the archetypes. I wanted to utilize the concept of sacred geometry in such a way that its underlying numbers could serve as a language for accessing the archetypes and the meaning behind their activity.

My search for a geometric number matrix began with the Pythagoreans, who, like the later Platonists, viewed mathematical forms (number) and geometric harmonies as visible expressions of Divine Intelligence.[7] Jung believed that "number" itself was an archetype, a symbol of an underlying principle of wholeness and unity.[8] If, as quantum physics suggests, the Universe is an ocean of vibration, then that which separates one manifestation of matter from another is the rate or frequency of vibration. The rate of vibration is a number. As Galileo declared, the all-pervasive language of the Universe is number. Number is the bridge between the physically knowable and the realm of intuition or metaphysical knowing. This helps explain how we can sense that we are being stared at. It is the vibratory signature of the heart of the person staring that our heart feels. Their staring is a conscious act directed at us, which creates an entanglement of vibration through the fabric of spacetime. Our heart is a counting system and can feel the slightest change in vibration through the matrix or geometry of spacetime. This is the reason geometry is sacred. It is sacred because the geometric matrix of spacetime is the result of the underlying Cosmic Song—the one the heart is connected to and sings with in harmony.

Some physicists are now exploring the possibility that sub-atomic particle interactions arise as consequences of this underlying vibratory geometry.[9] For example, interactions normally described by mathematical formulas thousands of terms long can now be described by a one-term expression using a computation based on the volume of a jewel-like "amplituhedron."[10] Theoretical physicist A. Garrett Lisi contended that all known fields and dynamics of spacetime were found through pure geometry.[11] This supported the ancient symbol of the heart, which was depicted in terms of geometry. If the heart is the bridge between our outer world and the inner world of the archetypes, then the clue to accessing the field of unlimited intelligence from which they arise must be found in the ancient symbol for the Heart Chakra.

The only thing I knew about the symbol of the Heart Chakra was that it was the Twin-Tetrahedron or the Star of David surrounded by twelve lotus petals. The other clue was that it was usually depicted as the color green:

Heart Chakra Symbol with Twin-Tetrahedron in the Center

Mythology is perhaps the best source for understanding how geometry relates to the archetypes. My first clue had already arrived synchronistically with the pinecone I received at the family reunion bingo game. Throughout history, the pinecone has symbolized the Third Eye, enlightenment, and the pineal gland or the "Seat of the Soul." The Egyptian Staff of Osiris depicts two intertwining serpents rising up to a pinecone perched on top of the staff. The pinecone, as a symbol for Osiris, set me off on a journey through the sands of Egypt. It is the myth of Osiris and Set.

The story is about the Egyptian god Osiris and his jealous brother Set. Osiris, also described as the "Lord of Love," reigned for twenty-eight years until the day Set fooled him into getting into a box, which he then shut and sealed with lead and, with the help of seventy-two conspirators, threw into the Nile River. After a long search, his wife Isis found the box with his remains embedded in a tree trunk in Byblos on the Phoenician coast. She opened the box and with Thoth's aid used a magical spell to bring him back to life. Osiris lived long enough to impregnate her before he died again, and Isis buried his body in the desert. One day while hunting, Set came across the body of Osiris, became enraged, and tore the body into fourteen pieces and scattered them across the land. When Isis caught wind of this, she set out to find all the parts and put them back together. She found everything except the phallus, which was missing because it had been eaten by a fish. The gods were watching and were so impressed with her devotion that they restored Osiris's life and he became a god of the afterworld.

Set, however, was still so mad that he also wanted revenge on Isis's son, Horus. Since the divine Horus was considered to be the sky, his right eye was known to contain the Sun and his left eye contained the Moon. Eventually Set, who by then was the patron of Upper Egypt, caught up to Horus, the patron of Lower Egypt. They battled, but neither side was victorious so the gods decided to break the tie and sided with Horus. Unfortunately for Set, he lost one of his testicles during the battle, which became the Egyptian explanation as to why Upper Egypt lost its fertility. Horus lost his left eye in the fight, reconciling why the Moon is now so much weaker and dimmer than the Sun. A new eye was created by a part of the Moon god, Khonsu, and the left eye of Horus was healed and made whole.

The Osiris myth is often considered a lunar myth. The give-away is the reference to Osiris's age of twenty-eight at the time of his death. The other clue lies in the fourteen body parts scattered by Set around the land. There are twenty-eight days in a lunar cycle (28 is the mean between the *sidereal* period of 27.3 and the *synodic* period of 29.5). The 14 different body parts scattered by Set represent the 14 days between the New Moon (scattered) and the Full Moon (made whole). To be more exact, half of the *synodic* period of 29.53 days (the Moon's orbit in relation to the Sun) is 14.76 days.

There are four main phases of the Moon: Full, Half, New, and Half again. Seven days separate each of these four phases. The use of seven days in a week may have originally been intended to represent the original seven planets observed by ancient peoples. Makers of early playing cards used 52 cards to make 365 days (7 x 52) and added the joker to make 365 days. When we multiply the 28 days of the lunar cycle by 13 we arrive at 364 days, which also requires a joker or an extra "day out of time." The "day out of time" was observed by many cultures as a day of celebration—of gratitude and forgiveness—a day that was a bridge between the closing of the year and the beginning of a new year. Today it is mostly about partying and starting the new year with a hangover, further evidence that we have lost our connection with Nature and her natural rhythms.

The early use of a 360-day calendar provides a sense of harmony in number and a possible source for the number of degrees in a circle, the symbol of unity. The 360-day calendar uses 30 days per month over 12 months. This is the basis of the zodiac, which also relies on 360 degrees and 12 houses of 30 degrees each.

The phases of the Moon in the Osiris myth become an archetype activated in a transformative process. The number 14, as the days between the Dark New Moon and the Light Full Moon, represents a journey of transformation similar to the concepts of the alchemists. Recall that Set tricked Osiris into a coffin and immediately sealed it with lead to suffocate Osiris. He did this with the help of 72 co-conspirators. The human heart beats 72 times per minute on average. The inclusion in the story of the number 72 informs us that it is the human heart that guides us through the transformative process.

The alchemist's vessel or alembic is hermetically sealed in lead, and the spirit imprisoned in matter is cooked and suffocated. On a psychological level, it is the process of introspection that suffocates or cooks our natural tendency to blame other people and outside events for our problems. It is also the cooking or overcoming of that part of our ego-self that sees the natural world and everything and everyone in it as separate from us. It is the feminine spirit, Isis, which reconnects Osiris to a deeper meaning and significance of his experiences—back to wholeness beyond time and space.

The numbers that stand out in the Osiris myth relate to our sense of time. There are 7 days of the week based on the Earth's rotation on its axis relative to the Sun. The number 13 is the number of Full Moons in a year. Multiply 13 by 28 days in a month and we get 364 (the number of days in the lunar year calendar). Putting the numbers together gives us the following series:

7   13   28   364

The numbers above are found in a remarkable geometry. When the numbers 7 and 13 are two sides of a triangle, the hypotenuse is 14.76 (half of the *synodic* period of 29.53 days or the number of days between Full Moon and New Moon):

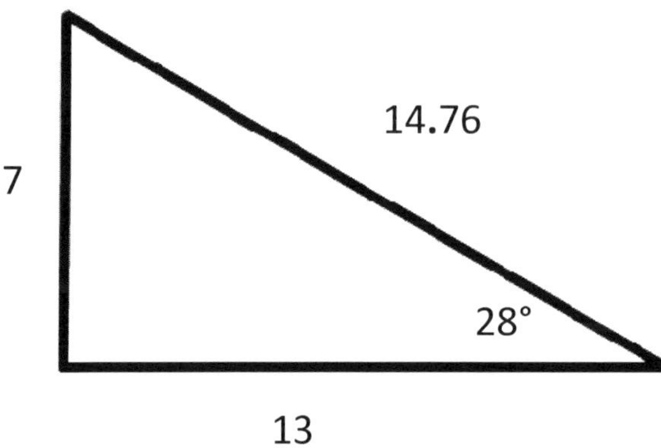

The Lunar Triangle of Isis

The Lunar Triangle of Isis is a key to understanding our connection to the harmony and mystery of the Universe, both seen and unseen. Because it is related to time, we can say that spacetime is the schoolyard on which our experiences act on us, impelling us to learn and grow.

The Lunar Triangle of Isis fits twelve times (not perfectly, but close) around the zodiac, providing a clue that our schoolyard has different stages of growth opportunities.

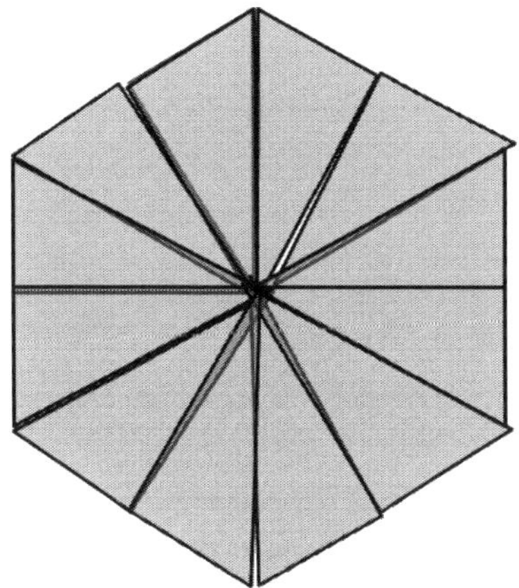

The Lunar Triangle of Isis
fits 12 Times Around a Central Point

According to the ancients, the Moon, her numbers, and her geometry were illuminating a path of personal transformation—a path of the heart. It is a path the ancients embedded in mythology and number. It was a secret path—one that required diligent personal effort and the willingness to go beyond one's self. Thankfully, the trials and tribulations of this Hero's Journey and its transcendent nature have been preserved for us in myth.

The Osiris myth, with its embedded numbers and Hero stages, tells us that our personal problems often contain a hidden geometry. If we can uncover this archetypal geometry, we have the opportunity to gain insight into a larger picture of our problem. This may be the first step in the assimilation and digestion of past traumas and repressed negative emotions, even if we have to dismember our past into bite-size pieces so we can extract the nectar of compassion, forgiveness, and heightened consciousness they provide.

Finding the hidden geometry behind our personal challenges is easier to accomplish once we understand the message behind each pattern. Each stage of the Hero's Journey connects with two other stages to form a triangle. The triangle geometry is perfect for providing information on the nature of our problem (the

Issue), the challenge we need to overcome (the Obstacle), and what is needed to grow beyond the problem (the Action):

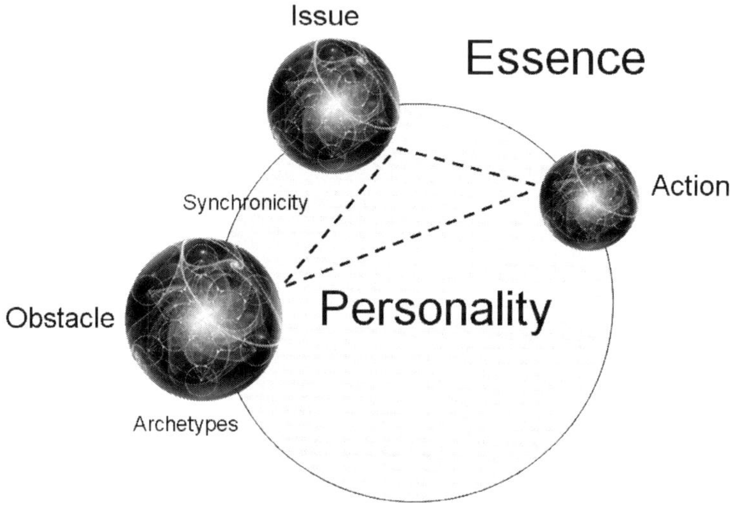

Archetypes work together in triads
(The Triad Dynamism of Archetypes)

A story of two monks, Tom and Bob, helps illustrate how triangles form the archetypal patterns of our Issues. One evening at the monk cafeteria, monk Bob inadvertently cut in front of monk Tom in the dinner line. Monk Tom, being a monk, took it in stride—at least he thought he had. Upon awakening the next day, monk Tom had a painful side ache. He immediately began making small figure-eights in the air just above his liver with his right hand. With his eyes closed, he felt into the pain and recognized that the emotion behind the pain was anger. He also immediately recognized that the anger originated with the episode with monk Bob the prior evening. The figure-eight motion acted like a möbius coil, which had the effect of cancelling out the negative energy he was experiencing in his liver. He also looked within himself until he found compassion for monk Bob and for himself. Within a few minutes, the pain was gone and he joined monk Bob for breakfast with a genuine smile.

The story of monks Tom and Bob gives us insight into how our conscious mind normally operates. Monk Tom's mind was aware that monks are "supposed" to act a certain way. We could call this monk Tom's societal conditioning. The problem was that he was actually upset that monk Bob cut in front of him. Anger is the emotion commonly associated with the liver according to ancient Chinese Meridian or Five Element Theory. Pain in the liver was the Issue causing monk Tom to look deeper. We know from the story that there was a component of food involved. We can imagine that the episode was a trigger for monk Tom that activated unresolved issues he had as a child around scarcity. In fact, monk Tom was an orphan and indeed had issues with food scarcity and issues of survival. His anger had nothing to do with monk Bob, per se. The problem was the activation of an earlier memory—an issue that monk Tom had not given himself permission to fully integrate on the emotional level. His mind was content to repress the feeling from the past so he could maintain his "good monk" image. But Tom, after all, was a monk, one who was connected to the inner knowing of his heart. As such, he trusted that synchronistic events, like someone cutting in front of him in order to stir up an old emotion, happened as a way of informing him that it was time to fully integrate his traumatic early-childhood experience. His repressed fear of scarcity from his early experience was the Obstacle preventing him from being truly authentic. Monk Tom was able to switch his emotion of anger to one of compassion. Compassion is an attribute of the heart. Tapping into the compassion of his heart was the Action he needed to take.

We now have enough information from monk Tom's experience to see the triangulation of the archetypal pattern that was activated in his situation with monk Bob. Monk Bob, incidentally, was an innocent bystander. We could say that it was monk Tom's archetypes that made monk Bob cut in front of him for the purpose of helping monk Tom. The triangulation of monk Tom's situation is found by connecting the Issue (anger in the liver—associated with the Solar Plexus Chakra) to the Obstacle (unresolved issues with survival—associated with the Root Chakra) and finally to the Action (finding heart-centered compassion through the Heart Chakra).

Monk Tom was able to shift the disrupted energy flow of his liver by first becoming consciously aware of the real problem and then shifting that energy into a positive pattern of compassion with the aid of the figure-eight.

Tibetan Monks have known about figure-eight energy flows for thousands of years. They discovered increased energy and vitality by stimulating these four basic energy flows:

1) A figure-eight pattern on the top of the head.
2) Figure-eight patterns on the front, back or sides of the head.
3) Figure-eight patterns on the front, back or sides of the torso.
4) Figure-eight patterns on the legs (front, back or sides).

Figure-eights can be made over any part of the body that is uncomfortable. I recommend making figure-eights over the body with the non-dominant hand. If you are right handed, then making figure-eights with the left hand seems to help synchronize the body's natural energy flow and reset any residual fight or flight sympathetic nervous system response that may be in a habituated alert state.

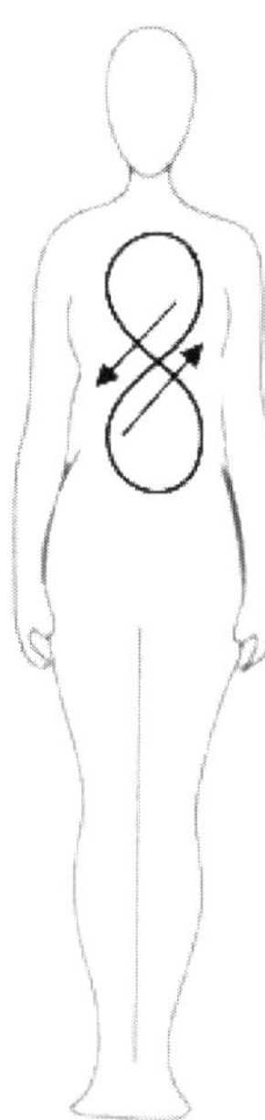

Smaller figure-eight patterns can be found in the body as all parts of the body are holographically related to all other parts. For example, the blood flowing through the heart takes on a figure-eight pattern as there is an intersection of venous blood passing through the right atrium, overlapping aortic blood coming through the left atrium.

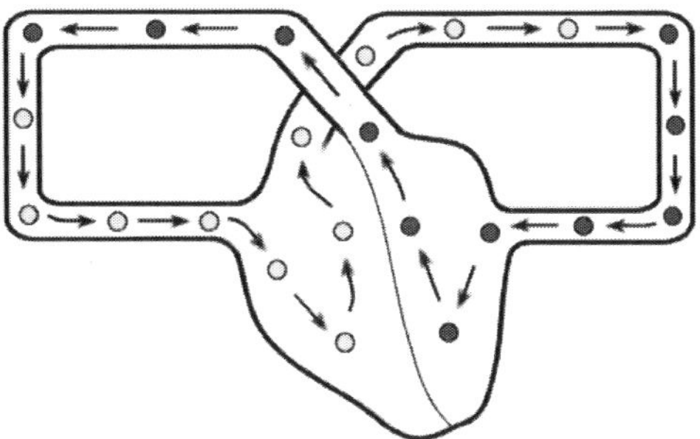

The Flow of Blood Moving Through
the Heart and Lungs in a Figure-eight.

The figure-eight also appears in the DNA antenna in our cells' energy production centers (mitochondria), which assumes the shape of what is called a supercoil.[12]

Supercoiled DNA molecule.

There is a tradition among Native Americans that when a gift is presented, the person receiving the gift moves the gift along a horizontal figure-eight pattern a few times in order to "clear" any old energy from previous owners. The figure-eight is an ancient symbol used to bring balance and harmony back into a space when the pattern is repeated.

Monk Tom used the figure-eight pattern to neutralize residual resonance patterns acquired from negative childhood experiences. Figure-eights are helpful in times of stress or emotional discomfort. I like to use them just before speaking to large groups of people. I also find it helpful to reset my nervous system when something starts to make me angry or upset. The motion is helpful in informing the brain that we are safe and not in any danger.

By triangulating monk Tom's liver pain using the Triangle of Isis, into Issue, Obstacle, and Action, we more clearly see the subconscious pattern activated by his encounter with monk Bob:

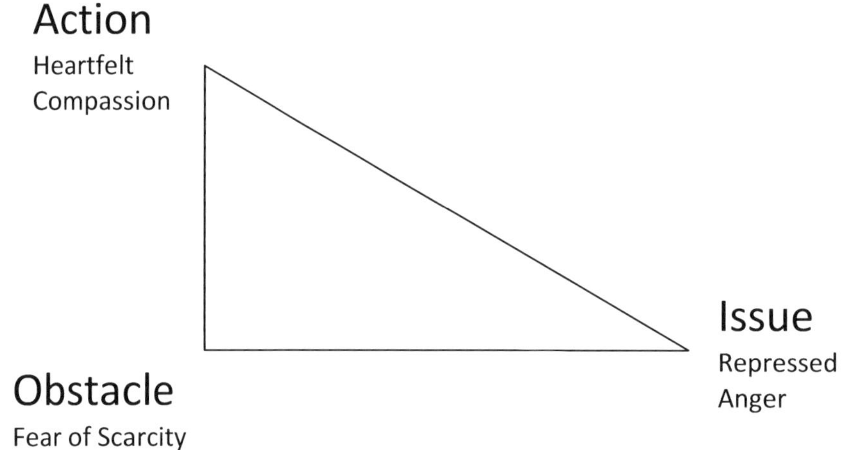

In a later chapter, by placing this triangle into the geometry of the heart, we will see how monk Tom's Issue, Obstacle, and Action were related to specific stages of the Hero's Journey. For now, it is important that we understand, through Janet's and monk Tom's examples, how we can access the wisdom of our heart to guide us through the deeper issues that occasionally seek resolution through unpleasant experiences. These two examples also demonstrate how Scalar Heart Connection can help us communicate directly with the activated archetypes responsible for our external discomforts.

Scalar Heart Connection offers a mini-session called "Ask Your Heart." Anyone can do the session any time. The program is available for free on the website www.scalarheartconnection.com and can also be downloaded as an app. It utilizes the same principles as found in the monk Tom example. The program begins by asking you to type in a problem or an issue that is causing an upset or discomfort. The following example shows how easy the program is to use and how valuable it is for helping to shift incompatible resonances around an Issue.

Christine was having financial worries and feelings of anxiety about her business. She used the Ask Your Heart App to gain insight into her problem. Her heart provided her with a number, which once entered into the program gave the answer that her Issue was the result of an archetypal activation in the Solar Plexus Chakra. She also received the number related to the Emotion, "Controlling." It was the feeling of needing to control the situation that was giving her anxiety.

Next, Christine's heart showed her the number related to the Negative Mind-brain Conditioned Response or Belief and the related statement, "I doubt myself." This was the Obstacle. Christine said she wasn't sure if she was making the right choice about staying in her business and doubted if she had anything to offer people. She recognized that she had grown up with a critical and terrible mother as well as an absent father, with the result that she doubted herself.

The program then asked Christine to tap into her heart's innate wisdom and to be shown a number related to the Unmet Heart Need that resulted from her early experience. She was shown the number related to "Sleep." At first glance this seemed quite odd to her. It is common that a positive resonance fails to imprint on us as a result of the overwhelming negative vibration of the negative mind-brain conditioning and beliefs. This meant that the negative emotion of "controlling" could be shifted with the positive resonance of "sleep." However, it is difficult for our conscious thinking brain to make the connection between the two, which is exactly the reason she didn't ask her brain, but her heart instead.

Christine said that she had been having trouble sleeping. She said she usually fell right to sleep, but lately she would lie awake thinking about all the stuff going on and try to force herself not to let stuff in the world consume her. Her mind made the connection between the anxiety of trying to control and the opposite, which is sleep—repose or relaxation.

The next step in the session was to ask the heart to show Christine a number related to the Positive Heart Message from heart-consciousness. This was the Action. Christine chose the number related to the statement, "I am creative and give birth to new ideas." She then received the insight that the inner Hero's Journey had brought her to the precipice of self-doubt to help her see that she had everything she needed within her all along. She said, "I just needed to have a situation show me I can do this. . . to trust that I am going to make the right decision and that I am courageous like a Hero." She created her personal Positive Statement from the information that her heart provided: "I am courageous, trusting in my own instincts, manifesting my own ideas and I bring about positive change for myself and others." She repeated this statement to herself while making small figure-eights over her heart and listening to one of the Quantum Healing Codes.

Christine happily reported, about six months later, that the session had helped her find the courage to close her retail space, even though it was hard on her ego. She set up a home office, and business has been booming ever since. She recalled how she mentioned in her session that part of her vision included wanting to work in wide open spaces with natural lighting. Her new space, she said, overlooked the mountains and she did most of her business poolside.

Christine's example shows how we can utilize the innate wisdom of our heart to guide us through difficult times. It also gives insight into the triangulation of the Issue, Obstacle, and Action. However, there is an even deeper archetypal pattern involved in her session. Later in this book we will see how the Lunar Triangle of Isis is used to reveal these patterns. But first, we need to understand how the archetypes throw problems at us, guide us through our Hero's Journey, and provide the right action needed to overcome our problems.

A classic example that captures the essence of the Hero's Journey is the story of *Eros & Psyche*, described in the next chapter. According to some, the myth of *Eros & Psyche* is a story about the growth of the soul. For others, it takes on an Oedipal flavor about psychosexual development. Yet for others, it is about the nature of the psychological potential of human development. All of these ideas may be appropriate. One of the great things about myths is that they are open to interpretation and can be applied in different ways based on the circumstances. I prefer the more Jungian interpretation that *Eros & Psyche* is about the process of individuation and how that comes about through the conscious encounter with the unconscious. But it can be more than that. As we are about to discover, the affair between Eros and Psyche can also represent the bonding of mind and soul. Either way, it is rich in metaphor and secret meaning.

NOTES:

1. Rupert Sheldrake, *The Sense of Being Stared At* (3rd Edition), (South Paris, ME: Park Street Press, 2013).

2. Julia Mossbridge, Patrizio Tressoldi, and Jessica Utts, "Predictive Physiological Anticipation Preceding Seemingly Unpredictable Stimuli: A Meta-Analysis," *Front. Psychol* 17(2012). http://dx.doi.org/10.3389/fpsyg.2012.00390

3. http://www.dailygrail.com/2014/3/Scientific-Research-Suggests-We-Unconsciously-React-Events-10-Seconds-They-Happen

4. Rollin McCraty et. al., "Electrophysiological Evidence of Intuition: Part 1. The Surprising Role of the Heart," *The Journal of Alternative and Complementary Medicine* 10 (2004), pp. 133–143

5. Marie-Louise Von Franz, *Psyche & Matter*, (Boston: Shambhala Publications, 1992), p. 21.

6. Dean Radin, *Entangled Minds: Extrasensory Experiences in a Quantum Reality*, (New York: Paraview Pocket Books, 2006).

7. Richard Tarnas, *The Passion of the Western Mind*, (New York: Ballantine Books, 1993), p. 50.

8. Marie-Louise von Franz, *Number and Time,* (Evanston, IL: Northwestern University Press, 1998), p. 45.

9. Natalie Wolchover, "Scientists Discover a Jewel at the Heart of Quantum Physics," *Quanta Magazine* Sept 17, 2013. http://www.simonsfoundation.org/quanta/20130917-a-jewel-at-the-heart-of-quantum-physics)

10. Nima Arkana-Hamed and Jaroslav Trnka, "The Amplituhedron," (arXiv:1312.2007v1 [hep-th]), 2013.

11. A. Garrett Lisi, "An Exceptionally Simple Theory of Everything," (arXiv:0711.0770 [hep-th]), 2007.

12. Maxim D. Frank-Kamenetskii, *Unraveling DNA*, (New York: Perseus Books, 1997).

CHAPTER 4

Mythology and Number

> The number seven is suitable and agreeable
> to holy and divine things.
> ~ Apuleius

The story of *Eros & Psyche* is found in the Latin novel *Metamorphoses* by Apuleius of Madaurus (c.125–c.180), otherwise known as "Lucius" Apuleius after the main character of his novel.[1] The title suggests an alchemical theme and, indeed, St. Augustine referred to the novel as *The Golden Ass*, hinting at the alchemical transformation of the main character. With the use of magic Apuleius accidently turned himself into a donkey and was later redeemed (transformed) after a series of unfortunate adventures back into a "new" man.

From an alchemical point of view, the label "Golden Ass" refers to the golden transformative vessel, in this case, the donkey. But it is the body of the human being that holds the key to transformation, pointing to our life experiences and their way of bringing us closer to understanding and re-connecting to the Cosmic Song.

Apuleius's journey began with a desire for freedom, represented by his desire to use magic to turn himself into a bird. His journey was interspersed with bizarre and pornographic stories embedded around the central theme of sexuality, love, and freedom. Von Franz suggested that these interruptions inserted throughout the novel are actually dreams.[2] In this way, unconscious content percolates to the surface of the main story in the way we have a story about ourselves while we are awake, interspersed with dreams that provide messages and insights to guide us along our journey.

The most famous of the inserted stories is *Eros & Psyche (Cupid & Psyche)*, although Apuleius doesn't label it as such. This inserted story starts in book four of the novel. The number 4 relates to the four stages of alchemy, as well as the four seasons and the four elements, all of which point to the journey towards ultimate unity or wholeness. We saw earlier in the Osiris myth that there are four phases of the Moon with seven days between each one. The story of Eros and Psyche takes up a total of three books or chapters. The story is essentially a Hero's Journey inside a Hero's Journey: a microcosm within a microcosm. Plato said the name *heros* is only a slight alteration of *Eros*, from whom the Heroes sprang.[3]

I find comfort in Lucius's exploits, especially when I make an ass out of myself. In Jungian circles, the story has been analyzed in such a way as to suggest that Apuleius had a mother complex. I think we all have a mother complex. I know I had one when mine left me at nursery school for the first time. Whether our mother complex is positive or negative may relate to how successfully we detached from that bond as we set out to find the lost Song. A negative mother complex can stem from our mother's reluctance or refusal to let us leave, as much as it arises from our refusal to go.

No one knows the origin of the *Eros & Psyche* story, adding to its archetypal mystique. Scholars do know that Apuleius's version was an adaptation of an earlier Greek rendition. The word "Psyche" (saɪki) is the Greek "Soul" or "Breath of Life." The word "Psyche" in Greek is also the word for butterfly. Aristotle perhaps originally associated "Psyche" with the white butterfly to denote the white Moon, as seen floating in the sky during the daytime. Naturally, when we think of butterflies we think of transformation—the metamorphosis of the caterpillar turning into a beautiful winged creature. The word cupid in Latin is *Cupido* or "Desire" or "*Amor*" ("Love") as the Greek *Eros*.

The Babylonian version of the story belongs to the category of astronomic observation and lunar myths, which include the descent of Ishtar and the life-death-rebirth theme of Venus and Adonis.[4] Apuleius, no doubt, was aware of the earlier mythology as the ultimate redeemer of Lucius, the Golden Ass, is Isis, the Great Moon Goddess.

The story of *Eros & Psyche* can be broken down into four lunar cycles; one cycle takes us from New Moon to Full Moon and back to New Moon. Within each of these cycles, the characters learn and grow psychologically and spiritually. The first cycle begins with Psyche growing (waxing) into a young and beautiful maiden whose popularity grows until men and women are so enamored with her that they forget to pay proper homage to Venus. They begin to refer to her as the New Venus. Psyche's beauty is so intimidating that no man seeks her hand in marriage. This is the first Full Moon of the story, as Psyche blossoms into a young woman.

We aren't told anything about Psyche's childhood. We only know that she is in the full bloom of her womanhood and expected to settle down with a husband and have children. This is the first cycle of our lives, where we tend to follow the expectations of others and haven't matured enough to stand up for what we really want. At this point in our lives, we ourselves may not completely know what we want.

Psyche's father, a king, fearing she will remain single, seeks the advice of the oracle of Apollo. Apuleius's choice of the oracle of Apollo instead of another wisdom source is obvious when considering that Apollo was the god of light and of music. His twin sister was Artemis, a goddess of the Moon, who carried a bow and arrows in the manner of Eros. Apollo's other epitaphs included "Lyceus" and "Lukeios," meaning "light," which happen to be from the same derivative as the name of the main character, Lucius. The meaning of the name Lyceus was also associated with Apollo's mother Leto, who was identified with the wolf. The oracle tells the father that Psyche is fated to marry a serpent-human-monster.

In the meantime, Venus becomes jealous of Psyche and seeks revenge for outshining her. Offended, Venus uses her son Eros to get revenge by using his arrows to make Psyche fall in love with the serpent-human-monster. Eros is young, immature, rash, evil mannered, with fire and arrows. If Psyche represents the spiritual essence of our soul or the animating spirit of our soul having an earthly experience, then Eros is the active energy of our mind, which reacts to will and desire. Eros, in his immature state, is concerned with the physical kind of love, thereby falling in love with Psyche in secret from his mother.

Psyche falls in line with everyone's expectations and goes ahead with the wedding to the unseen serpent-human-monster, not realizing Eros has taken its place without his mother's knowledge. Her wedding is described as a funeral wedding. When the ceremony is complete, Zephyrus, the gentle west wind, carries her away to a low place, a valley where she vanishes from the sight of the world, like the New Moon disappearing from view as it is consumed by the Sun. This is the completion of the first lunar cycle.

When Psyche enters the palace of her new husband, she finds herself in the presence of the Sun again in the beginning of the second lunar cycle. This is the honeymoon phase of her new relationship, where all expectations lie at the feet of the new partner, who, like Psyche, we imagine will make us complete and eternally happy. Apuleius informs us of this Full Moon phase by the reflection of the Sun against the palace gold and precious gems. Inside the palace, singing, ethereal servants fulfill every desire of Psyche. The palace is alive with music, but it is not the Cosmic Song. It is only an echo of the Cosmic Song, in the same way the palace is not her true home. The gold of the palace is a false kind of glitter, like the temporary joy we experience with new love, a new car, new house, new job, etc. When spirit is lulled to sleep by mind-brain consciousness, we tend towards relationships that are comfortable, convenient or of a purely sexual nature.

At night, when Psyche goes to bed, a sweet sound comes to her ears before her unknown husband arrives, and again when he leaves in the morning before dawn. Each time he leaves, the invisible voices come as a comfort and a great pleasure to Psyche. She begins to desire her husband more and more. She is pleased by her husband's nightly visits, but continues to think about her family. In other words, she has not individuated. She is unsure of herself, still seeking the approval and recognition of others, particularly her family. This indicates that the Moon is now waning again back to the depths of the unconscious, forcing Psyche to re-examine her life and priorities. She is still young and has yet to embrace the nature of her authentic self.

Confused and full of doubt, Psyche arranges to visit her sisters, who become jealous after seeing the palace and all its richness. They tell Psyche the reason her husband only visits her at night is because he is a serpent-monster. In the Babylonian myth, the serpent is the symbol of darkness. Hence, Eros represents the dark side of the Moon, the dark side of ourselves we keep suppressed in our subconscious. The embrace of Eros and Psyche by night illustrates the latent unity or wholeness unrealized within ourselves.

The beginning of the third lunar cycle is marked by Psyche discovering she is pregnant. Eros promises the child will be an immortal god if she keeps his secret and does not look at his face. Psyche hasn't experienced the true depth of love and is feeling trapped. Something inside her wants to see the truth. Seeking truth is an act of expanded awareness, indicating that the Moon is now waxing again on this third lunar cycle and approaching fullness (pregnancy).

Coincidently with the approaching Full Moon, Psyche's curiosity overcomes her and she brings a lamp to bed in order to see the face of her sleeping husband. She carries a knife in her other hand just in case her sisters are correct about his identity. The knife is that part of us that hasn't quite embraced our full potential and sense of self in the world, but is willing to decapitate what is holding us back.

When the light of the lamp reveals Eros's divine beauty, Psyche is overcome with admiration of his glorious body and divine countenance. She loses strength and falls on her knees. Beside the bed she sees the quiver and arrows of the great god, and takes one of the arrows and tests its sharpness with her finger. She pricks herself with the edge and drops of blood flow, and on her own accord, she falls in love with Love. She then embraces Eros and kisses him a thousand times. The Moon is now full again and Psyche has stepped into the fullness of herself. However, while smothering Eros with kisses, a drop of burning oil accidentally falls from the lamp onto the shoulder of Eros and he flies away. The dark side of the Moon is now nowhere to be seen.

The light of the Full Moon begins to wane a third time and Psyche wanders the Earth vainly looking for her beloved. She comes to a riverbank and contemplates drowning herself. There, she finds Pan sitting on the other bank. Pan manages to talk Psyche out of throwing herself in the water. He reminds her of her promise to serve and worship True Love.

Psyche leaves Pan and heads straight to each of her sister's houses, tricks them to ride Zephyrus to Eros's palace, and then has the west wind drop them both to their deaths. The good news is that Psyche no longer pays any attention to what other people think. The bad news is that Venus discovers that her son is in danger of death from the hot oil wound and she is furious with both him and Psyche. The goddesses Juno and Ceres notice her anger and come to calm her down, but to no avail. Venus rides her chariot up to the heavens to seek the help of her brother, Mercury, in finding Psyche. Four white doves carry the chariot and all kinds of birds follow, singing sweet honeyed notes, being the "tuneful choir of Venus." Here Apuleius reminds us of the four phases of the Moon, as the dove is the symbol of the Moon Goddess. Mercury issues a reward for the return of Psyche: "seven sweet kisses of Venus."

Juno and Ceres catch up to Psyche and convince her to throw herself at the mercy of Venus. Venus declares her marriage to Eros illegitimate and challenges her to prove her love for Eros with impossible tasks. Each time, Psyche is successfully aided: first by ants, then by a green reed of sweet music inspired with a gracious tune and melody, and then by Jupiter's eagle. Infuriated, Venus sends her to the underworld of Pluto with a box to retrieve a small amount of Proserpina's beauty (the Greek goddess equivalent is Persephone). Psyche's decent into the underworld, where she undergoes obstacles and more challenges, is paralleled by "The Twelve Labors of Heracles" or of Ishtar, who also belongs to the astronomical cycle of Babylonian lunar-myth.[5] The Moon's phase now darkens and disappears from the night sky as Psyche believes this final task is impossible and climbs a high tower with the intention of jumping to her death. The tower, inspired, provides her with the guidance she needs to make the journey, particularly the advice not to look inside the box once it contains the mystical secret of beauty. Of course, at the end of successfully accomplishing all the underworld tasks, she looks inside the box and falls into a deadly sleep.

Eros, meantime, now recovered, flies out of the chamber where Venus kept him and immediately goes to find his wife. He finds her asleep and wipes away the sleep from her eyes and sends her off to give the box to his mother. The reunion of Eros and Psyche marks the beginning of the fourth lunar cycle. Eros and Psyche are now in love on a level that transcends the physical. They are each complete and whole within themselves.

While Psyche heads off to return the box to Venus, Eros flies to heaven to petition his father, Jupiter, to unite him with Psyche for eternity. Jupiter, seeing that his son has matured and is sincerely in love with Psyche, throws them a grand Royal Wedding, the Union of the light and dark sides of the Moon. During the reception, it is noted that "Venus danced finely to the music." In time, Psyche gave birth to a daughter named Bliss.

As soon as the old woman finishes the story of Eros and Psyche, Lucius's troubles continue. Lucius, as an ass, has fallen from the human level down to that of an animal, where his experiences are bestial and sexually perverted. By the end of his ordeal, a cook and a baker purchase him. The cook and the baker, however, are in the service of Thiasus. Von Franz explained that Thiasus was the name of the orgiastic reunions in the Dionysian mysteries.[6] Apuleius, she said, was alluding to the secret meaning of the mysteries, which was not to release the beast in man, but to humanize the animal side already in us.

The final episode is a bit repulsive, even too repulsive for Lucius, who, realizing his own immoral behavior, escapes to "a secret place of the Sea coast," and falls asleep on the sand. Lucius falls asleep on the shore, just along the border of Universal consciousness (the ocean). He has reached the lowest point of misery through his personal tragedies and has surrendered to the Sea. He wakes up just as midnight arrives (midnight is the number 12) in time to see the Full Moon over the sea:

> I found good hope and sovereign remedy, though it was very late, to be delivered of all my misery, by invocation and prayer to the excellent beauty of this powerful goddess. Wherefore shaking off my drowsy sleep I arose with a joyful face, and moved by a great affection to purity myself. I plunged my head seven times [7] into the water of the sea; which number of seven [7] is convenable and agreeable to holy and divine things, as the worthy and sage philosopher Pythagoras hath declared.[7]

Lucius joyfully, through his tears, makes an invocation and prayer to the Great Moon Goddess in the four figures of Ceres (Greek Demeter), Venus, Artemis (Greek Diana), and the underworld goddess, Proserpina. He recognizes the one transcendental power behind this four-fold goddess and realizes that the goddess was behind all his misfortunes, guiding him back to himself.[8] The realization of the Self is an experience of Unity with the Infinite, beyond life or death.[9]

Lucius falls asleep again and "by and by (for my eyes were but newly closed)" appeared to him from the midst of the sea the divine figure of Queen Isis. She holds a cup of gold in her left hand and when she moves her right arm, triple chords "gave forth a shrill and clear sound." The alchemical vessel is a round cup, which represents the totality and unity of the Cosmos and in which the transformative process takes place.[10]

The transformative process, as myths inform us, takes place within the human body. It is the Hero Journey of the butterfly emerging from the dark chrysalis into the light. Myths also remind us of the music, the Song that guides us along our path, calling us to itself along the way. We begin the journey by unwittingly loving beauty in people and then learning to love the beauty that is unseen, the beauty of our own soul. Plato explained that there is a third nature of human beings, a "man-woman" called a "hermaphrodite." In Greek mythology, Hermaphroditus was the son of the Greek god Hermes and the goddess Aphrodite. Hermes was a god of transitions and a mediator between mortals and the divine.

The symbols for Hermes include the number 4 and the Caduceus, his shepherding staff that has spread wings at the top and two entwined snakes wrapped around the shaft. The two snakes are the seemingly opposite energies of Eros and Psyche. Eros is the downward flowing energy into physical desire and worldly love, where Psyche's energy naturally points upwards to divine love. By embodying both male and female energies, Hermaphroditus symbolizes their sacred union.

The clue to creating a geometry that accounts for all the numbers in the myth of Osiris as well as *Eros & Psyche* lies in the number 4. The number 4 is the symbol of an earlier Hermes—Hermes Trismegistus, the Egyptian Thoth and father of alchemy.[11] Thoth is the one who helped Isis with the magic spell that brought Osiris back to life the first time. And, Isis is also the goddess who came to the rescue of Lucius, the Golden Ass.

The number 4 is an alchemical symbol, often referred to as the Cross of Hermes:

The Cross of Hermes

The intersecting triangles at the base echo the alchemical motto, "As above, so below." This Hermetic dictum reminds us that we are microcosms of the macro-cosm, like fractals of a unified whole.

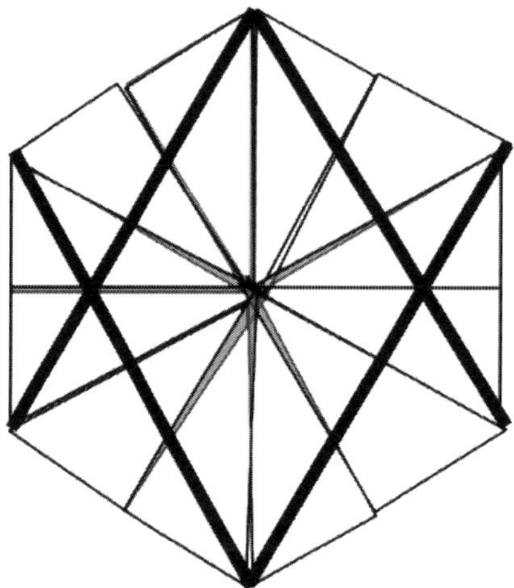

The Cross of Hermes within
the Geometry of the Triangle of Isis.

The upper numeral 4 is the sacred number of Hermes and represents the four directions and the union of the four elements: the sacred Union. The resulting square-ness in alchemical terms represents the physical body as the house of the soul (with four walls) as well as the vessel or golden cup in alchemical terms.[12] Apuleius symbolized our physical body as the alchemical vessel with the theme of the Box of Beauty. The box reminds us that eternal beauty does not exist in nature or in personal relationships. There is always an ugly side. Falling asleep is the state of being enamored with the beauty of matter—the great seduction. At the late point in the story where Psyche looks inside the box, she receives a mystical secret and falls asleep to the world. She transcends the opposites as she has proven she is in love with Love.

The microcosm is our inner Hero journeying back, like the prodigal son or daughter, to the macrocosm of Universe. It may also inform us that Earthly love is only a reflection of a higher spiritual Love or that we are a part of the Universe (the One) rather than separate. Separation is only a belief. On a more general level it may express the interconnectedness of all things. It does have one thing in common with Isis and that is the geometry of the Twin- or Star-Tetrahedron. One of the symbols of Isis is the eight-pointed star:

The Eight-Pointed Star of Venus

The Star-Tetrahedron in three-dimensions contains eight vertices or "stars."

The Interlaced Triangles Contain Eight Points or Vertices.

The Star-Tetrahedron is essentially two triangles interlaced. One triangle faces upwards and the other points downwards, as in the Cross of Hermes.

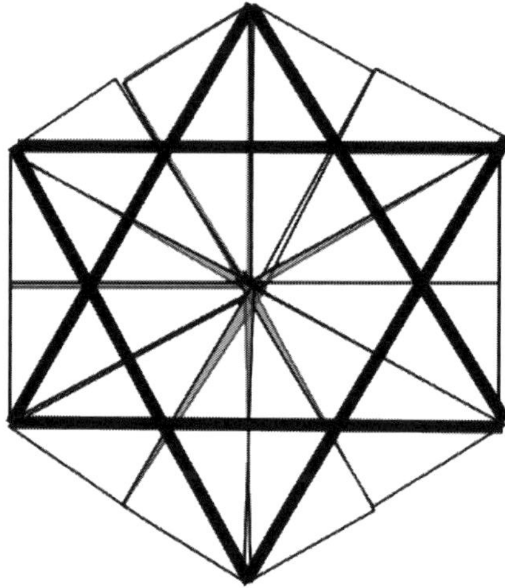

The Star-Tetrahedron fits within the Star of Isis.

There are also four components of the transformation process. The first two components can be viewed as Eros and Psyche representing the duality of mind-brain consciousness versus heart-consciousness. We also have a third energy, the friction and challenges of our life experiences. Our everyday experiences seem to be at odds with our innate desire for bonding and wanting to feel whole and complete. There is a saying that God purposely created the world imperfect; otherwise, we would become attached to our physical existence and not want to return to Her. The fourth element is the invisible guide that came to Psyche's rescue at every turn. It is that small voice of wisdom we hear when we are still, calm, and receptive to the Song. The Song is calling us back to Union with itself, creating disappointments for us on the one hand and then guiding us on the other. This is the goal of the courtship and ultimate Royal Wedding. This is why Hermaphroditus is associated with the institution of marriage and why the number 4 is the luckiest day to have a wedding.

The four walls symbolized in the Cross of Hermes represent the four stages in alchemy. The four stages aim to distill the duality of our nature into a unity or wholeness. This is the battle of our Higher Self versus our lower self. Moreover, the opposing four elements provide an ideal metaphor for this process of uniting the incompatible forces of Nature. Since the ultimate goal is a unity or wholeness, the circle represents the achievement of the goal. Oneness or Wholeness is therefore represented by the alchemist's distillation process whereby the gross and impure becomes the pure and subtle One. The man and woman (Eros and Psyche) in the figure below signify the hermaphrodite or alchemical union of the opposites.

Emblema XXI of Michael Maier's 1618 Atalanta fugiens.
'Here followeth the Figure conteyning all the secrets of the Treatise both great & small'.

In *Psychology and Religion,* Jung described the four alchemical stages in psychological terms.[13] He explained that in the first stage we naively participate in our environment without questioning. This is Psyche going along with whatever her father tells her. It is also Eros running around and acting out in a juvenile manner. During the second stage, when thinking and reasoning develop, we become aware of duality and the tension of relationships, of being criticized and criticizing others. This is Psyche listening to the opinions of her sisters and Eros falling in love with Psyche behind his mother's back. We can also become critical of the religious or philosophical beliefs we inherited. This can lead to the third stage where we begin to "see" a different reality than the one we inherited from societal beliefs and limitations. This is the level of insight and a growing awareness, or attaining a higher state of consciousness and rediscovery of the idea of Unity. However, our expanded awareness is still within the scope of mind-brain or ego consciousness and remains subject to our conditioned beliefs. Because we have no way to validate our new insights, we remain in the field of faith. We may try to share our intuition with friends and family, but then we risk their disbelief and criticism and fall back to our conditioned approach. On the other hand, if we can differentiate our conditioned beliefs from our insights, we become aware of an expanded field of revelations contained within the unseen matrix of Universal consciousness. This is the concept of *gnosis,* where we experience one or more aspects of the mysterious unknown through faculties that lie beyond the intellect.

Somewhere between the third stage and the fourth stage, we run into a kind of arrested development. Jung described the three as a defective quaternity or, at best, a stepping-stone towards the fourth.[14] In this case, we also begin to "see" aspects of ourselves we would rather not know about. Consequently, we may simply deny those parts of ourselves, run off into a fantasy, or blame others. Either way, we are prevented from progressing to the fourth stage.

The step from three to four requires that we face unpleasant insights. Jung referred to this as confronting our Shadow. The integration of our shadow side is mythologically characterized by the Hero's descent into the underworld. The lunar-myth portrays this transformational step as the Moon descending below the horizon in the night sky. Psychologically, it represents a process of integrating our insights with our daily lives without using our inner transformative work as an excuse to avoid the world. All of our hidden "shadow" elements are distilled and their sediment, that which no longer serves us, is released. This is the stage where Psyche is further purified and Eros descends after her. It is the final transformation of Eros, leading him to the approval and integration of Jupiter, his father.

Psyche and Eros emerge from the underworld with forgiveness in their hearts. There is no ill will towards Venus or Jupiter. At some point in our lives, we have to let go of the past and all our hurts and perceived failures and recognize them and thank them for the transformative roles they played. Most often, this is a distillation of our relationships with our mother or father from old and negative past memories. Facing the deepest and darkest aspects of our selves is scary and requires that we enter into the "belly of the whale." Jung said it is only here that one can find the "treasure hard to attain."[15]

The fear sometimes arises in the uncertainty of who we will become when we emerge from inside the whale and are no longer our old self. However, it is in this stage that we begin to overthrow the mind and its negative thinking, which has been controlling our lives. We have now given control back to heart-consciousness and its connection to Universal "knowing." Hence, the arrival at the fourth stage is a union with the One. This is the difference between living on the surface of our heart and living from within its depth. The Gnostic figure Maria Prophetissa said of this process, "Out of the One comes two, two becomes three, and out of the third comes the One as the fourth."

The number 4 in the Cross of Hermes contains two crosses. The one on the right looks more like a traditional Gnostic cross, while the one that incorporates the number 4 has the proportions of what we think of as the Christian cross. The cross refers to the concept of the Unity possible by integrating the fourth stage: overcoming the duality imposed on us by mind-consciousness. The central cross is proportional to the human body where the intersection corresponds to the human heart. The alchemical stage where we first realize there is something beyond our everyday life is the "nigredo" stage, where our former conscious perspective is blackened out.[16] This is where the shadow challenges first emerge. From here comes the "green" aspect of alchemy, suggesting that when we emerge from the shadow life begins anew. The Green Lion is a common alchemical symbol for this stage, as it suggests a triumph and acquisition of a limitless energy. The goddess Isis, who transformed the Golden Ass back to Lucius, wore green garlands interlaced with flowers. This is the "greenness" or ever-green, which continues to live and give life. It is a symbol of re-birth and transformation in the manner of the butterfly emerging from the darkness of the cocoon.

Green is nature's color and, as we saw earlier, is associated with the Heart Chakra. It symbolizes harmony, creativity, and abundance. The light frequency of green is in the neighborhood of 528 THz. The number 528 is coincidently related to the definition of the mile at 5,280 feet and harmonically relates to the diameter of the Moon, Earth, Sun, and the number of seconds in a day. When Psyche listened to the "green reed of sweet music," the inner guiding voice of her heart, she was able to complete all of the nearly impossible tasks set out for her by the shadow.

Love, represented by Eros, is the universal principle that holds all the atoms and molecules of the world together. Love is the unifying means that binds the opposite elements. Plato said the opposing elements explain our connection to the One. In *Timaeus*, Plato says nothing is visible or tangible in spacetime without fire and earth.[17] He then reminds us that these two opposing elements cannot come together without a unifying third. We can imagine this bonding force as the greening energy of Nature and the vibration of the Song. In terms of Eros and Psyche, it is a bonding of a lesser quality; a more carnal form of love:

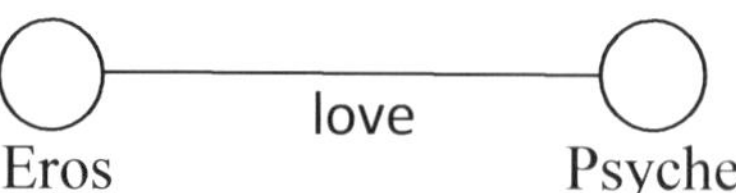

Plato, aware that something must bond the elements to heaven, adds a fourth binding force from the hand of the creator, Love (with a capital L):

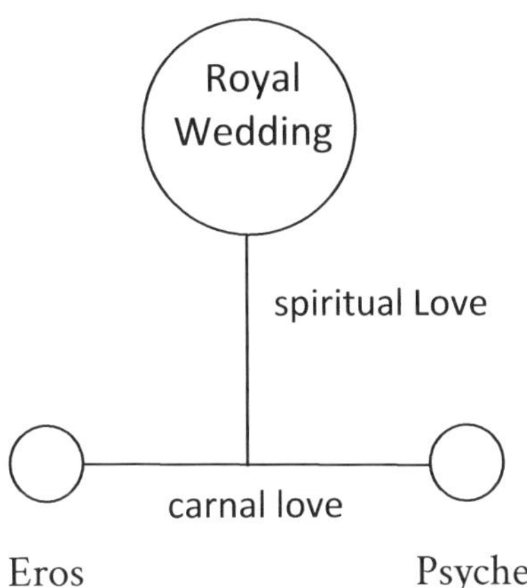

The transformation from carnal love to spiritual Love is represented in the story of *The Golden Ass* when the Goddess Isis directs her Priest to give Apuleius a wreath of roses (symbolic of Divine Love, not lust).[18] When Apuleius eats the roses he is transformed back into a human being.

Jung examined Plato's idea of the number four with a diagram showing Time as the fourth dimension:

Time, Jung said, is the immeasurable (relative at best), binding unseen force, needed for the characters in spacetime to interact.[19] The Fourth is the Unseen One guiding and activating the elements along the journey back to itself. It communicates in the language of symbols, dreams, numbers, and synchronistic events that inform us of its existence and ever-present guidance. If we surrender our ego-centered thinking and learn to extract the essence of our experiences with matter, we open ourselves to the reconciling forces of Nature. The story of Eros and Psyche fits the dual pyramid, quaternio scheme Jung presented in *Aion*:

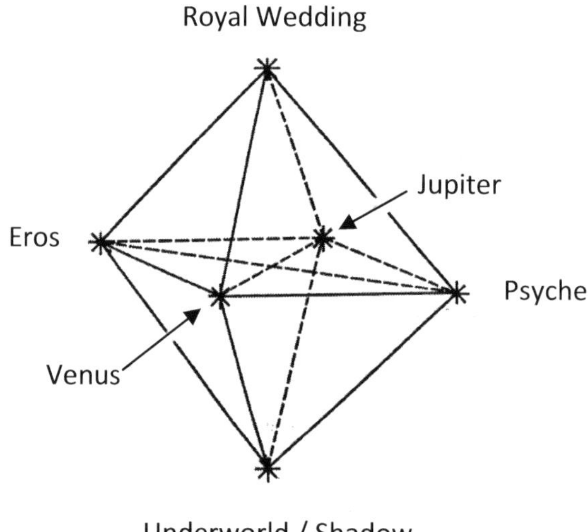

Venus is the Terrible Mother, who influences and challenges both the immature Eros and the naïve Psyche. She represents Soul working to mature the spirit ensnared in matter and bring 'her' back to spiritual/Self-awareness. Jupiter is the Great Father working to release matter from spirit by sublimating physical love to spiritual Love. He is the disapproving father of Eros, whose blessing is the ultimate obstacle between the union of Eros and Psyche. Psyche is spirit caught in the web of matter. Her energy naturally tends to flow upwards towards spiritual Union. Eros is consciousness solidified as matter (*maya*).

Another way to view the schematic is through the tertiary aspects of the tetrahedron:

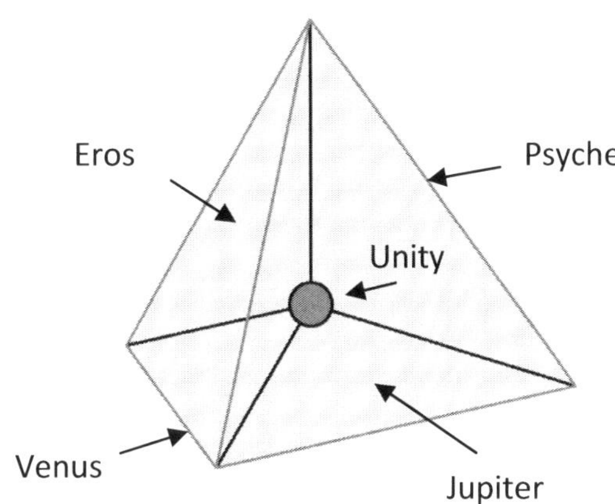

Each of the four faces of the tetrahedron is an isosceles triangle with three 60-degree angles. Each triangle face, therefore, contains 180 degrees (60° + 60° + 60°). When adding the degrees of all four faces we arrive at 720 degrees (180° x 4). The number 720 is a harmonic of the heart, which beats 72 times per minute. This indicates that the heart is at the center of the transformative process. It connects us to the unseen Unity through number.

Number bridges the two realms, the seen and unseen, because it represents the general structure of psychic and physical energy motions in nature and provides the key to the mysterious language of unitary existence.[20] The Divine marriage, the Royal Union, denotes the harmonious coming together of the cosmic rhythms—the Song.

Jung suggested that the zodiac is also the symbol of wholeness as the twelve months divide into four trimesters.[21] There are three months in each of the four seasons. This may explain why Apuleius began the story of *Eros & Psyche* in book four of the novel. Recall how the story takes Psyche through four cycles of the Moon waxing and waning. From one cycle to another, Psyche goes through a complete evolutionary transformation. Similarly, our life experiences offer us many microcosmic evolutionary cycles. We experience daily cycles, monthly cycles, annual cycles, and others as large as the orbit of Saturn. We can break our lives down into childhood, adolescence, adulthood, and old age. This is the reason we sometimes feel like we are experiencing the same problem repeatedly. Yet, we are able to respond to each similar problem with more wisdom. Hopefully, in time we will outgrow the problem, realize and digest its lessons, and then prepare ourselves for the next adventure.

NOTES:

1. Apuleius adapted the story from a Greek original of which the author's name is said to be Lucius of Patrae (the name of the lead character and narrator).

2. Marie-Louise von Franz, *Apuleius' Golden Ass*, (Washington DC: Spring Publications, 1970), p. I. 3.

3. Plato, *Cratylus*, 398 d.

4. I. Taylor, "The Myth of Cupid and Psyche," *The Academy*, June 18, 1887, No. 789.

5. Ibid.

6. Marie-Louise von Franz, *Apuleius' Golden Ass*, (Spring Publications, 1970), p. IX.10

7. Apuleius, *The Golden Ass,* Trans. W. Adlington [1566], (Horace Liveright, 1930, p. 248.

8. Marie-Louise von Franz, *Apuleius' Golden Ass*, (Washington, DC: Spring Publications, 1970), p. X.3.

9. Ibid, p. X.5.

10. Ibid, p. XII.2.

11. E. A. Wallis Budge, *The Gods of the Egyptians,* Vol. 1, p. 415.

12. Carl Jung, *Psychology and Alchemy*, Bollingen Series XX, (Princeton, NJ: Princeton University Press 1977), par. 338.

13. Carl Jung, *Psychology and Religion*, Bollingen Series XX, (Princeton, NJ: Princeton University Press, 1969).

14. Carl Jung, *Aion, Researches into the Phenomenology of the Self*, Vol. IX Part II, Bollingen Series XX, (Princeton, NJ: Princeton University Press), par. 351.

15. Carl Jung, *Psychology and Alchemy*, Bollingen Series XX, (Princeton, NJ: Princeton University Press, 1977), par. 438.

16. Marie-Louise von Franz, *Apuleius' Golden Ass*, (Washington, DC: Spring Publications, 1970), p. X.7.

17. Plato, *Timaeus*, par. 31 c-d.

18. Joseph Campbell, *The Power of Myth*, (New York: Anchor Books, 1991), p. 223-224

19. Carl Jung, *Aion, Researches into the Phenomenology of the Self*, Vol. IX Part II, Bollingen Series XX, (Princeton, NJ: Princeton University Press, 1979), par. 397.

20. Marie-Louise von Franz, *Number and Time*, (Evanston, IL: Northwestern University Press, 1974), p. 284.

21. Carl Jung, *Aion, Researches into the Phenomenology of the Self*, Vol. IX Part II, Bollingen Series XX, (Princeton, NJ: Princeton University Press 1979), par. 351.

CHAPTER 5

From the Many is One

> The goal of life is to make your heartbeat
> match the beat of the universe,
> to match your nature with Nature.
> ~ Joseph Campbell

My heart finds comfort in relationships, which is one reason I think of myself as a romantic. But three marriages have taught me that when we are not in tune with ourselves, we end up arguing and picking fights with our spouses. Perhaps in confrontation we are seeking to calibrate our heart to the vibration of true love. I say "true" love to distinguish our carnal concept from an unconditional type of love. When the saints and mystics say "God is love," I wonder if my heart is searching for the rhythm of that love. Perhaps all of our searching for love is actually a remembering from our heart of a unique kind of Cosmic Vibration. Maybe Dante's "dark wood," the theater we call our life, is an emanation, like the *New Testament* "Word," creating waves that ripple on the surface of God's coffee cup. Myths give us images of created things, like the Cosmic Egg, arising out of the sea of vibration.[1] These vibrating things then act out one part or another on the surface or, like a mirage, seduce unsuspecting, but amorous, sailors into their depths.

The small rippling waves on the water's surface, like a living, breathing, ever-changing holographic field, act on our senses to convince us of our reality that is our life, or a part of it. However, it may not be the complete picture of our reality, no more than our dreams are capable of including our awake-self reality above the surface of our dreamscapes.

We may never know what first bumped into the table that caused God's cup to wobble and consequently set this whole dark wood production into motion. The world's religions seem to agree it was God, but we don't know if he or she was pushed. The mystics tell us there is a Source of the vibration, the way a radio appears to contain music that we "know" comes from a distant, yet invisible, source.

We can imagine a basic vibration with just enough rippling effect to give the Cosmic Orchestra something to tune to. It might actually relate to the number 7, the number venerated by Lucius, the Golden Ass. It might not be such a coincidence that 7 is the number of days in the Genesis creation story. There are 7 heavens, 7 deadly sins, 7 virtues, 7 seas, 7 blessings, 7 colors of the rainbow, 7 chakras, and "seven sweet kisses of Venus." The human gestation period of 266 days is harmonically related to the number 7 (7 times 38 equals 266).

The number 7 is one of the sides of the Lunar Triangle of Isis, the one we discovered from the Osiris myth. The Lunar Triangle of Isis has sides equal to 7, 13 and 14.76. For those who are more visual, the "Eye of Horus" stands as a reminder:

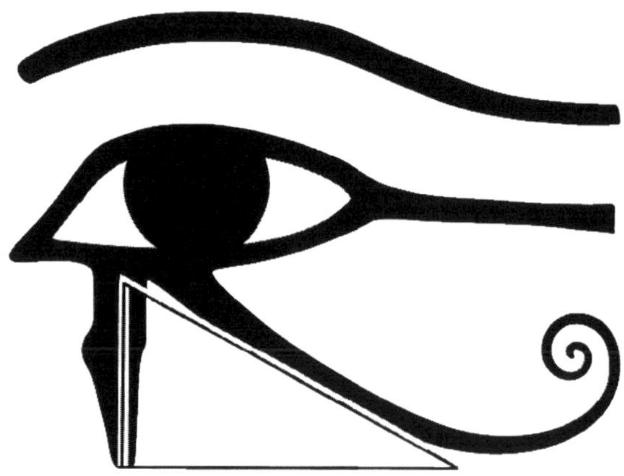

The Lunar Triangle of Isis is found
within the Geometry of the Eye of Horus
(Image by Jeff Dahl)

The number 3 is the number of the triangle (3 sides). It is also the base of the heart number 72 (3 x 24). The number 24 represents our concept of time in hours. The heart beats 4,320 times per hour. The frequency or note of A in Pythagorean Tuning is 432hz, which is based on a tuning ratio of 3:2.[2] The note of A tuned to 432hz is believed to line up to natural patterns, particularly to the resonance of our heart and emotional body.[3] The numbers 4 + 3 + 2 equal 9, the number of completion or wholeness. The numbers 4, 3, and 2 can also be presented as ratios of a whole circle as follows:

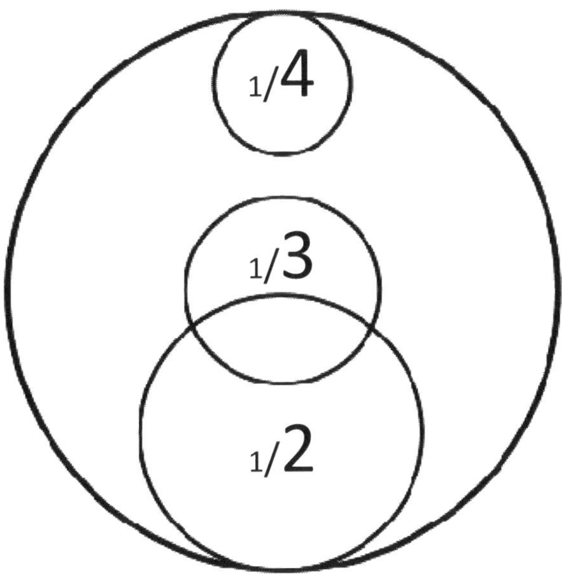

The Heart Number 4320 Expressed Geometrically

When we express the fractions ¼, ⅓, and ½ as decimals we arrive at the number 1.08, which is harmonically related to the numbers 108 and 1080:

$$\frac{1}{4} = .25$$
$$\frac{1}{3} = .33$$
$$\frac{1}{2} = \underline{.50}$$
$$1.08$$

According to some ancient schools of spiritual thought, there are 108 names for the Divine Mother. The radius of the Moon is 1,080 miles and the heart beats 1,080 times every fifteen minutes. Fifteen minutes is a quarter of an hour, just as there are four main phases of the Moon every 7 days (Full, Half, New, and Half again). In the story of *The Golden Ass*, Apuleius is transformed by the Great Mother in the form of Isis, who is also a Moon Goddess. Isis, as the Great or Divine Mother, is equivalent to Aphrodite, whom we encountered in *Eros & Psyche* in her Terrible Mother form as the mother of Eros. The Terrible Mother, as an archetype, is the negative side of the Mother Archetype. Jung said the Terrible Mother connotes anything dark: the world of the dead and anything that devours, seduces, and poisons.[4] In *Eros & Psyche*, she was Venus who put Psyche to impossible tasks and sent her to Hades to collect the Box of Beauty. Venus, as the Terrible Mother, imprisoned her son, Eros, in an effort to maintain control over him. Jung distinguished the traumatic effects of the Terrible Mother, as those characteristics that the mother actually possesses, from those which the mother only seems to possess as archetypal projection on the part of the child.[5] In other words, it can happen that our mom isn't really that horrible. She may do or say something horrible accidently, but the archetypes made her do it.

The Great Mother and the Terrible Mother are dual energies of the same archetype. She is the nurturing mother who looks after our every need and then deprives us until we have no choice but to jump out of the nest on our own. Eros and Psyche would not have embarked on their journey towards individuation without the torment inflicted on them by Venus.

In the end, the Loving Mother and the Terrible Mother will have helped shape us in ways that are essential to our evolution. From this perspective, we can forgive our mother for not being what she was not capable of being. She was either under the trance of an archetype—our archetype—or she was herself a daughter of a Terrible Mother. As Eric Neumann writes, "The hero is the person who overcomes the Terrible Mother."[6]

We overcome the Terrible Mother when we thankfully allow her to rip our ego-personalities to shreds. In this way, we find a new relationship with the Great Mother archetype—a relationship with our natural, authentic Self, the one that hasn't been molded by society, habit, and custom.

The Mother Archetype, the one forcing us towards personal growth, is naturally found within the geometry produced by the heart number 4320. We see this more clearly when we first connect the 4320 circles to the triangles of the Star-Tetrahedron:

The Heart Number 4320 is the Foundation of
the Twin Triangles of the Star-Tetrahedron.

The Lunar Triangle of Isis, The Great Mother, is found within the Star-Tetrahedron:

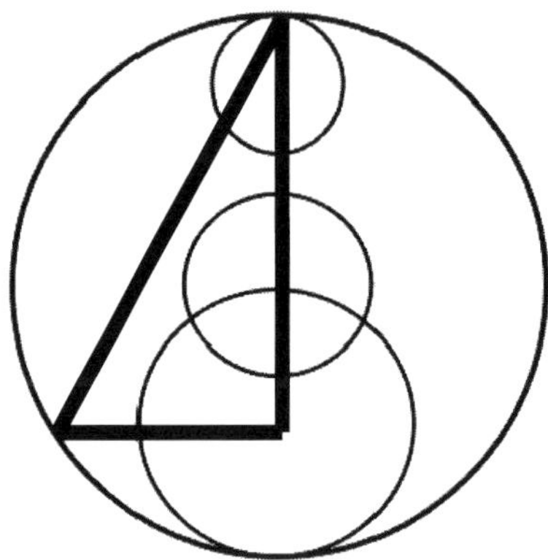

The Lunar Triangle of Isis within the 4320 Heart Geometry

The heart number 4320 and the Star-Tetrahedron are the foundation of the geometry of Metatron's Cube, which is also derived from the Flower of Life. Metatron's Cube is a classic sacred geometric pattern comprised of 13 equal circles with lines from the center of each circle extending to the centers of the other 12 circles.

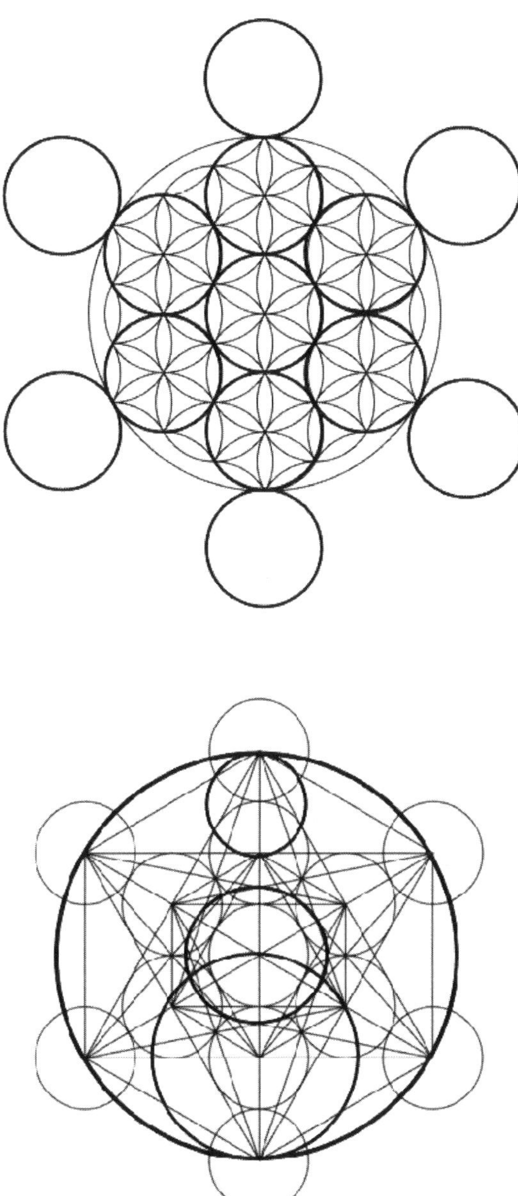

Metatron is considered an archangel in Judaism and in Christian folklore. Accordingly, he was Enoch, son of Noah, who was turned into an angel. According to Heinrich Cornelius Agrippa in his *Three Books of Occult Philosophy* (1533), Meratiron (Metatron) was equated to the vibrating Essence and Intelligence of the Divinity, and "fills the whole Universe, both through the circumference and center."[7] He was the messenger of wisdom—heart wisdom. Agrippa quoted our friend Apuleius, who was more than a novelist; he was also an insightful philosopher. One of his most philosophical books was *De mundo* ("On the World"), which no longer exists. Agrippa quoted him as saying, "There is but one God and one power, yet he is named by diverse names."[8] Agrippa, referring to Kabbalah tradition, said there are seventy-two (72) names of the Divine Essence (Cosmic Song) as certain properties, or archetypes, which flow to us for our benefit.[9] Agrippa referred to Metatron as "the prince of faces, whose duty it is to bring others to the face of the prince."[10] By "face" Agrippa is referring to the faces of the zodiac. Metatron's Cube can be seen as a matrix that utilizes the zodiac and its twelve stages of development as a tool for connecting us to our innate intelligence.

The numeric relationships found in the heart number 4320 add an uncanny dimension to its mystique. For example, the number 4320 is in synch with time and the Sun. The heart beats 8,640 times in two hours. There are 86,400 seconds in a day. The diameter of the Sun is approximately 864,000 miles. The Sun has its own rhythm if you consider its 11-year solar flare cycle; 11 times 72 equals 792 and 7,920 miles is the diameter of the Earth.

In half an hour, the heart beats 2,160 times (72 x 30), which is the diameter of the Moon. The numbers 3 and 11, therefore, connect the heart to the Sun, Earth, and Moon. The ratio of 3:11 is .2727, which we can round to .273. It takes the Moon 27.3 days to orbit the Earth in respect to the fixed stars.

The number 11 is considered a sacred number. Lucias's *The Golden Ass* is composed of 11 books. If you are not sure about the date of last year's Full Moon, just go back exactly 365 days and add 11. I don't know when this will ever come up in a conversation, but it is an interesting astronomical phenomenon. Astronomers don't think it is very magical, only the difference between our 365-day Sun year and the lunar year of 354 days (365 – 354 = 11). The Sun and Moon have this wonderful love dance between them: the Moon chasing, the Sun hiding. The number 11 also follows the number 10, which gives a sense of completion: 1 thru 10, and we start counting over again. Therefore, the number 11 announces a new beginning or a new evolutionary cycle. Without the Sun there would be no life on Earth, which is probably why 3,960 (the radius of Earth) divided by 360° (the archetypal number for wholeness) equals 11. This informs us that Earth is the evolutionary stage on which the Hero's Journey is acted out.

With the numbers 3 and 11, we get a glimpse of how number relates to everything in the Universe: heart (3 x 24); Earth (11 x 720); Moon (3 x 720); Sun (3 x 72 x 4). Therefore, we cannot avoid the conclusion that the heart is connected to the rhythm and number of the Universe, making it the portal by which we can communicate with the Cosmic Song.

I imagine that communicating with the Cosmic Song would give me insight into my Whole being. My mind has difficulty with the idea of Wholeness: the one who is one with the One. My mind always wants to know who is the One I'm supposed to want to be at one with. The thought of it is terrifying because it is a complete mystery and consequently my mind is happy to stay where it is—until my heart's agitation drives me to unrest, anxiety, depression, guilt, and on bad days, shame.

G. I. Gurdjieff, a spiritual teacher in the early- to mid-20th century, taught that most of us live our lives in a state of hypnotic "waking sleep." He also believed that it is possible to transcend to a higher state of consciousness and achieve our full human potential. Gurdjieff considered the circle to represent the process of unfoldment with the divisions around its circumference symbolizing the steps of the process of Self-discovery. These divisions can take the form of the twelve months of the zodiac or in the case of Gurdjieff, the Enneagram. Who we are within the circle is all our patterns of behavior. The church father Origen said we have more personalities within us than herds of cattle, herds of sheep and goats.[11] Jung echoed this sentiment when he said our "psyche is far from being a homogeneous unit—on the contrary, it is a boiling cauldron of contradictory impulses, inhibitions, and affects."[12] This is why, as Gurdjieff explained, we have so much trouble going on a diet. One of our personality affects thinks it is a good idea to lose some weight and vows to eat a half a grapefruit in the morning. By the time we arise and start breakfast, we find ourselves eating both halves of the grapefruit plus cereal, toast, and everything else we can find. The reason, he said, is clear: we didn't have a consensus of going on a diet from the other 999 personalities within us.

For the most part, we are unaware of the herds of wild animals within us until one or more gets their button pushed. We saw this happen to monk Tom when monk Bob pushed the scarcity button on one of monk Tom's subconscious personalities. Recall how one of Janet's personalities craved her father's attention and nurturing. There was also a personality affect in Christine's example that doubted itself to the point of creating worry and anxiety in the rest of her herd. These examples explain why Gurdjieff divided the human being into two parts: *essence* and *personality*.[13] Essence represents our true nature: who we are at the level of Unified or Whole Self.

Our personality is what Gurdjieff described as not really belonging to us because it has been acquired from the outside through parental and societal conditioning. The Attractor pulls us through life's challenges as the archetypes activate our negative personality behaviors and patterns so we can become aware of them and work to overcome their negative influences. In this way, the personality content within the circle motivates us towards an expanded realization of our Self that lies outside the circle. Buckminster Fuller reminded us that a circle has two sides. It has an inside and an outside. The inside of a circle is 360 degrees. The outside of a circle is also 360 degrees. Consequently, the Unified Self of essence and personality must be represented as 720 degrees (360 + 360). And, the number 720 is harmonically related to the average number of heart beats per minute: 72.

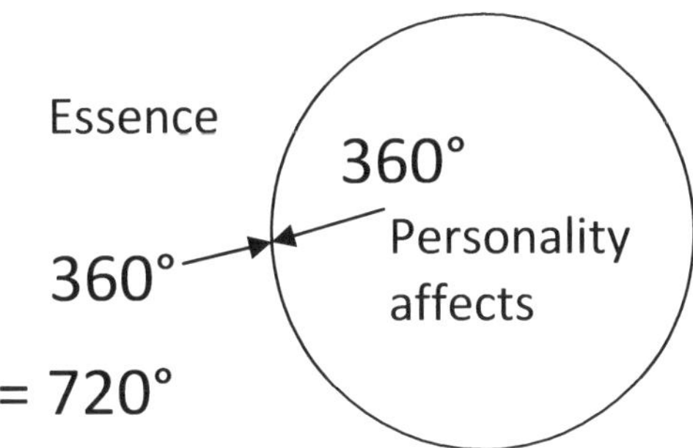

The realization of our true essence happens when our personality affects become passive and essence becomes active. It requires a loosening of our grip on what we believe about ourselves: our ego-identity that is tangled up with others' expectations. Untangling our essence from our personality requires conscious awareness of our conditioned behavior. This is not a simple task, as most of our conditioned responses are both habituated and subconscious. Heart-consciousness is connected to our essence and can bring our subconscious patterns to light, thereby helping us transform them.

The number 4320 reduces to the number 9: $4 + 3 + 2 + 0 = 9$. The number 9 is the symbol of completion or Unity. It can be seen as the ultimate goal of the Attractor. In other words, it is the Attractor and its archetypal dynamisms that lead humanity on a path of evolutionary consciousness. Numbers themselves have a qualitative influence over our life's remedial experiences, with 9 as the achievement of re-unification with our higher Self. The journey to wholeness was symbolized by G. I. Gurdjieff in the Enneagram. The Enneagram symbol relies on the trinity of 3 - 6 - 9 and incorporates the heart geometry of 4320:

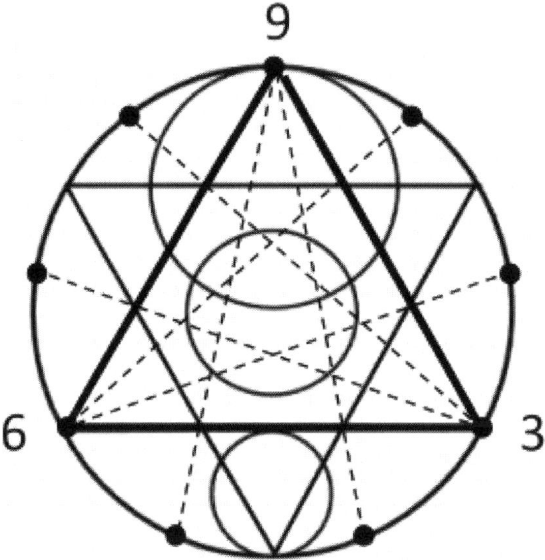

The Yin/Yang symbol represents Wholeness and Unity. The numbers 3 and 6 can be seen as representing each side of the Yin/Yang with 9 as the "S" curve oscillating between them.[14]

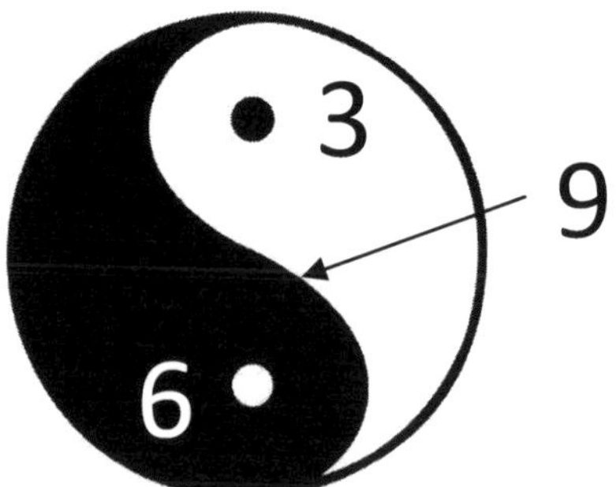

The oscillation that occurs between the 3 and 6 is the result of a doubling or octave of 3, which equals 6. Doubling 6 equals 12, and 1 + 2 = 3. Then 12 doubled equals 24, and 2 + 4 = 6. In this way, 3 and 6 go back and forth. We can also see that 3 cannot transform into wholeness (9) without 6 and vice versa. For example, if 3 forces its way onto 9, we get 3 + 9, which equals 12, and 12 is 1 + 2 = 3. Consequently, 3 turns back on itself without any progress towards wholeness. Likewise, 6 cannot integrate with wholeness (9) on its own as 6 + 9 = 15, and 1 + 5 = 6. This tells us that without the integration of our life experiences, both outwardly (6) and inwardly (3), we will not achieve wholeness (3 + 6 = 9). We can think of 9 as the Attractor or the Metatron archetype behind the dynamic energy flowing between the 3 and 6, with the ultimate purpose of bringing the opposites together (The Royal Wedding).

Similar to Gurdjieff's teachings, Scalar Heart Connection utilizes the transformative energy of the numbers 3, 6, and 9. Gurdjieff defined the number 3 as the *passive* element, 9 as the *neutralizing* element, and 6 as the *active* element. When the *active* element interacts with the *passive* element, with the help of the *neutralizing* element a specific result is achieved.[15] In terms of Scalar Heart Connection and the Hero's Journey, the number 3 represents the **Issue** at hand or the activated personality pattern, which generally shows up in our questionable behavior and negative mind-brain conditioned reactions. The number 9 represents the **Obstacle** or Negative Mind-brain conditioning that must be transcended. And the number 6 is the **Action** the Hero must take in order to accomplish his or her objective (the lesson of that particular stage, which is also an integration of our fractured personality-consciousness). The dynamics of our Issue, Obstacle, and Action are represented in the geometry of the 30 degree, 60 degree, and 90 degree triangle, as we discovered in the monk Tom and monk Bob story:

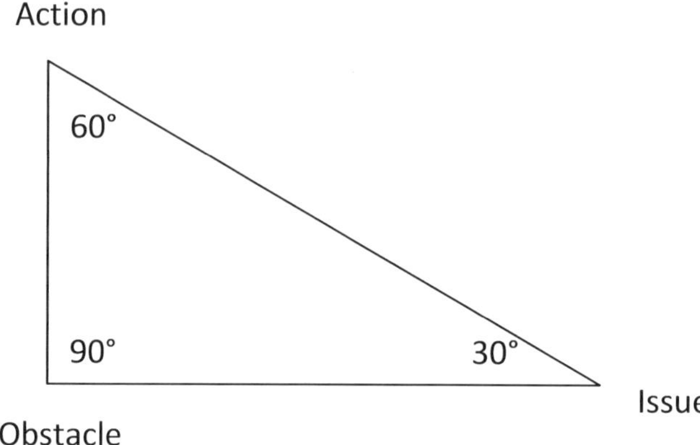

The 30-60-90 triangle is essentially the Lunar Triangle of Isis. As we will see later, this triangle is the key to communicating with the wisdom of our heart. It will bring to conscious awareness the true nature of our symptoms (Issue), what Negative Mind-brain Conditioned Belief is holding us back (Obstacle), and what our heart recommends we do about it (Action).

We are not alone on this journey. Every Hero's Journey has its Mentors. The Attractor is both the goal and the motivator of action. The Attractor also provides the Mentors, who help us along the way. Mentors often show up in our lives synchronistically. The portal to the intelligence of the Attractor lies within the heart. When we connect to the wisdom of our heart we are connecting to the dynamisms operating beyond spacetime. Our life's journey, seen as a process of Self-discovery, can be seen as a transcending spiral. This was the message for me in the pinecone I received as a gift at the family reunion: that the Fibonacci 3-6-9 series results in a golden mean (phi) spiral that fits exactly within the 4320 geometry of the heart (Metatron's Cube): 3, 6, 9, 15, 24, 39, 63, 102, 165, 267, 432. [16]

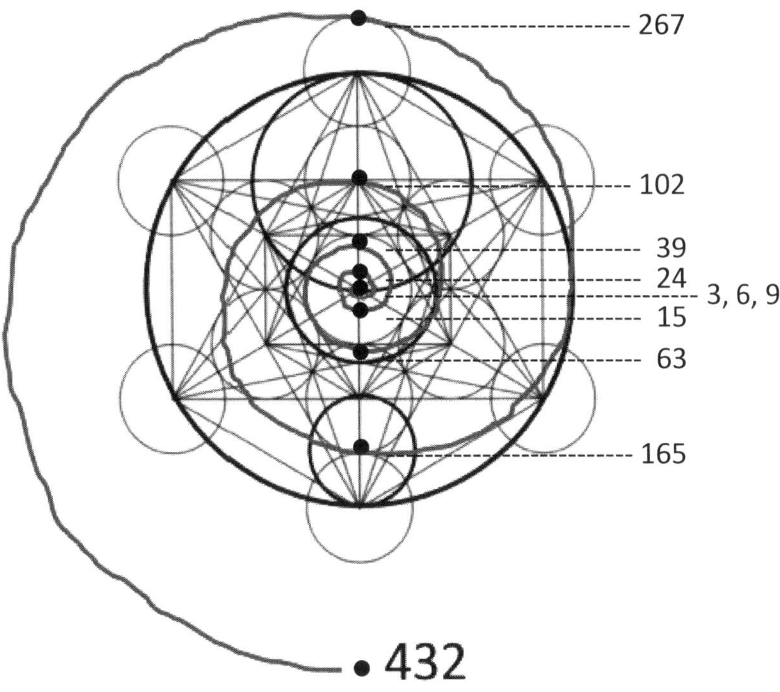

The Spiral of Life as a Journey from Personality to Essence
is Related to the Heart Number 4320.

The synchronicity of the pinecone revealed to me the spiral heart geometry that encourages us to endure life's challenges by learning to see them as opportunities for personal growth. Without suffering and obstacles there would be no forward progress along the spiral, no motivation to change. This doesn't mean we are here only to suffer. It means our life experiences teach us to find and connect with our full creative and joyful potential. It is a matter of waking up, as Gurdjieff points out, to our true and limitless being.

The Spiral of Life is an unfolding, directed by the archetypes. It serves as a metaphor for our evolutionary cycles and our journey through life's experiences for the purpose of reconnecting to heart-consciousness and the Song. The Attractor (Metatron) is pulling us towards the singularity of Unity with our higher Self.

Therefore, it would be more accurate to show the Spiral of Life three-dimensionally as ascending from the zodiac to a singular point in the middle:

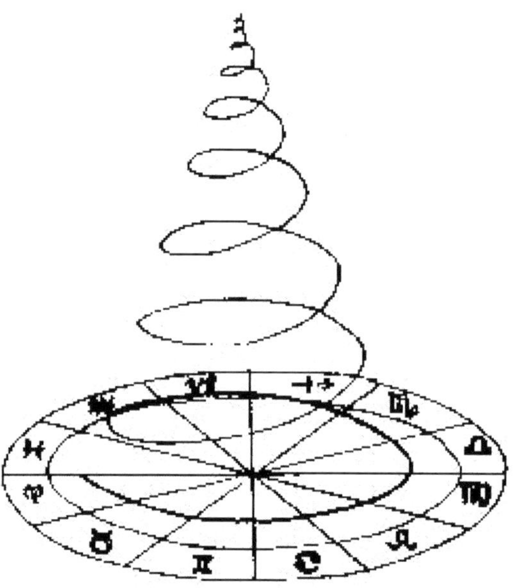

The Spiral of Life Journey Around the
Zodiac to the Singularity of Self

The zodiac is also a *mandala*. The word "mandala" is Sanskrit, meaning "circle." It is a spiritual and ritual symbol in both Hinduism and Buddhism used to represent the Universe. The word "mandala" has become a generic term for any diagram or geometric pattern that represents the cosmos. Jung felt that ultimately all mandalas point to the center or to the unity of the Self, while the fragmentary parts of our illusory or false self scamper to the outer edges. He realized through the mandala that all of his experiences had led back to a single point.[17] That single point represents the goal of our journey: to return to wholeness and live in harmony with the infinity of the Cosmic Song.

Harmony Mandala by Jo Blaine Thomas

The mandala has its place in mythology. For example, the Goddess Hestia, the Keeper of the Flame, the Fire of Knowledge and Wisdom, stands in the center of the hearth, the Great Round. Hestia's round hearth contains the sacred fire at its center. The Great round is in the shape of a mandala. Hestia's story is a living myth as it is ongoing. The ending is yet to be written. It is the story of how the feminine spirit of Hestia re-emerges from behind the patriarchal veil of reason, control, and oppression and re-ignites the flame of feeling, intuition, and the heart-felt inter-connection within ourselves and with each other. This is the adventure we are all taking collectively as we learn to reconnect with each other and with the global community.

Both globally and individually, we often find ourselves on the outer edges of our inner mandala, where we encounter conflicts and problems in our lives.

The more the archetypes shake our floor, the greater the urge becomes to seek comfort in the center of the Great Round. Often, as soon as we have seemingly solved one problem, another wave of dissatisfaction begins to take over. In this way, we are never satisfied. This process leads us from one layer along the spiral of unfoldment to the next. For many, this can be a cause of great anxiety and restlessness. Not aware of the process, we may try to cover up our inner conflicts with a variety of antidepressants and other mind-numbing substances. The problem with the numbing approach is that it only causes the unconscious to attempt to reach the individual by even more drastic means, such as an accident, loss of a job, divorce, or illness.

The Ancients assigned different characteristics to each of the twelve sections of the zodiac mandala. Each of the twelve months represents a stage of growth, which corresponds to one of the four seasons. This cycle can feel like a treadmill at times. We often feel like we have done a lot of personal work only to find ourselves back in similar situations repeatedly. Family holiday get-togethers can sometimes trigger responses in us that feel uncomfortably close to how we reacted in childhood. Sometimes we can anticipate the turn of events: who is going to say what to whom and how the family dynamics will erupt, all seemingly scripted beforehand. The truth is, each time we encounter a similar and unpleasant situation there is at least some small lesson we have gleaned from the previous experience. Each time we feel that we have returned to a similar situation, we may notice if we look carefully, that we have a higher, more aware, perspective. Think of this circular pattern as a spiral: the spiral of unfoldment. In this manner, we can imagine we are experiencing a personal crisis from at least one stair landing above where we were the last go-around.

Along the spiral journey, the Hero will encounter issues that keep him or her stuck in one stage or another. In order for the Hero to continue, it is necessary to overcome an obstacle. Once the Hero identifies the obstacle, they must then take some action in order to overcome the obstacle, which then resolves the issue so that the Hero may continue. The Triple Spiral motif from Newgrange, Ireland, best represents this idea of Issue, Obstacle, and Action.

The Triple Spiral representing Issue, Obstacle, and Action

NOTES:

1. The Egyptian primordial and formless God laid an egg in the primeval waters and from the egg emerged the first manifested form of God, who in turn created or emanated Ra-Tem-Nefertem, the carrier of the Divine Word or creative power.
2. The note of A at 432hz was a common tuning standard or "concert pitch" used to tune orchestras for a performance until the modern standard concert pitch of 440hz Was passed by the American Federation of Music in 1917 and by the U.S. Standards Bureau in 1922.
3. B.T. Collins, "The importance of 432Hz Music," http://omega432.com/432-music/the-importance-of-432hz-music
4. Carl Jung, *Symbols of Transformation*, Bollingen Series XX, (Princeton, NJ: Princeton University Press, 1990).
5. Carl Jung, *The Archetypes and the Collective Unconscious*, Bollingen Series XX, (Princeton, NJ: Princeton University Press, 1981), pp. 82-83.
6. Erich Neumann, *The Great Mother*, (Princeton, NJ: Princeton University Press, 1964), p. 168.
7. Henry Cornelius Agrippa, *Three Books of Occult Philosophy*, (San Bernardino, CA: Mystical World Reprints, 2012), p. 246.
8. Ibid.
9. Ibid. p. 248.
10. Ibid.
11. Marie-Louise von Franz, *Psyche & Matter*, (Boston: Shambhala Publications, 1992) p. 151. See Origen commentary on Leviticus 52.
12. Carl Jung, *The Archetypes and the Collective Unconscious*, Bollingen Series XX, (Princeton, NJ: Princeton University Press, 1981), pp. 82-83
13. G. I. Gurdjieff, *In Search of Being*, (Boston: Shambhala Publications, 2012), p. 39.
14. http://rense.com/rodinaerodynamics.htm (accessed June 21, 2014)
15. Ibid, p. 241.
16. The traditional Fibonacci Sequence begins with 1, 1, 2, 3, 5, 8… However, any sequence of numbers can be used as long as each subsequent number is the sum of the previous two.
17. Carl Jung, *Memories, Dreams, Reflections*, (New York: Vintage Books, 1989), p. 196.

CHAPTER 6

The Zodiac and the Matrix of Metatron

> There is the me I think is me and there is the me
> I portray to people around me, but like the Möbius coil
> without one side or the other,
> I am always what is inside my heart.
> ~ Indiana Jane Linsteadt

Throughout the story of *The Golden Ass*, Apuleius accounts for all the "faces" of the zodiac that were recognizable in his time:

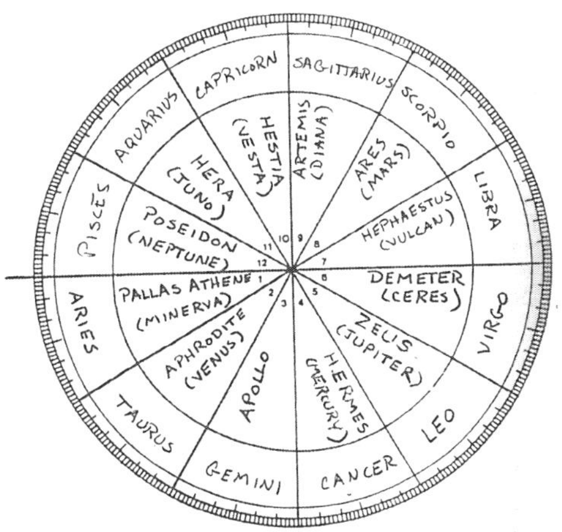

The Olympian Rulerships of the Zodiac.

In the story of *Eros & Psyche*, we saw the character of Venus in both her Aphrodite form and as the young maiden Psyche. Psyche's father consulted with the Oracle at Apollo before her marriage to the beast (Eros). Apuleius describes Eros with certain Mars qualities: wicked, with neither manners nor respect for the decencies, breaking up respectable homes, and so forth. Later, Venus introduces Vulcan as the father of Eros during her ranting about Eros falling in love with Psyche. Venus rants on about Eros's lack of respect for his stepfather Mars, accusing him of setting Mars after other women to make her jealous. After Venus sends Eros off to bring down Psyche she goes to the seashore to gloat, and at the touch of her rosy feet Neptune bobs up to the top of the waves along with his naughty wife with a lapful of aphrodisiac fish. Ceres and Juno show up later to help and save Psyche. Mercury is solicited to help Aphrodite find Psyche. Jupiter gives Psyche immortality at the end and they all live happily ever after. However, there are three faces missing from the story of *Eros & Psyche*: Diana, Minerva, and Vesta. Diana and Minerva make their way into other chapters, but Vesta (Greek: Hestia) is never directly mentioned.

Hestia's name means "hearth, fireplace, altar." The historian Cicero informed us: "The goddess whom they call Hestia. Her power extends over altars and hearths, and therefore all prayers and all sacrifices end with this goddess, because she is the guardian of the innermost things."[1] Hestia rejected the marriage proposal of Apollo, and swore herself to eternal virginity. In effect, she rejected Venus's passion for the physical and became her antithesis.[2] Hestia's eternal flame was hinted at in the lamp Psyche used to see the sleeping Eros. One of the Priests of Isis was also carefully described as holding a lamp. The careful exclusion of Hestia, after great care was taken to include all the other zodiac archetypes, draws attention to the symbolism of the lamp.

Von Franz explained that in mythology light symbolizes consciousness. And particularly, the light of a lamp represents that part of consciousness we can control. However, it seems that Psyche was unable to control her lamp, which von Franz said was due to the "burning" passion that the lamp also symbolized. In this sense, the lamp was the quintessential symbol for the whole story: Lucius's burning passion for power and sexual possession rather than seeking the deeper spiritual Love. Von Franz explained that Lucius must get "to know the goddess

Isis through personal experience and subordinating himself to the . . . mysteries of the soul."[3]

The faces of the zodiac wheel have mostly all changed or moved since the time of Apuleius. Additional planets have been discovered and incorporated. The new cast of characters is as follows:

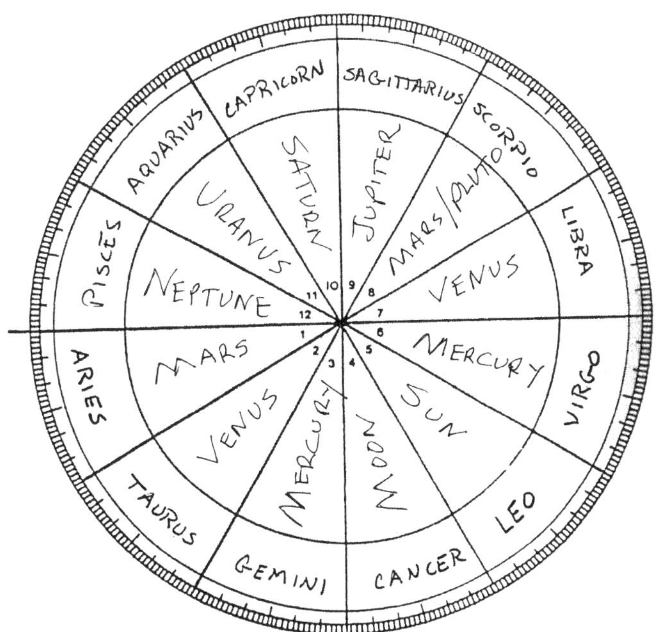

The zodiac can be divided into fourths,
which reflects the four phases of the Moon,
the four stages of alchemy, and the four seasons:

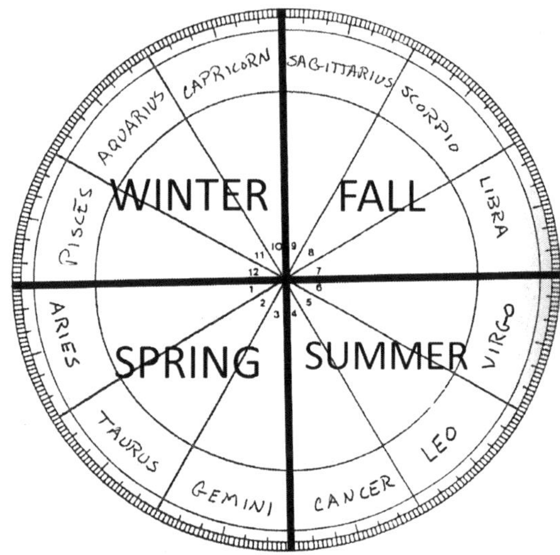

The planets have archetypal influences over the seven chakras or energy/emotional centers in the body:

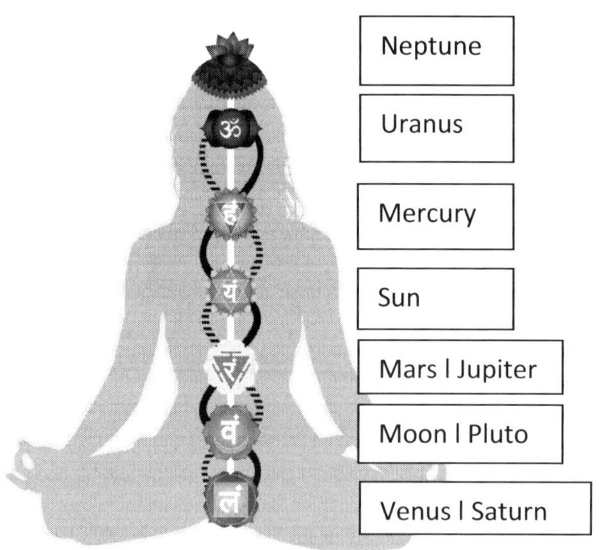

The word "chakra," derived from the Sanskrit word *"cakra"* meaning "wheel" or "turning," has its origin in Hindu texts. The word refers to the spiraling vortices of life force or cosmic energy found along the spinal column. These centers of bioenergetic activity emanate from the major nerve ganglia branching forward from the spinal column.[4] The chakras are also associated with major endocrine glands. Each chakra has its own unique frequency of vibration, harmonic pattern, and specific color, and each serves as an energy transformer providing sequentially stepped-down energy to various hormonal, physiological, and cellular processes in the body. [5, 6] The two flows of energy that comingle along the spine intertwine like the caduceus staff of Hermes:

The energy flow within the human body is a microcosm of a larger seasonal pattern of birth, transformation/growth, and death. The four phases of the Moon cycle are also analogous of the four seasons and the life cycle of plants. For example, the story of *Eros & Psyche* opens with Psyche as a newly planted seed in the dark soil of life. What nutrients the seed is able to extract from the soil determine whether it grows or stays dormant. Either we answer the Call to Adventure or we stay put in Dante's dark wood.

Under favorable circumstances, our seed will germinate in Spring and struggle towards the warmth of the Sun's rays bearing down on the topsoil. We can all relate to how our struggles with the obstacles of life serve to make us stronger. If or when we are successful in breaking through into the light above the surface, we begin to enjoy the warmth of the Summer Sun that provides our continued growth and development into green, fruit-bearing entities. Under the right environmental conditions (water, nutrients, sunlight) the fruit of our labors ripens just before the Harvest Moon marks the autumn of our life. The seeds we leave in the winter soil are the beginnings of new cycles of life and death—one dependent on the other.

Nature tends to repeat what works, so this same cycle exists in the human body. We find it in our digestive system, where the intestines sort out what is useful (nutrients) from what no longer serves us. The hepatic portal vein remarkably transports 95% of the bile salts back to the liver, where bile is recycled and used again to aid digestion. This area of absorption and elimination, like the seed in dark soil, is found at the Root or Earth Chakra, which is associated with our connection to the Earth and basic instincts needed for survival.

The next higher chakra is the Pelvis Chakra or Sacral Chakra, also known as the Water Chakra. The Water Chakra is the center associated with the womb, but also the kidneys. This is the center where imagination and creativity germinate and pour through our sense of being.[7] It is also an emotional center related to desire and sensory pleasures.

The next chakra is the Plexus Chakra (solar plexus), also called the Fire Chakra. It represents the fire or heat of the Sun. This is the center that fuels action and self-determination.

Once we are in full bloom and bearing fruit, we are in the Heart or Air Chakra, the center where we step into our sense of authentic identity in relation to the world.

Above the Heart center is the Throat Chakra, the center of creative expression—the harvest.

The Brow Chakra is the most active and open for those who have successfully born fruit and given their seeds back to the cycle of life. This is the stage of the Hero's Journey where the hero brings the gift of wisdom back to society for the benefit of humankind.

The full cycle of the zodiac houses and the Hero's Journey contains 12 stages. The only thing missing from the number 12 is the Hero. The number 13 is actually a better number to represent the Hero's Journey because it takes into account the Hero standing in the center. We can also think of the center as representing the goal of the Hero: Unity. The number 13 is also the number of Metatron's Cube, with 12 circles along the circumference surrounding the 1 circle in the middle.

Earlier, we saw how the geometry of the heart number 4320 is essentially the geometry of Metatron's Cube:

Metatron's Cube provides the template of the zodiac, where we can map out the twelve stages of the Hero's Journey. The zodiac, as an evolutionary symbol, incorporates the planetary influences similar to the "Helpers" in *Eros and Psyche*:

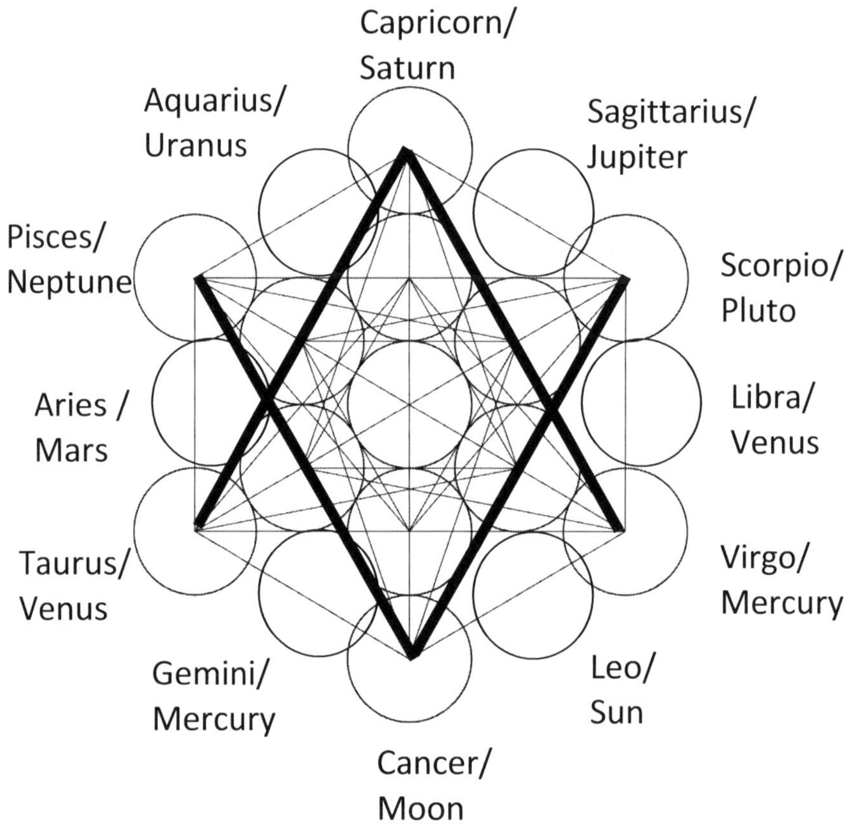

The Lunar Triangle of Isis, which is essentially the same as the 30-60-90 degree triangle, is also embedded in the geometry of Metatron's Cube:

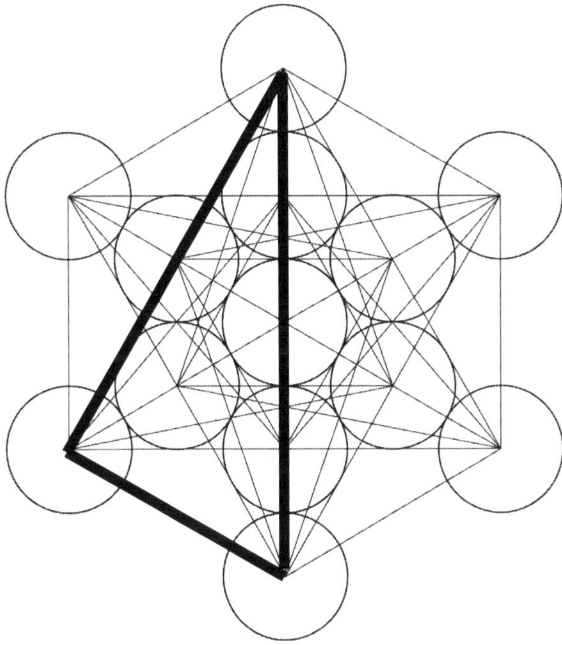

The Lunar Triangle of Isis within Metatron's Cube.

The Lunar Triangle of Isis as the geometry of Issue-Obstacle-Action provides a sense that there are further connecting patterns to be explored within Metatron's Cube. Indeed, we are about to discover 144 patterns. But first, we need to put our geometry to a test. If the zodiac represents a map of the faces of the archetypes that motivate human beings to change and grow, then we should be able to see this in action on a global scale. And, to ensure we are on scientific footing, we will examine the findings of Harvard graduate and California Institute of Integral Studies professor Richard Tarnas. In his book, *Cosmos and Psyche*, Tarnas, based on thirty years of research, demonstrated the existence of a consistent correspondence between planetary alignments and the archetypal patterns activated in human history and behavior.[8] One of the alignments Tarnas researched was that of Uranus and Pluto. These two planets are about change and transformation. As such, their alignments appear to impact the course of human history. The alignments below show Uranus and Pluto in opposition to each other during the French Revolution and conjunct during the turbulent 1960s:

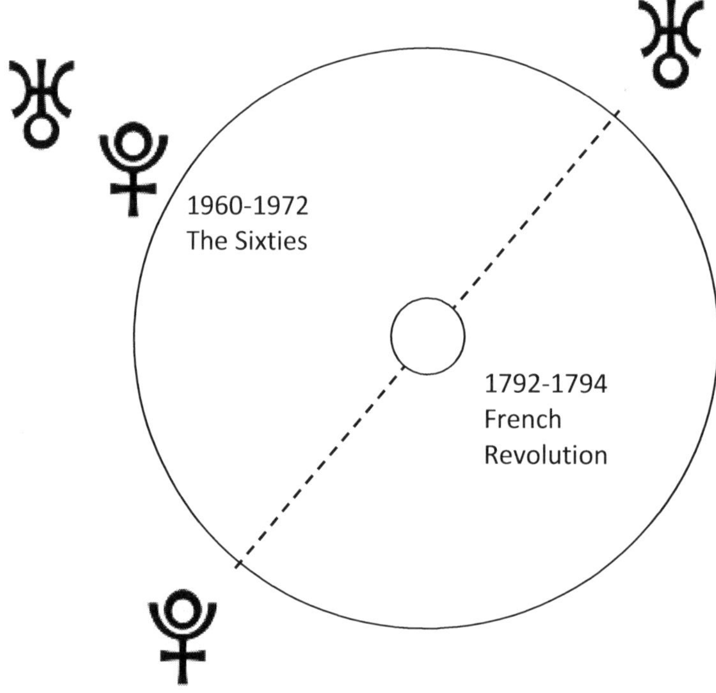

Uranus and Pluto Alignments During
the French Revolution and the Sixties.

The next Uranus-Pluto alignment after the sixties is 2007-2020, with a more exact alignment from 2012-2015. Tarnas said this alignment points to the possibility of "significant cultural and archetypal dynamics that include heightened impulses for radical social change and cultural creativity, accelerated technological and scientific advance, the empowerment of progressive and reformist political movements, intensified feminist, civil rights, and countercultural activity…"[9] In short, we are in for change.

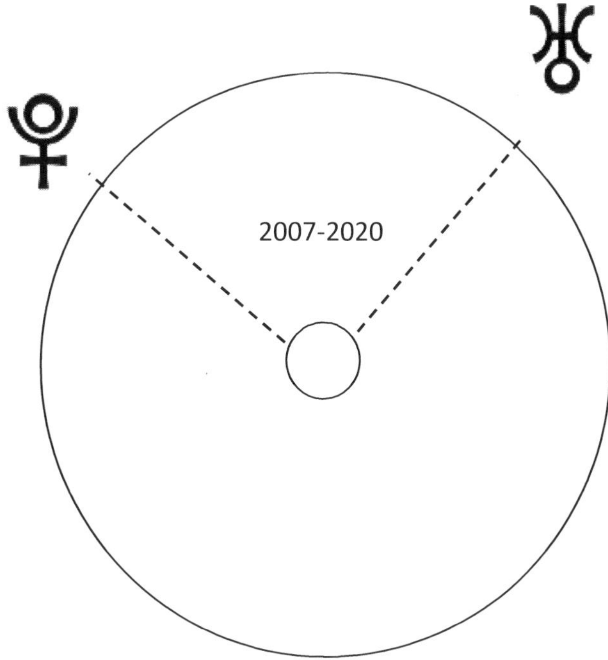

Uranus and Pluto in "Square" Alignment from 2007-2020

Jung also had the idea that civilization is influenced on a global level by the planets. However, he took into consideration an even larger cycle of planetary alignments—the Precession of the Equinoxes. He treated the archetypal influence of these alignments as if they affected the global community as one big "global pa-tient."[10] By the word "patient," he was referring to someone seeking psychological help (psyche-o-logical).

The Precession of the Equinoxes is the 25,920-year constellation parade that occurs above the sky:

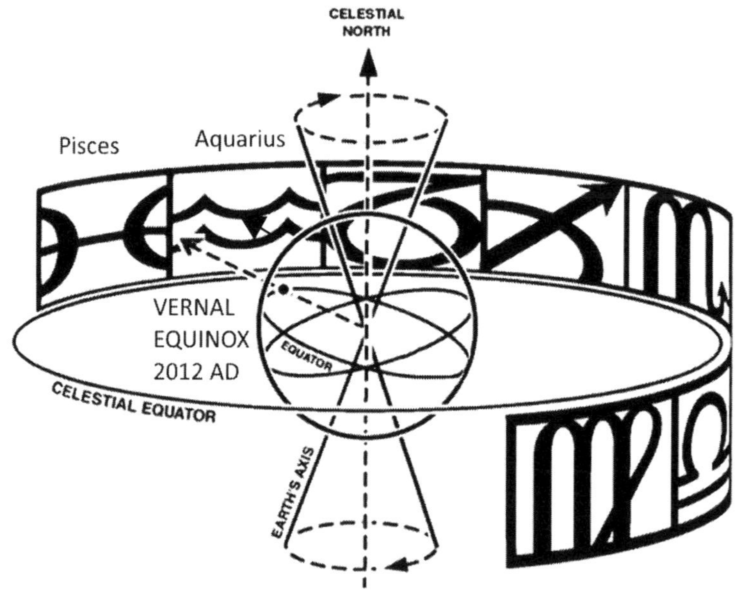

The Fixed Stars Appear to Parade Behind the Sun
in Reverse Order as Seen at the Spring Equinox.
(Image courtesy of Courtney Roberts, author of *The Star of the Magi*.
Illustration by Michael G. Conrad)

This Great Year calendar has influenced humanity from one Golden Age to another. We have now just entered the Age of Aquarius, which is the half-way point back to Leo, the Egyptian Golden Age. This means that every day from now forward brings the global community to ever higher states of conscious aware-ness. The Egyptians were aware of the Great Year cycle and there is reason to be-lieve that the Great Pyramid of Giza is a monument to The Hero's Journey back to the Golden Age. The geometry of the Great Pyramid, with its base angles of 51.8 degrees, is identical to the Heart Pyramid within Metatron's Cube:

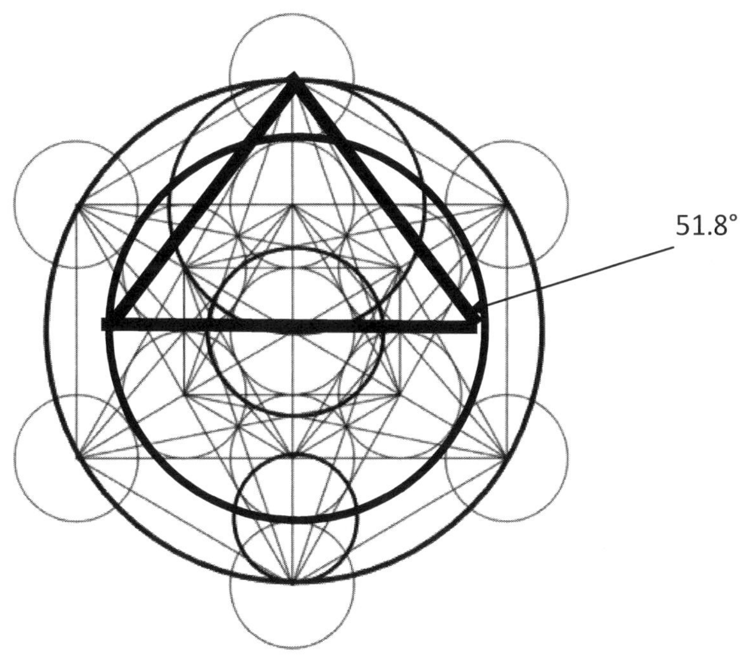

The Geometry of the Great Pyramid of Giza is Found in Metatron's Cube

If Tarnas and Jung were correct that our global patient is affected by the archetypal dynamisms whose faces appear in the night sky, then we should see a relationship between our position in Aquarius and the events activated around us. To test the concept that The Lunar Triangle of Isis serves as a guide, I have included the 30-60-90 degree triangle in the zodiac below:

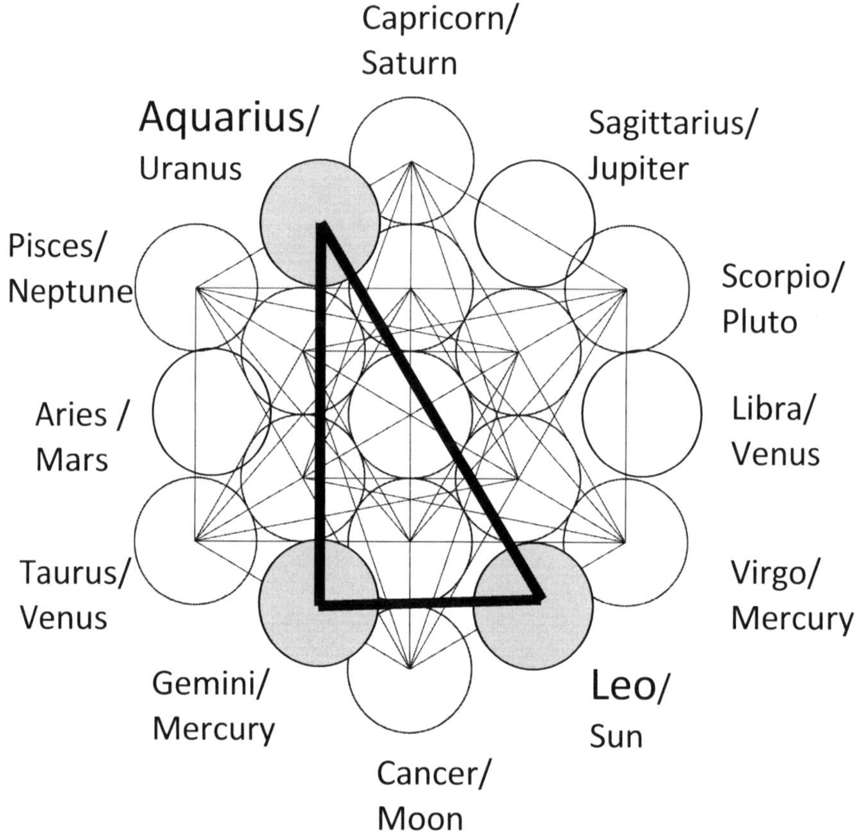

The current Age of Aquarius shown with
Gemini as the Obstacle and Leo as the Action.

Aquarius is associated with the energy of breaking out of old structures. Aquarius opens us to new ideas and the desire for freedom, where people may rebel against authority. Traditionally, Aquarius is about the expansion of consciousness. Aquarius is ruled by the planet Uranus, which is known for influencing sudden change. It is the planet of revolution and reform. Uranus is the pioneer of the solar system. These are the qualities Tarnas described as the influence we are now experiencing with the square alignment between Uranus and Pluto. According to the 30-60-90 degree triangle, the Obstacle or challenge for humanity during the Age of Aquarius is found in the house of Gemini, ruled by Mercury. Mercury is about the mind. In the house of Gemini, Mercury is more about the judging mind, the part of our thinking that has been culturally conditioned. The Gemini mind can be overly critical, to the point of being racist and generally intolerant of others, particularly of their religious or spiritual beliefs. The Action is found in the Fifth House of Leo, ruled by the Sun. The house of Leo is related to the Heart Chakra and informs us that our objective is to move out of judgmental thinking and into heart-consciousness, where we learn to accept others and ourselves.

The application of the 30-60-90 degree triangle in the Grand Year astrological chart of the "global patient" is like looking at the archetypal patterns on a macrocosmic level. Applying the Issue-Obstacle-Action triangle to our personal astrological chart provides us with a more microcosmic view. In this way, we can see how we are individually affected on a global as well as personal level. We can also apply the same concept for issues that arise on a monthly level, daily level, and even problems and challenges that come up for us hourly.

Using the 30-60-90 degree triangle will make more sense when we understand the archetypal significance of each of the twelve houses and their correlations to the twelve stages of the Hero's Journey. As we will discover in the next chapter, each house signifies a stage of personal or global evolution. If we can identify the archetypal pattern that is activated in our current situation, we can better understand some of the subconscious components that are trying to surface and come to light.

NOTES:

1. Cicero, *De Natura Deorum 2. 27* (trans. Rackham) (Roman rhetorician C1st B.C.)

2. M. Kajava, "Hestia Hearth, Goddess, and Cult," *Harvard Studies in Classical Philology,* 102, 2004, pp. 1–2.

3. Marie-Louise von Franz, *The Golden Ass of Apuleius: The Liberation of the Feminine in Man,* (Boston: Shambhala Publications, 2001), pp. 107-108.

4. Anodea Judith, *Eastern Body, Western Mind: Psychology and the Chakra System as a Path to the Self,* (Berkeley: Celestial Arts, 1996), p. 5.

5. R. Gerber, *Vibrational Medicine,* (Rochester, VT: Bear & Company, 1988), p.128.

6. Kiiko Matsumoto and Stephen Birch, *Extraordinary Vessels,* (Taos: Paradigm Publications, 1986), p.6.

7. D. Eden, *Energy Medicine,* (New York: Jeremy P. Tarcher/Putnam, 1998), p. 149.

8. Richard Tarnas, *Cosmos and Psyche,* (New York: Plume, 2007), p. 468.

9. Ibid.

10. Edward F. Edinger, *The Aion Lectures: Exploring the Self in C. G. Jung's Aion* (Toronto: Inner City Books, 1996), p. 12.

CHAPTER 7

The Twelve Houses of the Zodiac and Stages of the Hero's Journey

The Matrix of Metatron provides a blueprint that can aid us through our individual issues. To create this Hero's map, we first place the chakras and their corresponding planetary influences into their respective zodiac houses:

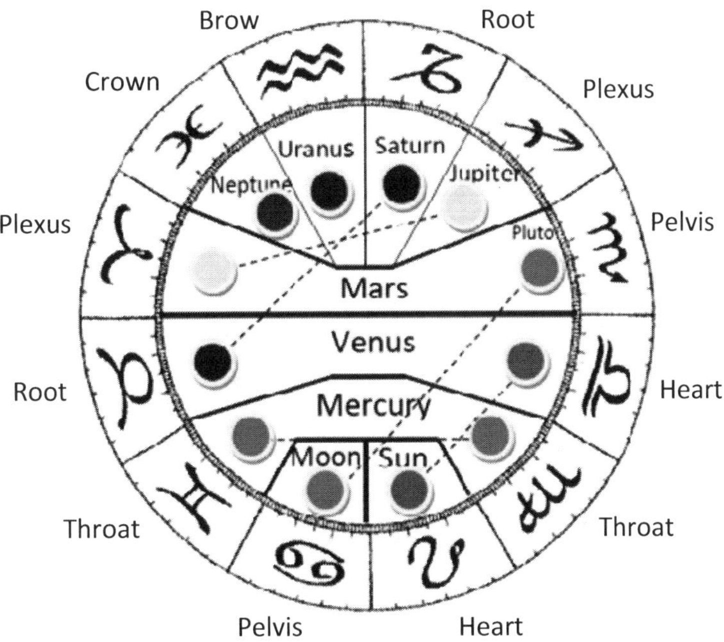

The Seven Chakras and their Corresponding Zodiac Houses

Next, we need to understand the archetypal energies of each of the zodiac houses and how they relate to the stages of the Hero's Journey. [1, 2, 3]

First House: Aries, ruled by Mars (SOLAR PLEXUS Chakra)

The first stage of the journey corresponds to the First House, the month or "house" of Aries, the Greek Ares (Roman equivalent to Mars). Aries is generally considered the son of Zeus (Jupiter) and Hera. The zodiac traditionally starts at Aries because it represents the beginning of Spring, the season of new birth and new beginnings. However, this new season is only a continuation of the seed lying dormant in Winter, represented by Pisces, where Aphrodite, the Goddess of Love, dances on the waters of the collective mind or world soul. Some poets and authors have claimed that Aphrodite had a relationship with Aries and their offspring was Eros. The poet Hesiod represented Eros as emerging from the sea foam with Aphrodite at the beginning of time to spur procreation.

Aries symbolizes the emergence of consciousness into the material world, characterized by self-awareness or self-identity. This is the stage of development dominated by instinctual motivations and actions. This is the house of "I am." Here, the "ego" begins to become aware of itself and strives to prove itself through its activities. It is the stage where we strive for everything we want and throw tantrums when we don't get them.

The story of *Eros and Psyche* began in Aries; Eros wanted action and wanted to win at all cost. He made a game of love and the more impossible the relationship, the more he cheated.

The Hero at this stage may feel anxious, frustrated, vulnerable, or dissatisfied with life's experiences. The influence of Mars in this house represents the aspect of personality that instigates action. It is about desire and the way we go about getting what we want. The Aries personality takes action and is often a leader. Aries is courageous and purposeful, responding to life's challenges. However, Aries people can be controlling, dominating others in their strong will to act. They can become angry, warlike, jealous, and competitive.

Home in Society—This is the Hero's home. The Journey begins in the Ordinary World that Aries has diligently created and dominates over.

Second House: Taurus, ruled by Venus (ROOT Chakra)

If we can characterize the energies of Aries as the boy-child aspect of self, then Taurus is the girl-child. This is the young Psyche under her father's protection and domination. Venus rules the Second House. In *Eros and Psyche*, Psyche was the new Venus, destined to become the daughter-in-law of the old Venus. Her beauty rivaled that of the older Venus, *and* she was mortal—having a human experience. The old and the new Venus are the same soul experiencing another lunar cycle of evolution. At this stage, Eros was still fooling around with his mother. According to Von Franz this was because he had a negative mother complex. Psychologically, we can look at this as our Mars identity trying to free itself from the Venus/Aphrodite of the Twelfth House (Pisces) as we embark on a new journey.

Taurus, the bull, plows the field and carries through with the actions of Aries. Taurus is more emotional, hence feminine, and is concerned with the emotional need to possess beautiful things. Thus, we found Psyche in the palace of Eros, surrounded by beauty and riches. While Aries is impetuous and can go into action for the sake of action, Taurus wants to know the value or purpose of the outcome of action. She is more concerned with the social expression of activity and is concerned with its aesthetic or spiritual implications.

Venus, ruler of Taurus, represents the aspect of personality concerned with personal values gleaned from the experiences gained from Mars. These values determine what we love and appreciate.

The Taurus personality can also be lazy in the field. Instead of plowing, she may become passive and spend her time grazing and enjoying the senses. In this case, she is unwilling to embark on the Hero's Journey, choosing instead to worry about her personal resources or she becomes preoccupied with comfort or security to the point that she is unwilling to leave the comforts of her home.

Call to Adventure—Taurus is the house of the Hero's Call to Adventure. Psyche's adventure began as soon as Zephyrus carried her to the valley beyond her ordinary world. She was comfortable in her palace and had everything she desired. Yet, she had a feeling of discontentment. She hadn't completely adjusted to the change. She felt inadequate. Her infatuation with Eros disrupted the comfort of the Hero's Ordinary World, presenting a challenge or a quest that must be undertaken.

Third House: Gemini, ruled by Mercury (THROAT Chakra)

The first two houses represent the aspect of self that contains the innocence of children. Ultimately, we are seeking to reconnect to this state of pure heart-consciousness. This is why the work of reconnecting to our heart is an alchemical process, an unfoldment and transformation back to our child-like innocence. However, the journey doesn't permit us to simply go backwards because it is too late. We have already entered the Third House of Gemini. Gemini represents the twins, ruled by Mercury—the mind of Eros. Here, we proclaim, "I think, therefore I am."

In Gemini, we become aware of duality. We become aware of masculine and feminine, light and dark, right and wrong. Eros visited Psyche in the nighttime and left before the arrival of daylight. There was a union between the two, but it was still immature and carnal. Their love had yet to grow into a more fulfilling spiritual kind of love. Psyche was not completely content with her husband's casual visits. She felt misunderstood and a victim of circumstances.

We have acquired so many experiences in Aries and Taurus that we now need to classify them so we can understand them. Mercury represents the ability of the mind to perceive what it becomes aware of through the senses. How we interpret these sensations is preconditioned by the culture in which we live, as well as the influence of the Aeon of our time.

Gemini can become caught in the duality of good and evil and erect intellectual structures that turn into judgments and dogmas. These rigid mental classifications can block further progress on the Journey as we become fixed in our own paradigm and unwilling to see beyond the horizon. The judgmental Gemini mind, influenced by generational beliefs, becomes fearful—fearful for survival, fearful of not being recognized, fearful of not belonging, etc.

Refusal of the Call—The Hero often refuses the call to take on the Journey because of fears and insecurities that surface from the Gemini mind. While

Psyche felt unsatisfied in her marriage arrangement, she refused to confront her husband in fear that things would change for the worse.

Fourth House: Cancer, ruled by Moon (PELVIS Chakra)

This is the house of emotions, where we can become further entangled with the material world. In Cancer we are looking for emotional security. This is where we store all of our emotional memories from the past. The risk is that we build walls around unpleasant memories or avoid them through mind-numbing substances and preoccupations. When this happens, we find a way to make ourselves as comfortable as possible in the world and then go to sleep. We go to sleep because we are afraid to continue on the Hero's Journey since that would require that we face our inner demons and the unknown.

Psyche became sentimental and wanted to see her sisters. Eros reluctantly allowed them to visit. The sisters, however, had their own agenda, and wanted to ruin Psyche's marriage out of jealousy. Psyche, on the other hand, didn't express her true feelings. Instead, she went along with her sisters' scheme to uncover the identity of the unseen husband. Psyche acted as if she were in junior high school, more concerned with what her friends thought than of her own inner happiness because she was emotionally immature.

The Moon serves as the archetype for the mother-image (Venus) showing us where our mother has most affected our emotional responses. It can relate to our mother's emotional state while we were in her womb. Our responses to these emotional states can relate to genetic and ancestral conditioning and are passed on if we don't confront and change them.

The motivation to take the Journey comes in many forms. Life's challenges have a way of forcing us into action, usually when we can no longer tolerate our current situation: an unworkable relationship, reaching the limit of alcohol or drug addiction, the loss of a job. All of these, and more, force us to re-examine our purpose and can wake us from our deep sleep.

Meeting the Mentor—For those who have not refused the call, the first encounter on the Journey is with a Mentor or protective figure. The Mentor can be that small voice of heart-wisdom from within. Psyche had many mentors and secret helpers in the form of the wind, ants, a reed, an eagle, and even the Moon Goddess herself in the forms of Juno and Ceres. The Mentor gives the Hero an amulet for protection, confidence, insight, and provides training to overcome the initial fears of facing the threshold of the Journey. It can also happen that the Helper appears to those who have initially refused the call or went to sleep and softens their hardened hearts.

Fifth House: Leo, ruled by Sun (HEART Chakra)

Leo represents the house of ego fulfillment. It is a full expression of our Aries identity, Taurus values, Gemini knowledge, and the emotions of Cancer. Leo is the sign of individuation or full self-consciousness. Leo represents who we truly are in our heart. It is here where we fully understand our life's purpose and express it with creativity and self-confidence. When we are not in tune to the energies of Leo, we can feel that life is a constant struggle. We may be unable to risk loving or feel that we are unlovable.

At this stage Psyche was determined to overcome her fears and learn the identity of her husband. She knew she was taking a risk, but stepped into her own personal power and took action. The light from the lantern that illuminated her sleeping husband's face was the light of understanding and higher states of consciousness. Once illuminated, she became conscious of the real nature of her love for Eros. She was also pregnant at this stage, like the Full Moon—pregnant with unlimited potential and awareness.

The Hopi Indians have a term for someone who is attuned to life's deeper meaning and is in touch with their higher purpose and potential. They are said to be of "One Heart." But those who permit evil feelings to enter or are only conscious of their own ego gratification are said to be of "Two Hearts."[4] This was the turning point for Psyche and Eros. Psyche risked revealing the serpent-monster and ruining what she thought was a good deal. If that were to happen, Eros and Psyche would have become two hearts. Instead, Psyche discovered a higher love and her union with Eros soon became an eternal Union.

Crossing the Threshold—The Hero finally commits to taking the Journey in the house of Leo. The Hero is now prepared to cross the gateway (the desert, deep sea, jungle, etc.) that separates the Ordinary World from the magnified power of the Special World. Eros still had some maturing to do so he ran home to mother. Psyche was now in love with Love and devoted her every breath to finding her beloved. She left the palace and embarked on the Hero's Journey.

Sixth House: Virgo, ruled by Mercury (THROAT Chakra)

Virgo represents the realization of the potential for perfection. The Leo ego must now learn to contribute to something outside itself. Mercury also rules Virgo, but in this new aspect of Virgo-mind we move from judgmental thinking to discernment or keen insight. Discernment allows us to see through the eyes of the heart. This allows us to analyze our behavior, actions, health, and ways of being that are related to the community beyond our individual personality. This is a form of the death of self, of ego-self. Virgo is the house where we serve as an apprentice to learn to be of service to others.

Mercury in Virgo communicates from the heart. However, the Mercury aspect of Virgo can become overly critical, projecting onto others what they don't like in themselves. They can become lost in details so much so that they lose the meaning or purpose of their endeavor.

When our Gemini-mind becomes too ego-conscious in Leo, we embark on a false Journey. In this case, we make our way along the Spiral of Life fooling ourselves that the inclinations of the higher houses towards service to others is about increasing our status in society. We are walking the Journey, but with Two Hearts.

Psyche was walking the Journey with One Heart. She has gone beyond her individual personality and was now devoted to her one true Love. She learned discernment by "seeing" life through the eyes of the heart.

The Road of Trials—Once the Hero crosses the threshold, they must survive a succession of tests and trials. The Hero encounters Allies and learns the rules of the Special World. The Hero discovers that agents of the supernatural are aiding them. A Sidekick may join them or they might gather a Hero team. Pan came to Psyche's aid and convinced her not to kill herself. Juno and Ceres also gave her advice as she wandered the world. This Initiation into the Special World tests the Hero's commitment to the Journey.

Seventh House: Libra, ruled by Venus (HEART Chakra)

In the house of Virgo, me-consciousness gives the reigns over to universal-consciousness or One Heart-consciousness. In Libra, we are no longer tied down by the wounds of the past. Instead, we embrace the non-personal world of the One Heart. This is the house of relationship, but it is more about relationship with others, the global community. This is the calling for relationship with our higher Self.

The Egyptians used the symbol of the goddess Maat, who, at the time of death, placed the human soul (heart) on one scale with a feather on the other. The soul was free to travel towards union with Self (soul) if the scale was not tipped by the weight of the ego-consciousness of Two Hearts.

The challenges the Hero finds in the Seventh House relate to the Journey of finding our true Self or our highest potential. When we are disconnected from our heart, we look for the world to define us and our place in society. We find ourselves trying to fit in and we lose touch with our feelings and our creative spirit. This feeling of untruth (the Egyptian feather of truth) can manifest as shame and guilt, leading us further away from our highest potential: reconnecting with our authentic Self (soul).

The balancing act of Libra is not to lose our identity in service to others nor dominate others.

The Approach to the Inmost Cave —The Hero must make the preparations needed to approach the Inmost Cave that leads to the heart of the Journey. Maps and battle plans are reviewed before the Hero is ready to face his greatest fear. Psyche didn't have a battle plan, but listened to the advice of Juno and Ceres and decided to turn herself in to Venus. This is one way to approach the inmost cave. Psyche surrendered her last ounce of ego and was willing to give her life in service to Eros and his mother. The Hero trusts in the guidance they have received so far and has risen above their own personal needs and ego fulfillment.

Eighth House: Scorpio, ruled by Pluto/Mars (PELVIS Chakra)

Traveling through Scorpio with Two Hearts can lead to Mars seeking fulfillment through deep emotional involvements from the past. When we enter the house of Scorpio with unresolved issues of guilt and shame, they can turn to anger and rage. We may then find blame with others or become greedy or lustful, or seek power and control. This can manifest as a desire for control over others, particularly desires otherwise repressed due to social or parental conditioning. The challenge is to transform the desire for personal power over others into desire for the common good of the group. This is where we can encounter our darker side.

How we see ourselves is also how we perceive ourselves in relationship to the outside world. When we are disconnected from heart-consciousness, we are left to create an identity based on our parenting, our earlier experiences, and how we learned to cope. But we are only encountering a make-believe world, one of personal perception and our need to belong or not belong. The way out for the Hero is to go deep into the feelings that underlie our coping conditioning. Most of us are so busy trying to perform, meet expectations—ours and others—that we don't take time for introspection. We normally go out of our way to avoid our true feelings. The result can be a life-long build-up of repressed memories until something happens to release the pressure.

The Hero with One Heart will find Scorpio to be the house of deep, transformative power. It is the house of unselfish love where one sacrifices their own ego-centeredness. This is why it is referred to as the house of death and re-birth.

Great Ordeal or Belly of the Whale —This is the central ordeal of the Journey where the Hero is swallowed by the unknown and appears to have died. The Hero goes inward in order to be born again. Venus challenged Psyche with impossible tasks to prove her sincere love for her son, Eros. The final task took Psyche to the underworld, ruled by Pluto. She obtained the mystical secret in the box and headed home, but curious, she opened the box and fell into a deadly sleep. This was also a death of the old Eros. He had matured and came to realize, through the Hero's Journey, that he was in true love with Psyche. This is the death of our old self and the transformation into a new person. A new Self emerges, who is positive, loving, joyful, and harmonious with the rhythm of life.

Ninth House: Sagittarius, ruled by Jupiter (SOLAR PLEXUS Chakra)

Sagittarius is the domain of the broader social realm—social service, organization, institutions, etc. Sagittarius is the house of higher learning and nobility. If the death of self-centered desires of Eros is not completed in the Eighth House, the person of Two Hearts will enter Sagittarius and expand their field of influence without regard for the needs of others. We will be tempted to project everything that is not right or balanced in the lower houses onto large groups of people. Without connection to our One Heart, we may express our insecure, me-self in grandiose outer expressions. Because we are isolated in me-consciousness we may constantly feel separate or even rejected, causing us to act in ways to gain success or to have people like and approve of us.

Jupiter (Zeus) is expansive and brings in broader horizons of philosophy, religion, and spirituality to the Ninth House. Jupiter is the planet of luck and travel. However, Jupiter can make the person of Two Hearts feel like a victim, manic-depressive, or proud and messiah-like.

In mythology, Jupiter as Zeus killed his father (Saturn) because his mother (Moon/emotions) told him the father was eating the children. But this was the view of the father through the eyes of the Gemini-mind. The person of Two Hearts still sees everything through the influence of unprocessed emotions stemming from the past (Fourth House). Through the eyes of Two Hearts we continue to be judgmental.

The Journey of the Hero ultimately teaches us that our preoccupation with the outside world still leaves us feeling hollow, no matter how much accolades we receive, riches we have, or power we possess. Our child-self, our One-Heart-self, on the other hand, never needs to prove anything. It only needs to know it is loved. When we know we are loved at the most visceral and sensual level, we open to our own uniqueness, which is then expressed and acknowledged. This is the image of the Centaur of Sagittarius aiming his arrow upwards towards the Divine. The Ninth House under the influence of Jupiter urges the Hero on to greater heights of spiritual attainment.

Reward—The Hero has survived death, overcome his greatest fear, slain the dragon, and has now earned the reward. For Eros and Psyche, their reward was the Royal Wedding conducted by Jupiter. Jupiter gave Psyche the drink of immortality and Eros became her everlasting husband.

Tenth House: Capricorn, ruled by Saturn (ROOT Chakra)

Capricorn is traditionally the house of career and social identity, where we achieve the goal of becoming a responsible member of society.

Saturn is the dark lord residing on the ringed planet of limitations, boundaries, and restrictions. Saturn represents the way we respond to the archetypal father image. The father image can reflect how we respond to authority, social structures, and boundaries. However, this is the view of the father through the eyes of the Gemini-mind and the Double Heart. The person of One Heart knows there is no such thing as the dark father. The person of One Heart understands that the dark father is a manifestation of the wounds we have suppressed from our encounters in the world of experience. Our suppression of feelings caused us to lose touch with our soul-Self leading to the projection of our problems onto the dark father, which in its essence is the need for a sense of self-worth.[5]

The Hero of One Heart experiences the father-image with an ecstatic "knowing" of universal love. The Hero connects to the father as the source of the soul (love). The Hero then becomes a portal of that love manifesting in the world. This is the goal of Scalar Heart Connection.

The Road Home—The Hero is now aware of the true nature of the Father and seeks his way back to his true home. Eros petitioned his father, Jupiter, to let him marry Psyche so they could be united eternally.

Eleventh House: Aquarius, ruled by Uranus (BROW Chakra)

Aquarius helps us break out of the structures of the Tenth House. Aquarius opens us to new ideas and higher ideals. The person with Two Hearts may find themselves operating on a more conscious level of awareness of the power of group. They tend to be concerned with the freedom of individuals and may rebel against authority without a responsible plan for the future. If we have not connected to our heart in the earlier houses, the wisdom we attain in our social role is the type that comes with old age, not the wisdom that comes from heart-consciousness.

Uranus is the first of the transpersonal planets and can bring on sudden change. It is the planet of revolution and reform. The change is usually one of separation. Uranus is the pioneer of the solar system.

The Hero in the Eleventh House breaks free of ego-self and returns to his or her true Self, our soul-Self. This is the story of the Prodigal Son, where we no longer want to be separate. We want to return to the Father, the Source. We rebel against the structures, rules, and expectations of society so we can merge into the oneness and wholeness of being—the being of One Heart. Ultimately, when we accept the Father, we are also accepting ourselves.

Transformation—The Hero is reborn or transformed.

Twelfth House: Pisces, ruled by Neptune (CROWN Chakra)

Pisces is where we come to the end of our lives and all our ego structures collapse into chaos and we are left facing ourselves. We either die to ourselves and reunite with our true Self or we plunge back into the cycle and start again in the house of Aries. In Pisces, we dissolve the last ego-crystallizations of separateness. When we enter the house of Pisces with Two Hearts and are not prepared for the dissolution of ego-consciousness we may tend towards activities of escapism. The ultimate goal of Pisces is about universal love—the kind of love that expects nothing in return.

Neptune is the ruler of the great ocean of the collective unconscious. Neptune entangles us in his net, making his victims lose their way. Those of Two

Hearts become ensnared and sink into a deep sleep or into addictions and denials. Those of One Heart slip through the net and figure out they don't have to conform to anyone's expectations. This is the image of the two fish of Pisces. The one fish swims downwards into the ensnarement of the rational world. The other develops faith and trust in a higher power and swims in the direction of intuition.

Return with the Elixir—The Hero has been transformed, purified, and returns to his or her true home. Venus danced at the wedding of Eros and Psyche. In time, Psyche gave birth to a daughter named Bliss.

Putting it all together, we arrive at Metatron's Matrix:

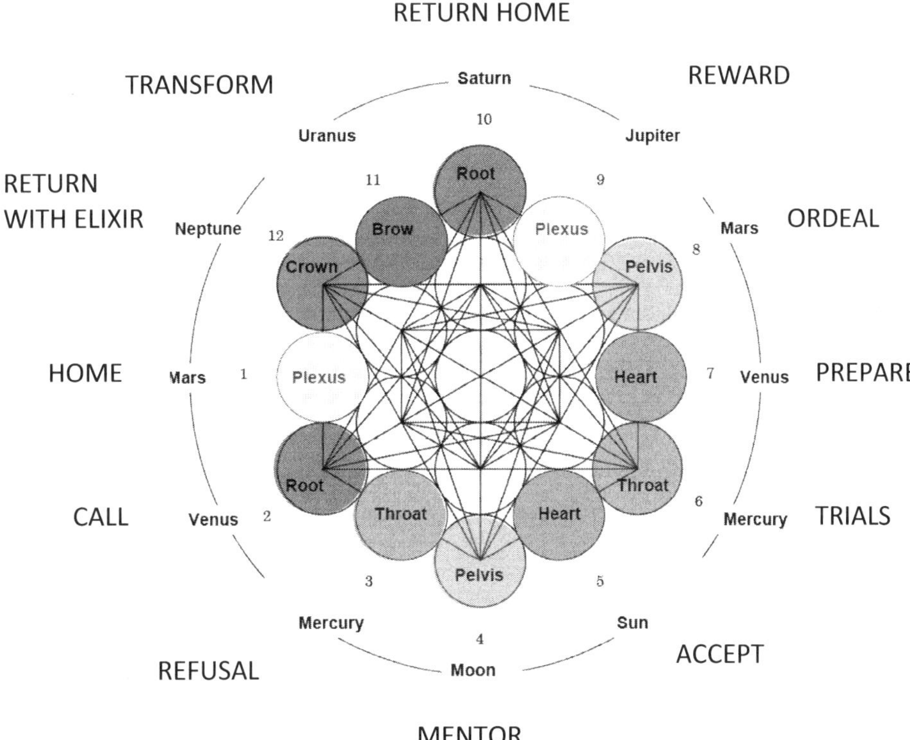

NOTES:

1. Marc Bregman, *Hubris of the Heavens, Archetypal Dreamwork and Rudhyarian Astrology,* (Montpelier, VT: North of Eden, 2008).
2. Joseph Campbell, *The Hero with a Thousand Faces,* (Novato, CA: New world Library, 2008).
3. Jinni Meyer and Joanne Wickenburg, *The Spiral of Life, A Psychological Interpretation of the Birth Chart,* (Petaluma, CA: CRCS Publications, 1987).
4. Frank Waters, *Book of the Hopi,* (New York: Penguin Books, 1977), p. 10.
5. Marc Bregman, op. cit.

CHAPTER 8

The Number 7 is the Soul of Nature

> The mind is like an iceberg, it floats
> with one-seventh of its bulk above water.
> ~Sigmund Freud

How we react to problems and people that we encounter has a lot to do with unconscious responses we learned from our earlier experiences, our conditioning. Sigmund Freud has been quoted as saying, "The mind is like an iceberg, it floats with one-seventh of its bulk above water." [1] The other $6/7^{th}$ needed to make ourselves whole and complete lies beyond our conscious, aware mind.

When we connect with our inner self, our heart-conscious self, we can then connect with the hearts of others and to the Earthbeat of our planet. The melody of the Cosmic Song vibrates through every cell of our body. We are that melody, and at the same time we are a unique note in the Cosmic Orchestra. When we are sad, lonely, depressed, uncertain, worried, anxious, or stressed, our individual song becomes out of tune and out of synch with the Cosmic Symphony. Our awareness of the divine essence fades.

In the 1990s researchers found that a healthy, happy heart produces beautiful music. Medical doctor and musician Zachary Goldberger, along with colleagues at the Beth Israel Deaconess Medical Center in Boston, put the variable heart rate to music. They translated the subtle and varied time intervals between heartbeats into integers and then mapped the integers into musical notes, which became the basis for a CD Goldberger, under the name of Zach Davids, released with the title "Heartsongs." The recordings revealed that healthy people had pleasing, dance-like melodies as opposed to the unpleasant sounds made by pathological hearts that had lost their inherent complex mathematical fractal features.[2] In biological systems, disease and aging are associated with the degradation of these fractal structures. [3, 4]

Fractals are geometric objects or processes that have self-similar structures on multiple scales of space or time. Examples include branches of a tree that are miniature replicas of the whole, as well as the branching patterns of cells of the nervous system, and blood and lung vasculature. This replication of geometric patterns is evident in Plato's triangles. If we look at the fabric of spacetime as an interconnected lattice of vibrating triangles (tetrahedrons), then one triangle is a fractal of the whole. In this sense, when one triangle is out of tune, it affects all the triangles that make up the whole.

Every vibrating system in the Universe is able to entrain with every other vibrating system because the fabric of spacetime vibrates. Therefore, the rhythm of the Whole controls the rhythm of the parts. Entrainment is possible when the variances of the frequencies found amongst the separate parts adjust until at a certain threshold the oscillations begin to synchronize spontaneously. The progressive transformation of the Hero follows a similar pattern. The obstacles and challenges reduce the Hero's ego-centered actions until a threshold is reached and then Psyche spontaneously opens the box.

When people come together in crowds and focus on a shared intention, like wanting the home team to win, the human parts synchronize into a crowd, which then begins to behave as though it had a life of its own. Entrainment occurs between people, particularly between people in a close relationship. Psychologists recently connected romantic couples with electrodes and monitored their heart rates and respiration. They found that both partners showed similar physiological responses, as would coupled oscillator models, like synchronized pendulum clocks. They noted, however, that it was the woman who tended to adjust her heart rate and respiration to her partner's. In contrast, when two individuals were not in a partnership, their hearts and breathing did not show synchrony.[5]

Being out of tune reflects in the inner chamber of our heart, which is connected harmonically and geometrically to the fabric and wholeness of spacetime. This is how we know the feelings of others without speaking or know when a friend is about to call before the phone rings. It also explains how we know when someone is staring at us. The resonance chamber of the heart, which reflects our thoughts and feelings, "knows" what the Cosmic Song knows. The Cosmic Song knows its own notes. It knows the notes it played in the past, what is playing now, and what it will play in the future. If we can re-connect to our heart, we can develop our sixth sense, the sense of "knowing." This will aid us in uncovering the $6/7^{th}$ of our iceberg hiding under the water of the unconscious.

The fraction $1/7^{th}$ stated numerically is:

$$.142857142857142857142857142857142587142857142857….$$

The fraction 7/7 contains the number of the heart (7) and represents Wholeness (7 divided by 7 equals One). The number 1/7, which is an infinite number, points to the infinity of Universal Intelligence. It is the remaining 6/7 that helps us achieve the goal of connecting to this infinite Intelligence, even when we are not aware that we have such a goal. While we all have our own ways of connecting to Source, the heart can be helpful in guiding us through the uncharted waters where icebergs float hidden in the depths of the unconscious.

The number .142857 is also embedded in the lunar myths as well as within the Lunar Triangle of Isis. The numbers 7, 13, and 28 are the cycles of time in terms of days and months. Recall that the playing card deck has 52 cards based on 4 suits of 13 cards each. The annual lunar cycle of 28 days times 13 Moons is 364 days. The number 52 is also 14.2857% or .142857 of the whole—364.

From *The Mystic Test Book* by Olney Richmond [6] we find an ancient view that the number 7 represents the soul in nature, although we have already gleaned this from Apuleius. Richmond revealed an ancient secret when he placed the numbers that make up 142857 around a hexagram. Furthermore, he explained that the result was a roadmap around the houses of the zodiac—a map guiding the heart of the Hero.

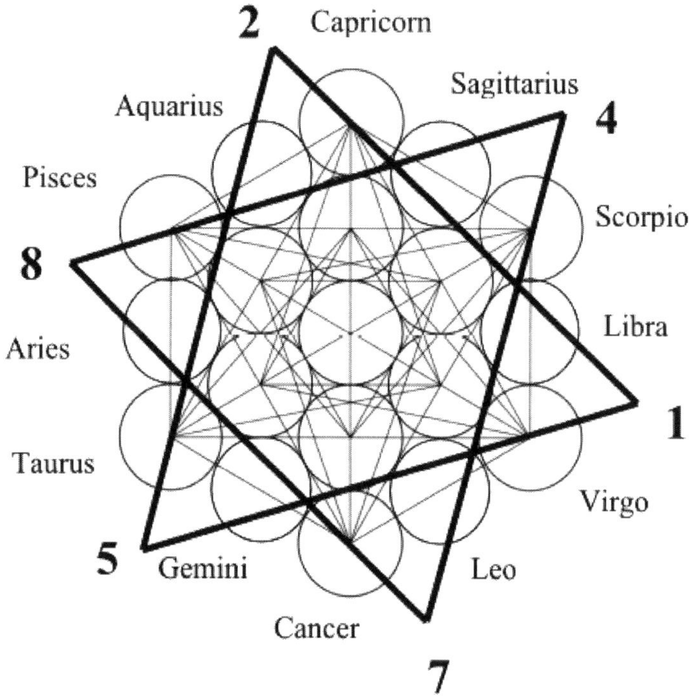

The numbers on opposite sides of the interlaced triangles add to 9, the number of completion. For example, the numbers 1 and 8 are in opposition to each other. The numbers 8 + 1 add to 9. In the same way, 5 + 4 = 9, and 7 + 2 = 9 (notice 72).

Each of the six tetrahedrons surrounding the houses above corresponds to two zodiac signs. We can imagine the signs to be moving around a large hexagon clock. By the end of 2012, the sign of Aquarius moved into the triangle influenced by the number 2. Therefore, on a global level, as in Jung's "global patient," humanity has entered the influence of Aquarius and the archetype of the number 2. In Richmond's illustration, the number opposite 2 is the number 7, which is now influencing the house of Leo:

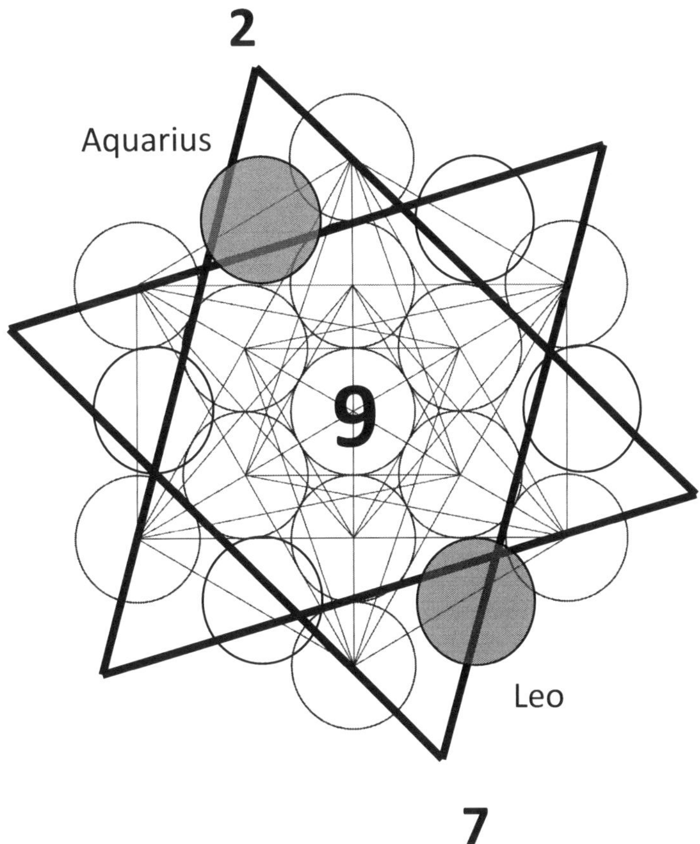

From the tradition outlined in *The Mystic Test Book,* we find that the number 2 relates to union or partnership in work or in friendship. This number 2 calls us to pay attention to the needs of others in our lives, and to tune into cooperation. This tells us that the number 2, along with its energy of cooperation and connection with the needs of the larger community, will influence our external experiences, motivating us towards growth. This indicates that we can anticipate this larger global issue to influence the issues our life experiences bring to us. This is also telling us that we can expect to be influenced by an innate opposition or obstacle.

From the diagram above, we find that the number 7 is opposite the number 2. The number 7 represents challenges in love and feelings in close relationship. It is about allowing others to be who they are without placing demands on them. It is asking us to be ourselves, free to be who we are and to experience being free of fear and attachment. It is the number of higher spiritual experiences. The number 7 influences the House of Leo, which is directly opposite Aquarius. It represents the challenge of the global community for the 21st century.

The numbers 142857 also appear prominently in Gurdjieff's Enneagram:

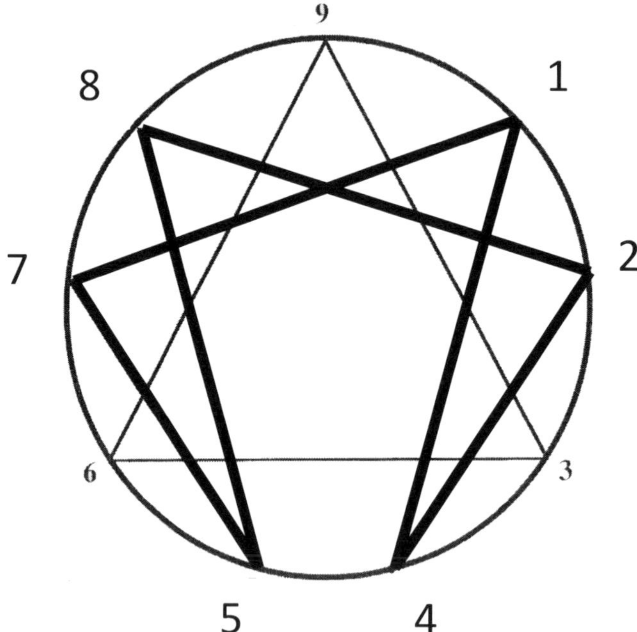

When we connect the dots in the sequence of 1 to 4 to 2 to 8 to 5 to 7, we end up with a flow diagram similar to the figure-eight:

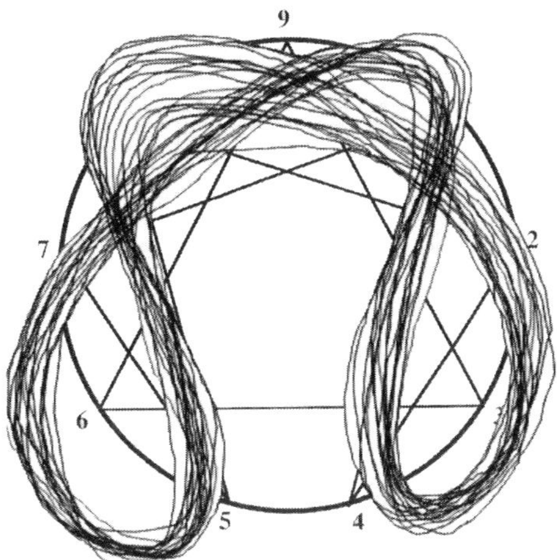

The flow of the figure-eight superimposed over the Enneagram represents the way we flow through our life's experiences. It teaches us that all our lessons, good and bad, are equal. Everyone will eventually experience each of the archetypal patterns and know their truths. This is the lesson of the number 142857.

Agrippa, in *Three Books of Occult Philosophy*, supported the magical quality of the number 142857 when he said of the four Elements: "each of them is three-fold, that so the number of four may make up the number of twelve; and by passing by the number of seven into the number of ten, there may be a progress to the supreme Unity."[7] The number 12, the number of houses in the zodiac, is 3 times 4, which takes us back to the idea of the journey through the four seasons (there are 3 months in each season). The number 7, the number of the heart, goes into the number 10, 1.42857 times (1.42857 x 7 = 9.999999…). As we will discover in the following chapter, the number 142857 plays an important role in the vibration that creates Metatron's Cube in three dimensions. It also gives us a clue as to how we can utilize the Matrix of Metatron to help us shift our limiting beliefs into positive ones by changing the vibration of our resonance.

NOTES:

1. The Freud iceberg quote most likely originated with Gustave Fechner. According to Ernest Jones in Vol. 1 of his biography of Freud, Fechner "likened the mind to an iceberg, which is nine-tenths under the water" (G.T. Fechner, 1860, *Elemente der Psychophysik*, Bd. II, S. 521, translation E. Jones, *Sigmund Freud: Life and Work*, Vol. 1, Hogarth Press, 1953, p. 410).
Jung credits Dr. G. Stanley Hall: He "uses a very striking symbol when he compares the mind to an iceberg floating in the ocean with one-eighth visible above the water and seven-eighths below." *Psychology of the Unconscious,* (New York: Moffat, Yard, and Company, 1917) p. xxxvii.

2. The Margret & H. A. Rey Institute for Nonlinear Dynamics in Medicine (ReyLab), http://reylab.bidmc.harvard.edu/heartsongs/index.shtml

3. Ary L. Goldberger, Luis A. N. Amaral, Jeffrey M. Hausdorff, Plamen Ch. Ianov, C.-K. Peng, and H. Eugene Stanley, "Fractal Dynamics in Physiology: Alterations with Disease and Aging,"Proc Natl Acad Sci USA 2002; 99[suppl 1], 2466- 2472.

4. Ary L. Goldberger, C.-K. Peng, and Lewis A. Lipsitz, "What is Physiologic Complexity and How Does it Change with Aging and Disease?" *Neurobiol Aging* 2002, 23, pp. 23-26.

5. Jonathan L. Helm, David Sbarra, and Emilio Ferrer, "Assessing Cross-partner Associations in Physiological Responses via Coupled Oscillator Models," *Emotion,* 2012, August, 12(4), pp. 748-62.

6. Olney Richmond, *The Mystic Test Book,* (Chicago: Temple Publishing Co, 1893).

7. Henry Cornelius Agrippa, *Three Books of Occult Philosophy,* (Mystical World Reprints, 2012), p. 25

CHAPTER 9

Quantum Healing Codes

Everything we call matter is all vibration.
What we call beauty is the harmony of all we experience.
~ Hazrat Inayat Khan

In my last book, *Scalar Heart Connection*, I explained the significance of the Quantum Healing Codes, specifically how they contain the vibrations that give rise to the geometry of Metatron's Cube in three-dimensional space. These codes or tones relate to the geometry of Metatron's Cube and to the specific emotional centers that are out of balance, over- or under-activated, or generally not supporting the healthy vibration of that center. Listening to the codes helps to connect the positive resonance of a new belief into the scalar field of potentiality, which recodes the new resonance in the body. You will perhaps recognize how the codes or "notes" 396, 417, 528, 639, 741, and 852 are embedded in the magic number of Freud's iceberg: 1 4 2 8 5 7. I became aware of this relationship when I noticed that the numbers 142857 are missing the numbers 3, 6, and 9:

$$1 \ 2 \ \_ \ 4 \ 5 \ \_ \ 7 \ 8 \ \_$$

The missing numbers, 3, 6, and 9 come together as the first and fourth codes in the Quantum Healing Codes. The code 396, the first code, relates to the radius of Earth (3,960 miles) and is a harmonic of the heart number 72. The color red, associated with the Root Chakra, is the frequency 396 THz.

By rearranging the numbers 142857 in terms of the Quantum Healing Codes, they create the remaining codes: 417, 528, 741, and 852. Richmond arranged these numbers around the zodiac and placed the codes 396 and 639 inside the center. According to *The Mystic Test Book*, the numbers 3, 6, and 9 relate to:

    3: Separation from Source (split or fall)
    6: Making peace, intuition, purpose
    9: Completion, helping others, universal love, sharing knowledge

The frequency or note 396 cps equates to the color red; the note 528 cps corresponds to the color green (528 THz). We saw the color green in *Eros & Psyche* as the "green reed of sweet music" and Lucius wore green garlands. We also saw earlier that the Green Lion in alchemy suggests the stage where the Hero acquires a limitless energy—the greening and ripening energy of Nature. The ancient symbol for the Heart Chakra is the color green and also contains the geometry of Metatron's Cube:

Indian Yoga Heart Chakra Symbol

The symbol for the Heart Chakra is a microcosm of Metatron's Cube. The heart is the center chakra and is symbolized by the color green, which lies at the center of the visible light spectrum; the heart speaks the language of the archetypes. It is the feeling center that informs us and guides us on our journey through expanded consciousness. The heart is connected to the vibration of spacetime, to the motives of the archetypes, and therefore knows our past, present, and future.

The code 528, the frequency of the Heart Chakra, reveals the heart's connection to the Earth and Moon through number. The combined circumference of the Earth and Moon is 31,680 miles. The number 31,680 is a harmonic of both 396 and 528. The number 31,680 divided by 528 is equal to 60—time.

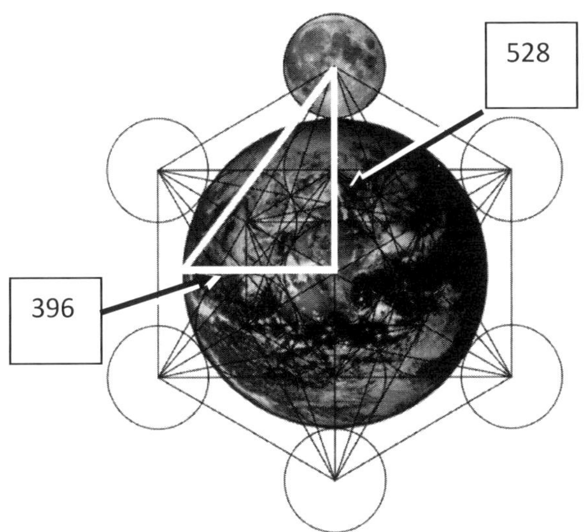

All these numbers work out the way they do because of the definition of the mile: 5,280 feet. No one knows precisely how the mile came to be 5,280 feet. It became the standard in England in 1593 by an Act of Parliament, during the reign of Queen Elizabeth I. The statute states: "A Mile shall contain eight Furlongs, every Furlong forty Poles, and every Pole shall contain sixteen Foot and an half." The Furlong was the distance a team of oxen could plough without resting, and was standardized to be exactly 40 rods. A rod or Pole was 16.5 feet. Therefore, a mile is 16.5 rods times 40 (a furlong) times 8 or 5,280 feet. Inquisitive minds now want to know the origin of the definition of the foot. What we do know is that a rod of 16.5 feet times 40 is 660 feet (a furlong). The hypotenuse of the triangle with sides 528 and 396 happens to be 660 exactly. This may not have been known to the farmers in 1593, but it is curious how the triangle made up of sides 396, 528, and 660 fits within the geometry of Metatron's Cube:

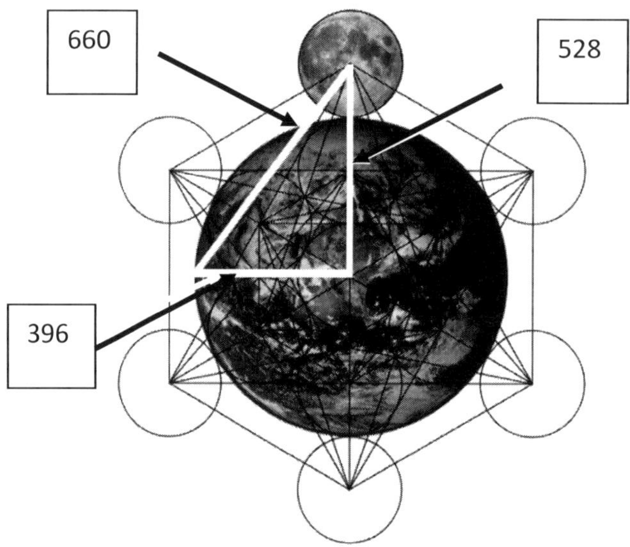

The notes 396 and 528 when played as a musical chord form a ratio of 4:3 or a Perfect Fourth. This tells us there is inherent harmony in the world when we live on Earth through heart-consciousness. We can imagine the discord our cells feel when we are out of tune in our relationship to the inner and outer worlds.

The other frequencies within the Quantum Healing Codes fit within the geometry of the Heart Chakra. This helps explain why the heart knows when the other chakras are out of tune:

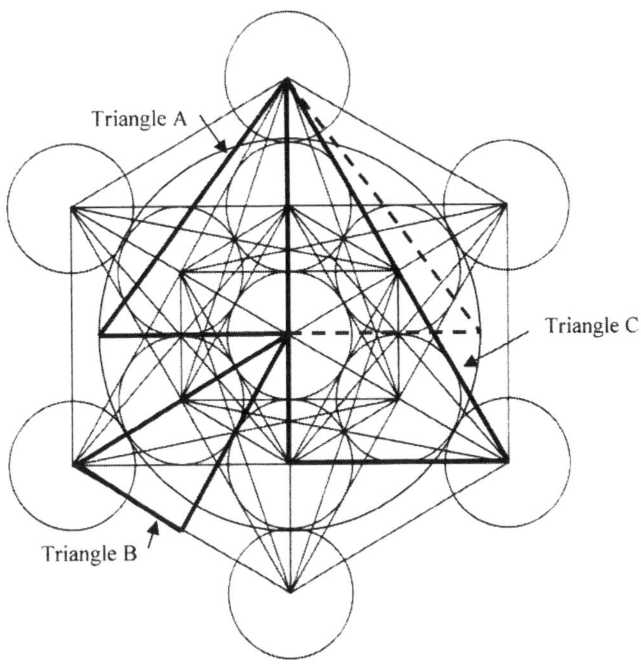

Triangle A is Frequency 396 and its Octaves;
Triangle B is Frequency 396, 417, 639;
Triangle C is Frequency 417, 639, 741.

The magic number 142857 as found in the Quantum Healing Codes as 417, 741, and 852 and used as the sides of a triangle, creates a triangle virtually identical to the Lunar Triangle of Isis:

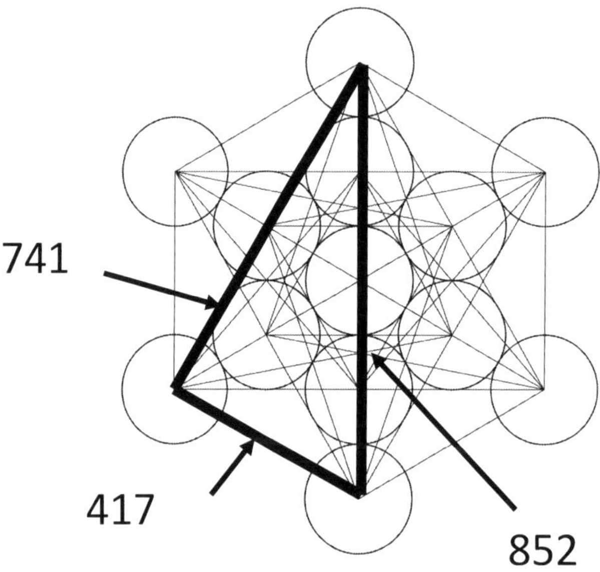

142857 Contains the Code for Creating the Lunar Triangle of Isis

On a smaller scale, the Quantum Healing Codes also contain the geometry of the Lunar Triangle of Isis with the harmonics of codes 396, 417, and 639:

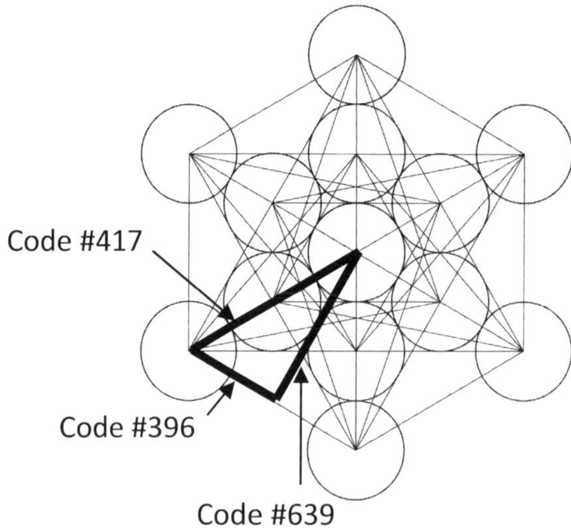

The triangle formed by the codes 396, 417, and 639 fits exactly twelve times around a circle, as we have seen earlier. This is equivalent to the geometry of the twelve houses found in the zodiac and the same pattern we achieved from the Lunar Triangle of Isis:

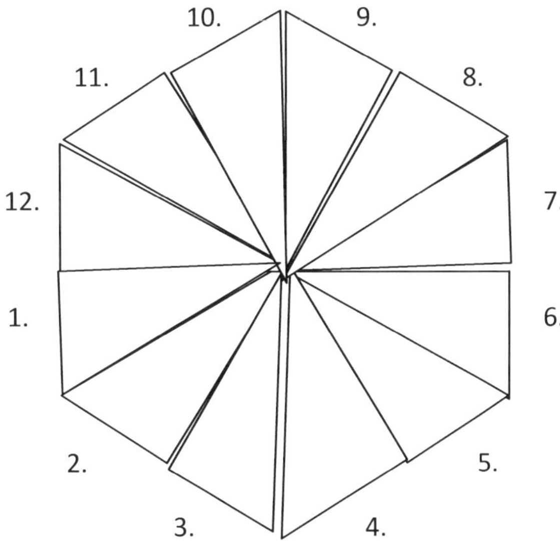

When we place the codes around the zodiac we begin to see how the codes relate to the various houses of the zodiac:

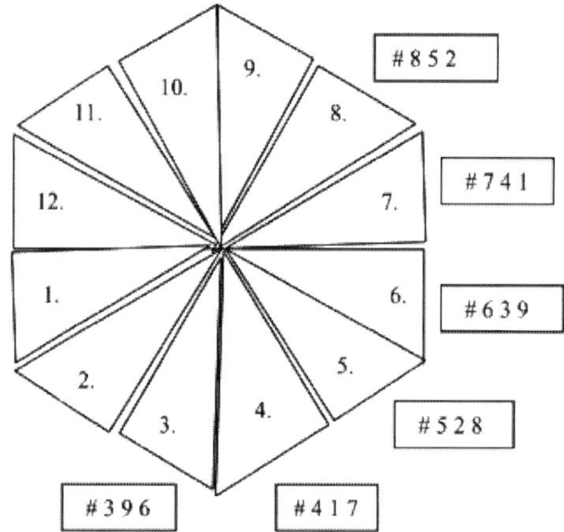

Quantum Healing Codes and the Zodiac Houses.

The codes and their corresponding zodiac houses are as follows:

Code	House	Attributes
3 9 6	3rd – Gemini	Mind, intellect, judging.
4 1 7	4th – Cancer	Emotions, childhood memories.
5 2 8	5th – Leo	Heart, creativity, self-expression.
6 3 9	6th – Virgo	Mind, discernment.
7 4 1	7th – Libra	Heart, compassion, relationships.
8 5 2	8th – Scorpio	Emotions, transformation.

The codes 396, 417, and 528 and the corresponding houses are arranged to support our lower, carnal needs in contrast to higher, more spiritual qualities of wholeness and concern for others and the global community, characteristics of the other three codes:

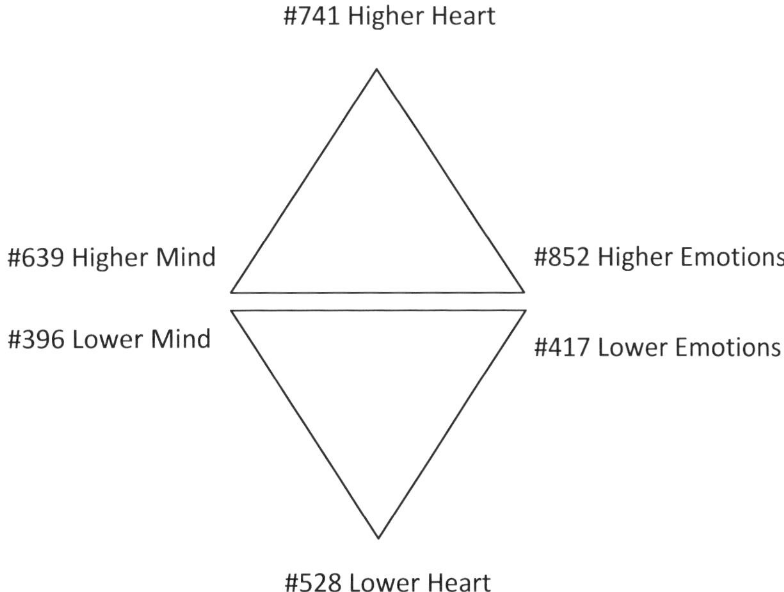

This pattern of codes and zodiac attributes reveals a diagram that can be interpreted as the Hopi concept of the person with Two Hearts. The people of Two Hearts signified a state of spiritual disunity, where the upper heart of love and compassion was ruled by the lower heart of ego-centeredness. When our life's journey brings us to a place of deeper understanding, compassion, and service to others, our Two Hearts state becomes One Heart.

The upward triangle represents the spiritual. The downward facing triangle refers to the physical. The heart knows what we are thinking. If our thought-forms are about survival, safety, reproduction, and other worldly desires, then we are activating the downward pointing triangle. This downward flow concerns itself with receiving and activates our "gut" responses, where anger, fear, greed, and envy reside. The upward heart has the quality of an outward flow, characteristic of the heart's physical circulation. The upward flow manifests as unconditional love and desires only to unite its fullness with others and the Infinite.

The Matrix of Metatron and the musical harmony of the Quantum Healing Codes provide the roadmap and the compass to guide us on our personal journey. The only things missing are the guides along the way. The guides are our Mentors that provide insight into the deeper nature of the archetypal messages that have jumped out in front of our path. When we can identify the archetypal pattern that is activated in our current situation, we can better understand some of the subconscious components that are trying to surface and come to light.

CHAPTER 10

Finding our Heart Mentors: Archetypal Patterns of the Codes

On the growing edge of our cultural awareness
lies the discovery that
the split between body and spirit is
only ever resolved through the heart.
~ Gary S. Bobroff

Perhaps our heart will never be at peace until we learn to let go of our individual determinations and open the Box of Beauty, thereby falling into resonance and conformity with the Cosmic Vibration. Ultimately, there is no escape from a heart agitated in multiplicity. It suffers and pains after this One vibration, the fundamental note of the Cosmos.

A Sufi master once explained that all things arising in creation inwardly agitate to rejoin their origin.[1] This suggests that one way to solve our problems is to start by paying attention to what our suffering is revealing. This is the beginning of opening our heart to the resonance or at-one-ment with the Cosmic Vibration.

If we could learn to extract the essence of life's experiences, we might find them to be the source of growth and evolution. We may not know what we are growing toward, but our heart's excitement will tell us we are headed in the right direction.

The previous chapters described the evolutionary houses of the zodiac and how the Hero's Journey fits within these archetypal energies. The story of Eros and Psyche provided insight into how we can use this evolutionary wheel to our benefit. The benefit arises when we find our Mentors.

Every Issue presented to us by our iceberg also comes with mentors who guide us toward the positive Action. Our Journey also makes us stronger by placing Obstacles and challenges in our path—sometimes daily, or so it can seem.

The triangles created by the Quantum Healing Codes provide a clue to the planetary or archetypal influences of the Issue, Obstacle, and Action. In this way, the Quantum Healing Codes act as mentors guiding the Hero through the challenges to be faced and overcome along the Journey.

The triangle created by each code extends from one astrological house or sign to another in its own unique Issue, Obstacle, and Action configuration. For example, the code 417 connects Cancer, Aries, and Libra:

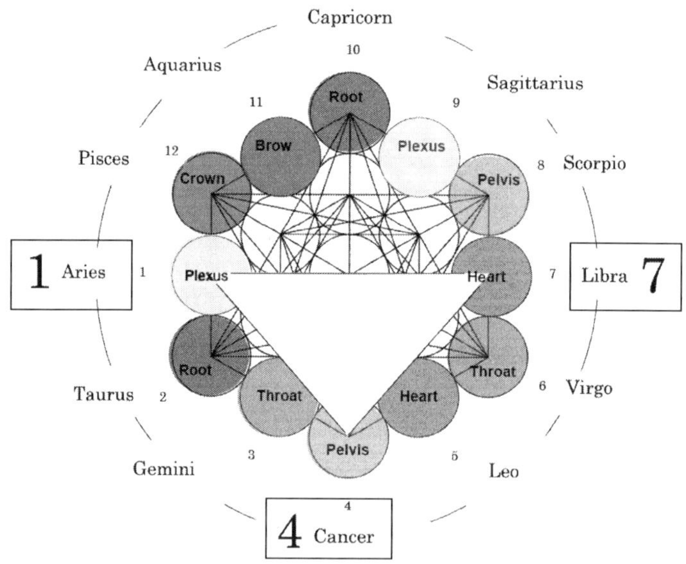

Quantum Healing Code Archetypal Pattern 4-1-7

In the example of the 4-1-7 pattern, the Issue is in the 4th House of Cancer and is about the emotions or issues related to childhood. The Obstacle is found in the 1st House of Aries and is about ego/survival related activities. The Action the Hero must take is related to the 7th House of Libra where the Hero is called to rise above the wounds of the past and embrace the selfless world of heart-consciousness. This archetypal pattern is essentially a tertiary configuration of the Houses.

As we rotate the triangle around all the houses, we end up with a series of tertiary configurations. These configurations are archetypal patterns that every Hero must surmount along the Spiral of Life Journey. Each triangular pattern points to the Issue, makes us aware of the Obstacle, and shows us the positive Action necessary to learn, transform, and continue on our Journey.

Below is a summary of the Quantum Healing Code Archetypal Patterns. The first number always refers to the Issue. The second number is the Obstacle. And, the third number is the Action.

Code	Chakra	House	Hero Stage	Issue	Obstacle	Action
3 9 6	Root	1, 2, 3	Home Call Refuse	Lower Mind	Higher Action	Higher Mind
4 1 7	Pelvis	4	Mentor	Lower Emotions	Lower Actions	Higher Heart
4 2 6	Plexus	4	Mentor	Lower Emotions	Lower Community	Higher Mind
5 2 8	Heart	5	Accept	Lower Heart	Lower Community	Higher Emotions
6 3 9	Throat	6	Trials	Higher Mind	Lower Mind	Higher Action
7 4 1	Brow	7	Prepare	Higher	Lower	Lower

				Heart	Emotions	Action
			(Reward) (Transform)			
8 5 2	Crown	8	Ordeal (Road Home) (Return with Elixir)	Higher Emotions	Lower Heart	Lower Community

Quantum Healing Code Archetypal Patterns

The table above assigns the first three houses to the first code, 396. This emphasizes that the first three houses lay the foundation of our self-image, our behavior, and what we believe about our abilities to succeed in life. The First House is where we take on the sense of self, our ego, and we are occupied with the needs of our physical body and survival on the level of the tribal community. The Second House represents what we value or the things we want to gain in life. The Third House is where we discover duality. It is where we view ourselves as separate, with our own will-power to do things on our own. The Third House represents the mind-brain and consequently the stage of the Hero where we refuse the Call to Adventure because we are too comfortable with our home, our things, or our sense that we can do it on our own (when we feel like it).

The personality qualities within the first three houses that make up the code and archetypal pattern 396 are concerned with a more physical relationship to Earth. Indeed, Earth is the theater for these traits to interact and stimulate us to grow and evolve. Perhaps Universe created Earth with a radius 3,960 miles as a constant reminder of our true task on this plane.

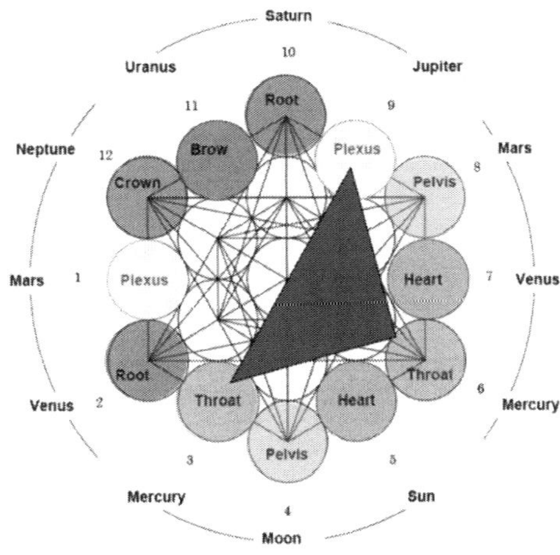

3-9-6 Pattern

Code	Chakra	House	Hero Stage	Issue	Obstacle	Action
3 9 6	Root	1, 2, 3	Home Call Refuse	3rd House Lower Mind	9th House Higher Action	6th House Higher Mind

The table above shows that when the Issue or stage of the Hero is in the Third House it is a call for the Hero to examine their lower-mind's tendency to judge others or see things from only one perspective—their own. The Obstacle standing in the way of the Hero's evolutionary/transformative advancement is that he or she may still need to learn to embrace the higher Action of compassion, which is the lesson of the Ninth House of Sagittarius. The Action the Hero needs to take is related to the Sixth House of higher-mind: Virgo, ruled by Mercury.

The code 396 is assigned to the Root Chakra, because the element of the Root Chakra is Earth and because it is the lowest of the chakras—the starting point. It is also associated with elimination. It is related to the alimentary canal: everything we put into our mouths and everything that goes out the other end. It is the animal instinct of finding sustenance—killing something to eat. It is also concerned with having a place to sleep and warm clothing, the basics of life. Once we are fed and have the basics covered we can get on to the business of creating more beings like us, the instinct of procreation.

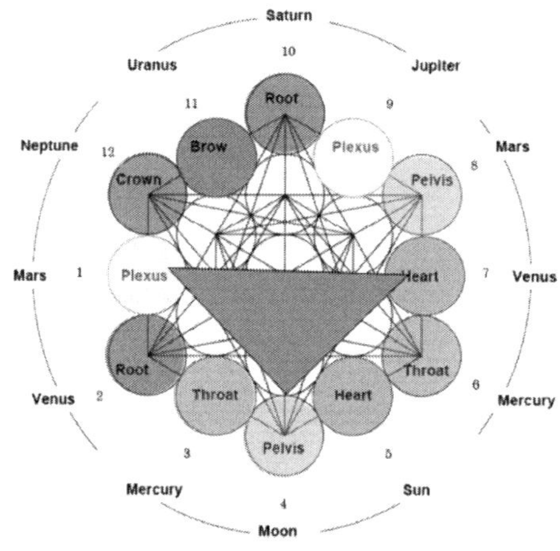

4-1-7 Pattern

Code	Chakra	House	Hero Stage	Issue	Obstacle	Action
4 1 7	Pelvis	4	Mentor	4th House Lower Emotions	1st House Lower Actions	7th House Higher Heart

When the 4-1-7 pattern is activated it is easy to become entangled in childhood memories, which can lead to conditioned beliefs of low self-worth. We are called to be courageous, heartful, and purposeful, responding to life's problems through positive action, and to rise above the wounds of the past and embrace heart-consciousness.

The center of procreation is in the Second Chakra, located at the area of the pelvis. This is where we typically experience the force of the libido, which is the same energy of the Root Chakra; it is only a question of where it is focused.

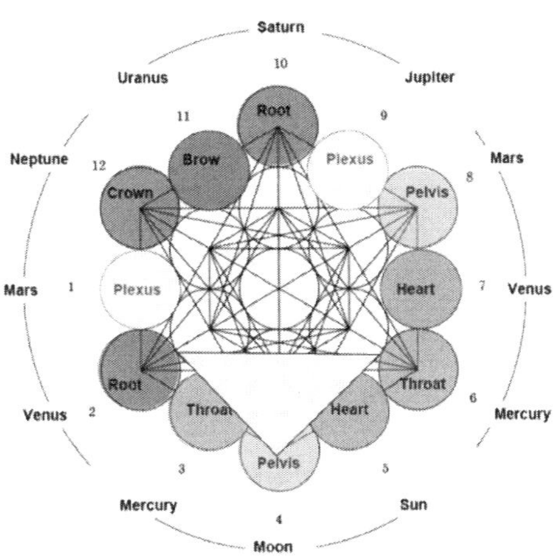

4-2-6 Pattern

Code	Chakra	House	Hero Stage	Issue	Obstacle	Action
4 2 6	Plexus	4	Mentor	4th House Lower Emotions	2nd House Lower Community	6th House Higher Mind

The Quantum Healing Codes don't have a 4-2-6 frequency per se. This code is the octave below 852. The code 852 is the Crown Chakra and is related to the color violet. The Solar Plexus Chakra is associated with the color yellow, although none of the early Vedic writings attribute colors to the chakras. Still, the opposite or complimentary color to violet is yellow and since 426 is the octave below 852 (violet) we can feel comfortable that 426 is a reasonable substitute code for the solar plexus. Indeed, when we take a closer look at the archetypal pattern this code displays it becomes obvious that it is appropriate.

When we become entangled in childhood memories (4th House), we can lose sight of what is valuable and truly useful for our personal development. We are called upon to re-examine our worries and anxieties about personal comfort and personal gain (2nd House) and learn to be of service to others (6th House). The solution to the anxiety and worry about survival may lie in becoming aware that the source of our desires and conflicts is coming from the lower chakras and to then move into the fourth chakra, the heart—the center of compassion and connection.

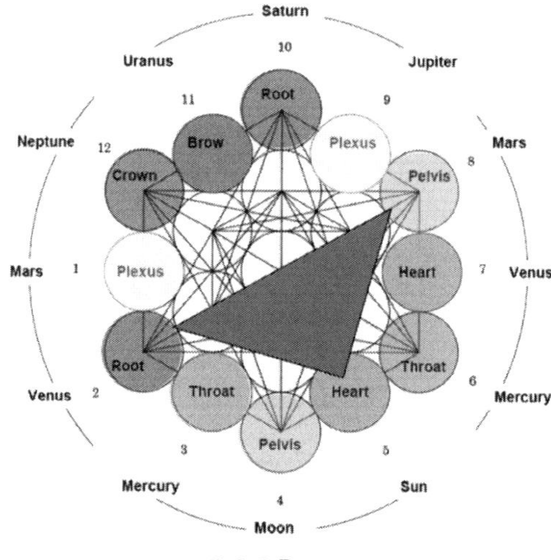

5-2-8 Pattern

Code	Chakra	House	Hero Stage	Issue	Obstacle	Action
5 2 8	Heart	5	Accept	5th House Lower Heart	2nd House Lower Community	8th House Higher Emotions

We know our Issue is in the 5th House when we feel we are not expressing our full power and are holding a sense of low self-esteem. We can become too concerned with fitting in and lose sight of what is truly valuable (2nd House). We are called to re-examine and overcome feelings of guilt or shame coming from unresolved issues of the past (8th House) and to be reborn into our vital and positive sense of well-being.

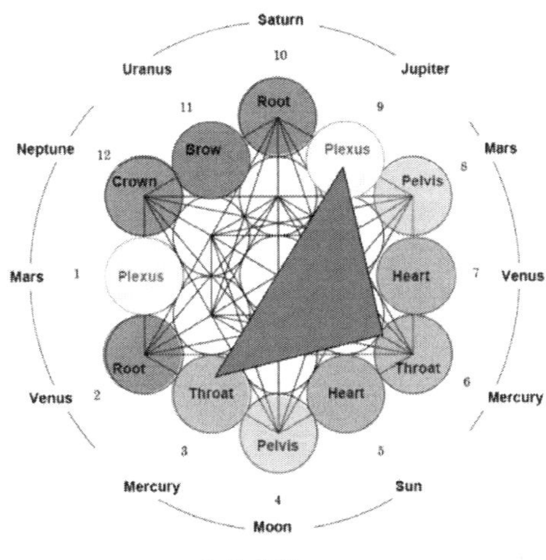

6-3-9 Pattern

Code	Chakra	House	Hero Stage	Issue	Obstacle	Action
6 3 9	Throat	6	Trials	6th House Higher Mind	3rd House Lower Mind	9th House Higher Action

Issues in the 6th House are generally about health (mental or physical) and the sense of well-being, which help the Hero analyze personal behavior and actions, leading to an awareness of the potential for perfection. Self-introspection helps the Hero grow beyond judgmental thinking and teaches discernment and intuitive knowing. This is a form of death of self (the ego-self); the Hero serves as an apprentice to learn to be of service to others.

The Obstacle for the Hero is in the 3rd House and is related to their own mind-brain conditioning that judges others according to various perceived differences. The Hero's cultural prejudices can block the progress on the Journey towards wholeness and a state of unconditional love. Only by expanding the heart wide enough can the Hero encompass all illusions of differences.

The Hero must realize that they don't have anything to prove, and know they are loved for who they are at the deepest core: connected to Divine energy (9th House). The Hero can then express his/her creative uniqueness and gifts in positive, life-enhancing ways.

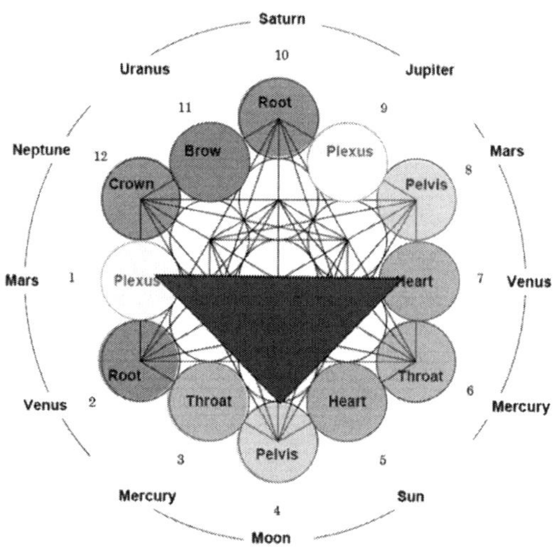

7-4-1 Pattern

Code	Chakra	House	Hero Stage	Issue	Obstacle	Action
7 4 1	Brow	7	Prepare (Reward) (Transform)	7th House Higher Heart	4th House Lower Emotions	1st House Lower Action

Issues with relationships (7th House) or feeling isolated can arise when we get bogged down with unresolved issues or suppressed feelings from the past (4th House). We are called to embrace a sense of identity in relation to others without feeling the need to control others or situations (1st House). It is a lesson in trusting the heart and our connection to the Divine.

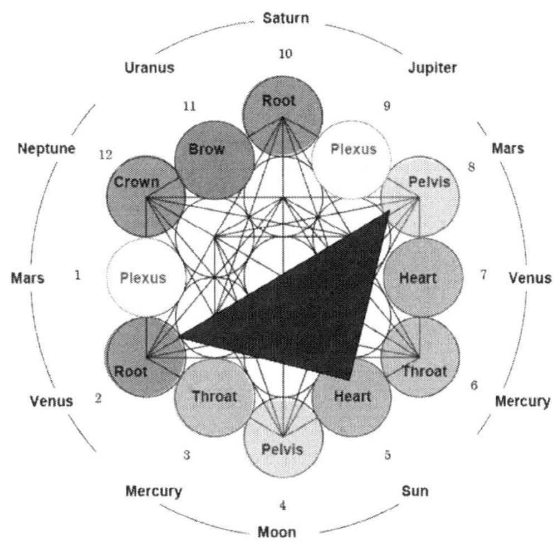

8-5-2 Pattern

Code	Chakra	House	Hero Stage	Issue	Obstacle	Action
8 5 2	Crown	8	Ordeal (Road Home) (Return with Elixir)	8th House Higher Emotions	5th House Lower Heart	2nd House Lower Community

The Issue of unresolved feelings from the past can turn to anger and rage (8th House). The Hero may blame others, become greedy, or seek power and control. The Hero is called to transform desire for personal control over others into desire for the common good of the group. The Obstacle is about self-identity and how the Hero expresses their full creativity and self-confidence (5th House). The Hero must learn to embrace their higher purpose without being lost in their own ego gratification. The Hero learns to release worries and anxieties about personal comfort, pre-occupation with having enough (personal resources) and the need to control (2nd House). The Hero strengthens their sense of self-worth and becomes mindful of the needs of others.

The 8-5-2 pattern is a bit tricky. While the pattern is related to the lofty Crown Chakra, the action takes the Hero back to the Root Chakra. This is the Spiral of Life in action. If the Hero is not able to overcome preoccupations with ego self-identity, they start the Journey over again. And while this sounds discouraging, it is not. The Hero starts again but from a higher perspective and that is progress.

NOTES:

1. Shabistari, *The Garden of Mystery,* Trans. Robert Abdul Hayy Darr,
   (Cambridge, UK: Archetype, 2007).

CHAPTER 11

The Archetypal Hero Patterns

If you only knew the magnificence of the 3, 6, and 9,
then you would have the key to the universe.
~ Nikola Tesla

It would be too simple if all our problems could be placed into seven archetypal patterns and that was the end of it. Human beings are too complex to be categorized so simply. While the Quantum Healing Code Archetypal Patterns provide an energy blueprint for an overall archetypal activation, there are often deeper subconscious layers involved in the Issues that prevent us from resonating with true heart-consciousness.

If the Quantum Healing Code Archetypal Patterns provide an overall picture of the real message behind our problem or Issue, the Archetypal Hero Patterns add a sort of personalized twist to our story. There are 24 Archetypal Hero Patterns. They were born from the 142857 geometry we saw earlier in Freud's iceberg. The 6 Quantum Healing Code Patterns and the 24 Archetypal Hero Patterns provide 144 possible combinations—enough to account for the majority of the challenges we will face in our lifetimes.

We can't help but notice that the number 144 is the number of two hearts: 72 + 72. The harmonics or octaves of 144 contain such numbers as 396 (Earth radius and Quantum Healing Code), 432 (Pythagorean Tuning and heartbeats in an hour), 639 (Quantum Healing Code), 864 (diameter of the Sun), 2160 (diameter of the Moon), 3186 (combined circumference of Earth and Moon), and others.

The Archetypal Hero Patterns are found by using the Lunar Triangle of Isis, which is the fundamental geometry of Metatron's Cube. This same triangle manifests from the Quantum Healing Codes 417, 741, and 852, which form a 30° 60° 90° triangle. Recall that 3, 6, and 9 were the missing numbers from the magic number 142857.

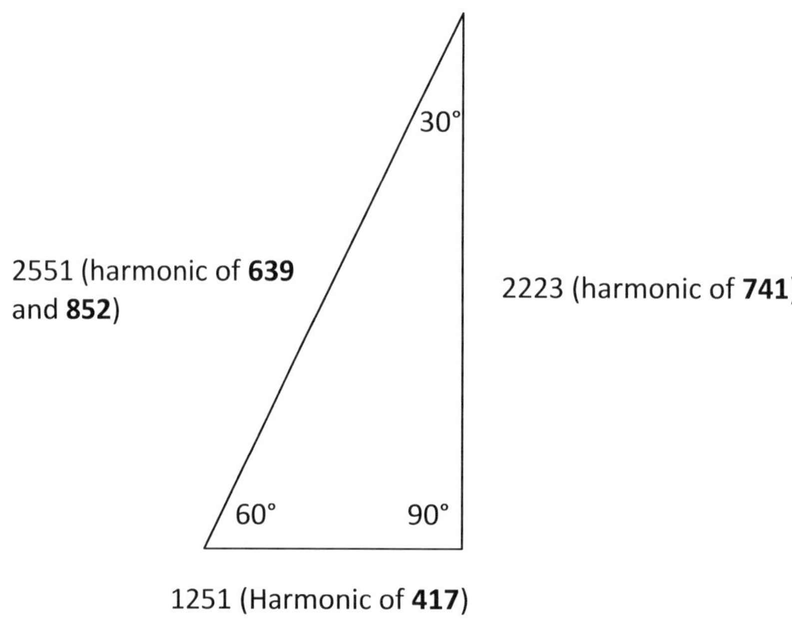

Note below how perfectly this triangle fits within the geometry of Metatron's Cube:

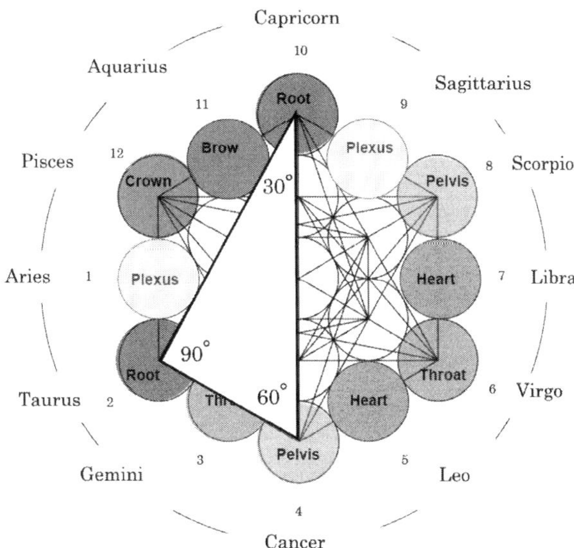

The Hero Triangle as the Basis for the Archetypal Hero Patterns

Referring again to *The Mystic Test Book*, the numbers 3, 6, and 9 relate to separation from Source, making peace, and completion. We can restate this in terms of the Hero's Journey as follows:

3: Issue - Separation from Source (split or fall)
6: Obstacle - Making peace
9: Action - Completion, helping others, universal love, sharing knowledge

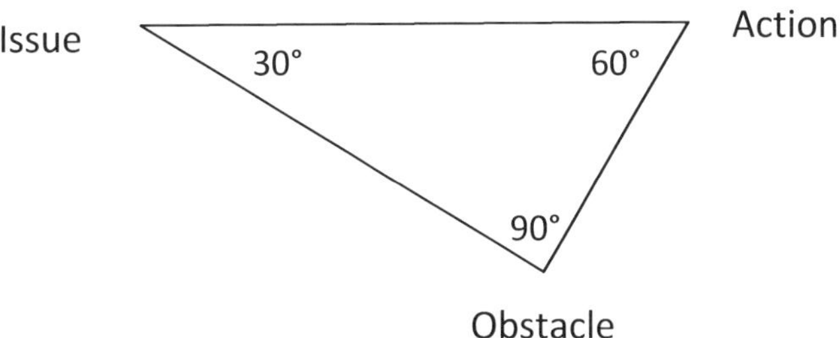

In the example above, the 30° angle in the Hero triangle points to the Issue lying in the Root Chakra in the Tenth House. In addition, the 90° angle presents the opposition or the Obstacle. The 60° angle, therefore, represents the Action the Hero must take in order to shift the Issue.

Astrologers will notice that the 90° angle encompasses two houses instead of the traditional three houses that ordinarily create a square as we found in the triangular patterns of the Quantum Healing Codes.

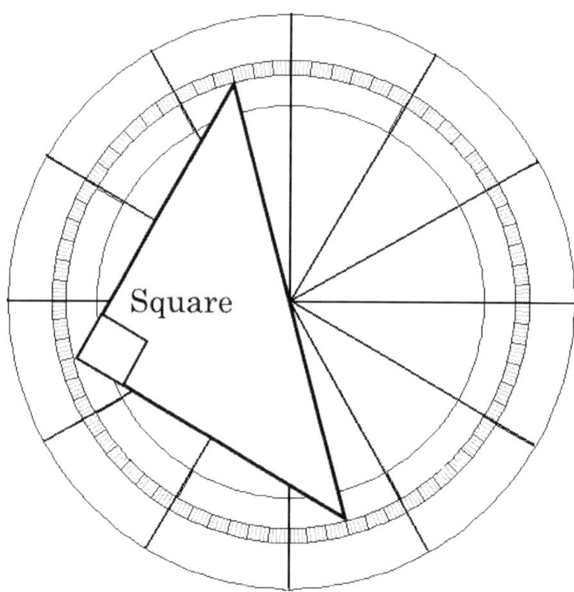

Traditional Square Aspect Between Planetary Influences

The square found in the Hero triangles is not the traditional square in astrology. Planetary influences aspected over three houses (90 degrees) can act at cross purposes. They may force us out of complacency, but too much tension can create immobilizing stress. The square in the Hero triangles is 60 degrees apart, which creates a sextile relationship between the two planets or houses involved. In the case of the 30-60-90 degree triangle, the sextile represents the mediating function between the Obstacle and the Action. It is still an Obstacle or challenge for the Hero, but it is more of an opportunity or positive harmony inspiring growth and increased awareness. The sextile also brings helpful people and mentors to our aid.

In the 30-60-90 degree triangle there are 120 degrees between the Issue and Obstacle. This is a trine in astrology. The planetary influence of a trine allows us to accept ourselves, others, and situations. It provides the confidence we need to meet life's challenges head-on with courage, trust, and faith.

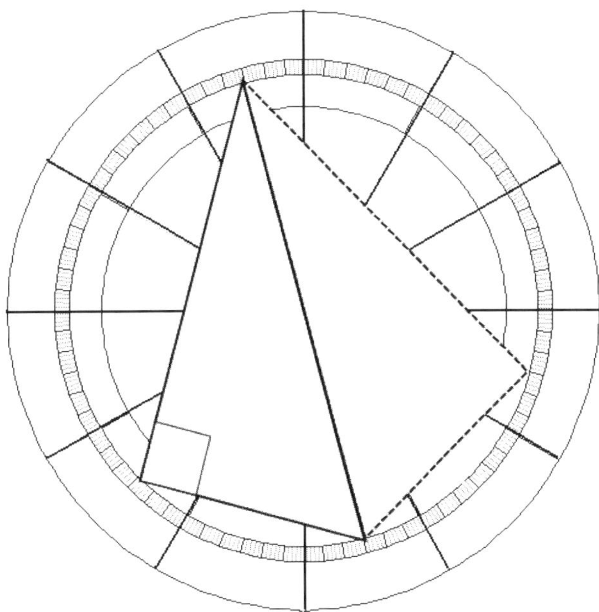

The Square in the Hero Triangle has the Mediating Effect of a Sextile

As we rotate the triangle around all the houses, twelve sets of triangular patterns become the Archetypal Hero Patterns. Flipping the 90-degree triangle from one side of the Action to the other (see dotted triangle above) gives an additional twelve triangular patterns for a total of 24 Archetypal Hero Patterns. Together, the 144 archetypal patterns characterize how the Hero is attempting to reconnect with their Higher Self and overcome the discordant resonance patterns that impose limitation.

Each of the Archetypal Hero Patterns is described in the following chart:

Archetypal Hero Patterns

1.

1-5-7	
Issue 1	Issues arise for the Hero related to the emergence of self-awareness in the material world or concerns about survival, taking action, or getting what they want. The Hero can experience anger, competitiveness, jealousy, etc.
Obstacle 5	The challenge is about self-identity and how the Hero expresses their full creativity and self-confidence. The Hero learns to embrace their higher purpose without being lost in their own ego gratification.
Action 7	The Hero is called to rise above the wounds of the past and embrace the selfless world of heart-consciousness. They are asked to find their sense of true Self and highest potential by stopping to try to fit in. They learn to live harmoniously with others.

2.

1-9-7	
Issue 1	Issues arise for the Hero related to the emergence of self-awareness in the material world or concerns about survival, taking action, or getting what they want. The Hero can experience anger, competitiveness, jealousy, etc.
Obstacle 9	The ultimate challenge for the Hero is a personal search for higher meaning and purpose. The Hero gains a broader view by moving beyond the limitations of ego-self. They are challenged to travel, have new experiences, attend schools of higher learning.
Action 7	The Hero is called to rise above the wounds of the past and embrace the selfless world of heart-consciousness. They are asked to find their sense of true-self and highest potential by stopping to try to fit in. They learn to live harmoniously with others.

3.

2-6-8	
Issue **2**	The Hero is concerned with their emotional needs, possessions, and beautiful things. They may become lazy or passive, enjoying the senses – making it difficult for the Hero to accept the challenge of growth and evolution as they would rather stay in the comfort of their own space.
Obstacle **6**	The Hero is challenged to learn discernment by "seeing" life through the eyes of the heart. The Hero moves out of judgmental thinking and analyzes their behavior, actions, health, as they learn to go beyond their individual personality. The Hero learns to be of service to others.
Action **8**	To move forward, the Hero may need to overcome unresolved feelings of guilt or shame, blaming others or trying to control others. The Hero is called to go deep into the feelings that they have learned to ignore. The Hero emerges transformed or reborn into a state of unselfish love and willingness to sacrifice their ego for the sake of others.

4.

2-10-8	
Issue **2**	The Hero is concerned with their emotional needs, possessions, and beautiful things. They may become lazy or passive, enjoying the senses – making it difficult for the Hero to accept the challenge of growth and evolution as they would rather stay in the comfort of their own space.
Obstacle **10**	The Hero begins to feel caged-in and restricted by their own or other's boundaries, leading to depression or worry. They are called out of their comfort zone or find it difficult to achieve career or social goals. Ultimately the challenge for the Hero is to become a vehicle for manifesting love into the world.
Action **8**	To move forward, the Hero may need to overcome unresolved feelings of guilt or shame, blaming others or trying to control others. The Hero is called to go deep into the feelings that they have learned to ignore. The Hero emerges transformed or reborn into a state of unselfish love and willingness to sacrifice their ego for the sake of others.

5.

3-7-9	
Issue **3**	The Hero is caught in duality, right or wrong, good and bad, where they over-think or become judgmental. They may interpret their experiences through the lens of cultural conditioning and react from fear; fear for survival, fear of not being recognized, not belonging, etc. Their mental rigidity and insecurity prevent them from accepting the call to adventure.
Obstacle **7**	The Hero is challenged to find harmony in relationship with themselves and others. The Hero no longer relies on the outside world to define them or tries to fit in.
Action **9**	This is accomplished by realizing they don't have anything to prove. They know they are loved for who they are at the deepest core: connected to Divine energy. The Hero can then express their creative uniqueness and gifts in positive life-enhancing ways.

6.

3-11-9	
Issue **3**	The Hero is caught in duality, right or wrong, good and bad, where they over-think or become judgmental. They may interpret their experiences through the lens of cultural conditioning and react from fear; fear for survival, fear of not being recognized, not belonging, etc. Their mental rigidity and insecurity prevent them from accepting the call to adventure.
Obstacle **11**	The Hero's challenge is to break out of old structures, personality crystallizations or conditioned behaviors that hold them in limitation. They are asked to be open to new ideas and higher ideals leading to expanded levels of awareness of the global community. The Hero must break free of ego-self and return to his or her true or Higher Self.
Action **9**	This is accomplished by realizing they don't have anything to prove. They know they are loved for who they are at the deepest core: connected to Divine energy. The Hero can then express their creative uniqueness and gifts in positive life-enhancing ways.

7.

4-8-10	
Issue **4**	The Hero may look for emotional security by ignoring unpleasant memories from the past or through mind-numbing substances and preoccupations. Life's challenges have a way of forcing them to re-examine their purpose and can wake them from their sleep.
Obstacle **8**	The Hero's challenge is to integrate deeply hidden memories, feelings, and psychological energies into their conscious sense of identity and personality. Repressed and unresolved issues can turn to anger and the need to control others. Social conditioning has taught them how to cope without getting in touch with their true feelings. The Hero transforms suppressed energies into desires for achieving group goals.
Action **10**	The Hero is called to re-unite with their sense of self-worth and break out of their self-imposed limitations and restrictions, becoming a responsible member of society. The Hero reconnects to the wholeness of unconditional love for themselves and others.

8.

4-12-10	
Issue **4**	The Hero may look for emotional security by ignoring unpleasant memories from the past or through mind-numbing substances and preoccupations. Life's challenges have a way of forcing them to re-examine their purpose and can wake them from their sleep.
Obstacle **12**	The ultimate challenge is to re-unite with their true Self by dissolving their sense of separateness and victimization. The Hero must disentangle themselves from Neptune's net of addictions and denial.
Action **10**	The Hero is called to re-unite with their sense of self-worth and break out of their self-imposed limitations and restrictions, becoming a responsible member of society. The Hero reconnects to the wholeness of unconditional love for themselves and others.

9.

5-1-11	
Issue **5**	The Hero may hold back from fully expressing their individuality, their power, and full potential. This may manifest as problems with creativity, self-expression, self-confidence and/or a sense of purpose.
Obstacle **1**	The Hero is challenged to embrace his or her sense of identity and self-will. The call is to be courageous and purposeful; responding to life's challenges through positive action.
Action **11**	The Hero must break out of old and negative or limiting beliefs and overcome the emotional suppression of old wounds from their encounters with the world. They are called to share their wisdom and spiritual knowledge with the community and contribute to the outside world, knowing they belong to the whole.

10.

5-9-11	
Issue **5**	The Hero may hold back from fully expressing their individuality, their power and full potential. This may manifest as problems with creativity, self-expression, self-confidence and/or a sense of purpose.
Obstacle **9**	The ultimate challenge for the hero is a personal search for higher meaning and purpose. The Hero gains a broader view by moving beyond the limitations of ego-self. They are challenged to travel, have new experiences, and/or attend schools of higher learning.
Action **11**	The Hero must break out of old and negative or limiting beliefs and overcome the emotional suppression of old wounds from their encounters with the world. They are called to share their wisdom and spiritual knowledge with the community and contribute to the outside world, knowing they belong to the whole.

11.

6-2-12	
Issue **6**	Issues with health (mental or physical) and sense of well-being help the Hero analyze their behavior and actions leading to an awareness of their potential for perfection. Self-introspection helps the Hero grow beyond judgmental thinking and teaches them to become discerning and intuitive. This is a form of death of self (our ego-self) where the Hero serves as an apprentice to learn to be of service to others.
Obstacle **2**	The challenge is in discerning what is truly valuable and useful for the Hero's evolution and the benefit of others from what they value for their own personal gain. The Hero learns to release their worries and anxieties about personal comfort, pre-occupation with having enough (personal resources) and to become grateful for that they do have. The Hero is called to strengthen their sense of self-worth and to become mindful of the needs of others.
Action **12**	The Hero reconnects to a sense of belonging to the whole by dissolving their sense of separateness and victimization. The Hero disentangles from Neptune's net of addictions and denial.

12.

6-10-12	
Issue **6**	Issues with health (mental or physical) and sense of well-being help the Hero analyze their behavior and actions leading to an awareness of their potential for perfection. Self-introspection helps the Hero grow beyond judgmental thinking and teaches them to become discerning and intuitive. This is a form of death of self (our ego-self) where the Hero serves as an apprentice to learn to be of service to others.
Obstacle **10**	The Hero begins to feel caged-in and restricted by their own or other's boundaries, leading to depression or worry. They are called out of their comfort zone or find it difficult to achieve career or social goals. Ultimately the challenge for the Hero is to become a vehicle for manifesting love into the world.
Action **12**	The Hero re-connects to a sense of belonging to the whole by dissolving their sense of separateness and victimization. The Hero disentangles from Neptune's net of addictions and denial.

13.

7-3-1	
Issue 7	Issues with relationships is also about how the Hero sees themselves in relation to others. A lack of harmony and connection with others leads to isolation and loneliness or feelings of shame and guilt. These issues can also be a calling for relationship with the Hero's Higher Self and a reconnection with their authentic Self. Before the Hero can continue his or her Journey, they learn to live harmoniously with others.
Obstacle 3	The challenge is their own mind-brain conditioning that judges others based on their differences. Their cultural prejudices can block their progress on the journey towards wholeness and attaining a state of unconditional love. Only by expanding the heart wide enough can the Hero encompass all illusions of differences.
Action 1	The action necessary relates to learning to embrace the sense of identity in relationship to others without becoming controlling or dominating. It is still about desire, but how we go about getting what we want in a heartful and compassionate manner.

14.

7-11-1	
Issue 7	Issues with relationships is also about how the Hero sees themselves in relation to others. A lack of harmony and connection with others leads to isolation and loneliness or feelings of shame and guilt. These issues can also be a calling for relationship with the Hero's Higher self and a reconnection with their authentic Self. Before the Hero can continue his or her Journey, they learn to live harmoniously with others.
Obstacle 11	The Hero's challenge is to break out of old structures, personality crystallizations, or conditioned behaviors that hold them in limitation. They are asked to be open to new ideas and higher ideals leading to expanded levels of awareness of the global community. The Hero must break free of ego-self and return to his or her true or Higher Self.
Action 1	The action necessary relates to learning to embrace the sense of identity in relationship to others without becoming controlling or dominating. It is still about desire, but how we go about getting what we want in a heartful and compassionate manner.

15.

8-4-2	
Issue **8**	Unresolved feelings from the past can turn to anger and rage. The Hero may blame others, become greedy, or seek power and control. The issue for the Hero is a calling to transform desire for personal control over others into desire for the common good of the group.
Obstacle **4**	The challenge calls the Hero to look deeply into unresolved issues from the past, particularly from childhood, where the Hero was taught to suppress their feelings. It is a call to re-examine their purpose and to wake up to that small voice of heart-wisdom from within.
Action **2**	The Hero releases worries and anxieties about personal comfort, preoccupation with having enough (personal resources) and the need to control. The Hero strengthens their sense of self-worth and becomes mindful of the needs of others.

16.

8-12-2	
Issue **8**	Unresolved feelings from the past can turn to anger and rage. The Hero may blame others, become greedy, or seek power and control. The issue for the Hero is a calling to transform desire for personal control over others into desire for the common good of the group.
Obstacle **12**	The ultimate challenge is to re-unite with their true Self by dissolving their sense of separateness and victimization. The Hero must disentangle from Neptune's net of addictions and denial.
Action **2**	The Hero releases worries and anxieties about personal comfort, preoccupation with having enough (personal resources) and the need to control. The Hero strengthens their sense of self-worth and becomes mindful of the needs of others.

17.

9-1-3	
Issue 9	Higher learning, big projects that reach out to the social realm, travel, and expanded ideas are the realm of Jupiter (broader horizons). If the Hero is not centered in heart-consciousness they may feel rejected or isolated and unable to move forward with big ideas.
Obstacle 1	The Hero is challenged to embrace his or her sense of identity and self-will. The call is to be courageous and purposeful; responding to life's challenges through positive action.
Action 3	The Hero is no longer influenced or discouraged by the judgments of others or by self-doubt. They utilize all the knowledge they have acquired through life's experiences to move forward with courage and trust.

18.

9-5-3	
Issue 9	Higher learning, big projects that reach out to the social realm, travel, and expanded ideas are the realm of Jupiter (broader horizons). If the Hero is not centered in heart-consciousness they may feel rejected or isolated and unable to move forward with big ideas.
Obstacle 5	The challenge is about self-identity and how the Hero expresses their full creativity and self-confidence. The Hero learns to embrace their higher purpose without being lost in their own ego gratification.
Action 3	The Hero is no longer influenced or discouraged by the judgments of others or by self-doubt. They utilize all the knowledge they have acquired through life's experiences to move forward with courage and trust.

19.

10-2-4	
Issue **10**	Depression and despair or obstacles and social structures/barriers can affect the Hero's sense of self-worth and their ability to contribute to the global community.
Obstacle **2**	The challenge is in discerning what is truly valuable and useful for the Hero's evolution and the benefit of others from what they value for their own personal gain. The Hero learns to release their worries and anxieties about personal comfort, pre-occupation with having enough (personal resources) and to become grateful for that they do have. The Hero is called to strengthen their sense of self-worth and to become mindful of the needs of others.
Action **4**	Life's experiences have a way of forcing the Hero into action. The Hero is called to re-examine their purpose and overcome their fears stemming from childhood memories and suppressed emotions.

20.

10-6-4	
Issue **10**	Depression and despair or obstacles and social structures/barriers can affect the Hero's sense of self-worth and their ability to contribute to the global community.
Obstacle **6**	The Hero is challenged to learn discernment by "seeing" life through the eyes of the heart. The Hero moves out of judgmental thinking and analyzes their behavior, actions, health, as they learn to go beyond their individual personality. The Hero learns to be of service to others.
Action **4**	Life's experiences have a way of forcing the Hero into action. The Hero is called to re-examine their purpose and overcome their fears stemming from childhood memories and suppressed emotions.

21.

11-3-5	
Issue **11**	Chaos, indecision, and uncertainty are the hallmarks of change. The Hero's life may change suddenly or they may rebel against authority and old structures.
Obstacle **3**	The challenge is their own mind-brain conditioning that judges others based on their differences. Their cultural prejudices can block their progress on the Journey towards wholeness and attaining a state of unconditional love. Only by expanding the heart wide enough can the Hero encompass all illusions of differences.
Action **5**	Instead, the Hero reconnects with their inner wisdom (their feelings) and their creative spirit. They promote generosity, warmth, love, and play.

22.

11-7-5	
Issue **11**	Chaos, indecision, and uncertainty are the hallmarks of change. The Hero's life may change suddenly or they may rebel against authority and old structures.
Obstacle **7**	The Hero is challenged to find harmony in relationship with themselves and others. The Hero no longer relies on the outside world to define them or tries to fit in.
Action **5**	Instead, the Hero reconnects with their inner wisdom (their feelings) and their creative spirit. They promote generosity, warmth, love, and play.

23.

12-4-6	
Issue **12**	The Hero may lose their way or become ensnared and sink into escapism and denials. They may feel stuck trying to conform to others expectation.
Obstacle **4**	The challenge calls the Hero to look deeply into unresolved issues from the past, particularly from childhood, where the Hero was taught to suppress their feelings. It is a call to re-examine their purpose and to wake up to that small voice of heart-wisdom from within.
Action **6**	The Hero is called to analyze their behavior and tendency to be overly critical of themselves and others. They take action to grow beyond the preoccupation with their individual personality and learn to be of service to others.

24.

12-8-6	
Issue **12**	The Hero may lose their way or become ensnared and sink into escapism and denials. They may feel stuck trying to conform to others expectation.
Obstacle **8**	The Hero's challenge is to integrate deeply hidden memories, feelings, and psychological energies into their conscious sense of identity and personality. Repressed and unresolved issues can turn to anger and the need to control others. Social conditioning has taught them how to cope without getting in touch with their true feelings. The Hero transforms suppressed energies into desires for achieving group goals.
Action **6**	The Hero is called to analyze their behavior and tendency to be overly critical of themselves and others. They take action to grow beyond the preoccupation with their individual personality and learn to be of service to others.

Metatron's Cube provides a template or a Hero's map for methodically uncovering the negative or chaotic thought vibrations that are disrupting peace of mind and affecting what is being manifested in our outer life. By mapping out the emotional aspects associated with each chakra, we have a means for identifying both the subconscious content holding us in negative patterns and the positive aspects required to shift our perspective. When we change our perspective, we change our reality.

When we feel emotionally out of balance, we can use Metatron's Cube as a means to connect to the heart's innate knowing. The process of Scalar Heart Connection allows us to do a session on ourselves as well as for and with someone else. The system relies on a matrix of numbers that allows the heart to communicate what our mind-brain needs to hear and integrate in order to create a new outcome.

Let's go back to the earlier example of Christine's example in chapter three. Recall that Christine was having financial worries about her business. Her heart told her that her mind-brain was stuck in a habituated pattern of responding to stress by wanting to control the situation. The process revealed that the deeper, unconscious belief was one of self-doubt. Once the Archetypal Hero Patterns were identified, the heart could tell Christine which of the 24 patterns were activated behind her Issue. To find her Archetypal Hero Pattern, we needed to use the expanded version of the Scalar Heart Connection process. This expanded version is available online to people who have taken the Scalar Heart Connection Workshop.

Using the expanded version, Christine intuited through her heart that she needed number 17, which is the 9-1-3 pattern. From the above chart of patterns, we find the following information:

17.

9-1-3	
Issue **9**	Higher learning, big projects that reach out to the social realm, travel, and expanded ideas are the realm of Jupiter (broader horizons). If the Hero is not centered in heart-consciousness they may feel rejected or isolated and unable to move forward with big ideas.
Obstacle **1**	The Hero is challenged to embrace his or her sense of identity and self-will. The call is to be courageous and purposeful; responding to life's challenges through positive action.
Action **3**	The Hero is no longer influenced or discouraged by the judgments of others or by self-doubt. They utilize all the knowledge they have acquired through life's experiences to move forward with courage and trust.

The triangle of the 9-1-3 pattern looks like this:

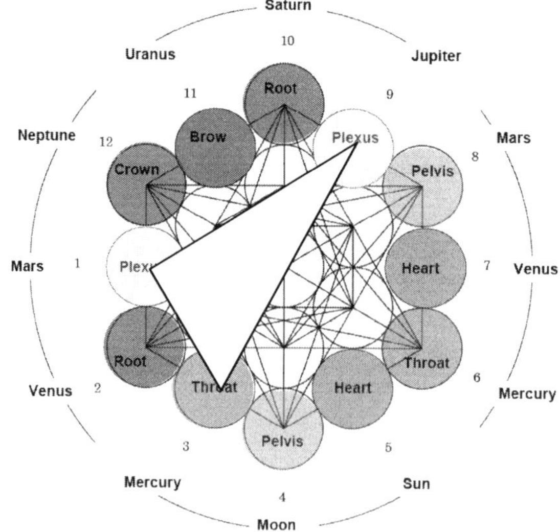

This pattern informed us that Christine's Issue was an archetypal activation of the 9th House, which indicated that the broader issue was more about her feeling rejected or isolated and unable to move forward with big ideas. She was afraid of closing her retail space because she couldn't see the future and didn't trust her own abilities (self-doubt coming from critical mother and absent father).

From the standpoint of the Hero's Journey, which we will explore in the following chapter, this is the stage where the Hero obtains the Reward. Christine was being asked to seize the moment, grab the gold, embrace expanded ideas, and reap the reward of being her true and authentic Self. To accomplish this, Christine needed to overcome the Obstacle, found in the 1st House. Here, Christine was challenged to be courageous and respond to life's challenges through positive action.

Up to this point, Christine was not taking action. Instead, she was frozen in a state of anxiety and worry. This is the Hero stage of being Home in the Ordinary World. Christine, like most of us, preferred to stay where things were familiar. From the perspective of the Hero's Journey, this prevents us from moving forward, exploring new frontiers, and truncates our opportunities for personal growth. But Christine needed not worry, because the archetypes have a way of moving us out of our comfort zone. In Christine's case, the motivation was the uncomfortable emotions of anxiety and worry stemming from her false belief that she needed to be in control.

The Action Christine needed was to take the first step. The Action in the 3rd House is the Hero's Refusal of the Call. The Hero refused to take that first step because she was overtaken by self-doubt. She was paralyzed. The Third House, Gemini, is the house of the mind, ruled by Mercury. Specifically, Gemini is where the mind judges and criticizes and can be held sway by what they imagine other people think of them. Gemini is the sign of the twins, representing the mind's perception of duality: right or wrong, good or bad, success or failure, etc. Recall that the heart gave Christine the Positive Heart Message, "I trust my heart's innate intelligence to nurture and take care of me." This was her Action. It was the Action of no longer being influenced or discouraged by the judgments of others or by self-doubt. It was about utilizing all of the knowledge she had acquired through life's experiences to move forward with courage and trust. And, as we learned, Christine did just that; she closed her retail space and started to work from home and her business is now booming.

Christine was able to change her reality by changing how she thought and felt. She changed what she thought and felt by calling up from her subconscious the belief that she was not good enough. Not being good enough was a belief that her mind-brain consciousness had kept repressed because it conflicted with the self-image her mind-brain was projecting to others. Unfortunately, the negative belief was part of her field of vibration. Consequently, the negative was what continued to manifest in her life. As soon as she became aware of her mind's deception, she was able to digest the feeling of doubting herself, realizing that the source of the feeling was only a perception she had projected onto her parents. The belief was only going to be as real as she made it. She now chose not to believe it. This new belief changed the vibration of her thought habit and feeling patterns. Her new resonance pattern, free of self-doubt, created a new reality.

It's often said that it takes a hundred years for new ideas to be generally accepted. It has been over a hundred years since quantum physicists were first scratching their heads over experiments whose outcomes were being influenced by the observers of the experiments. The general theme was the notion that subatomic waveforms of energy show up as particles in places where someone is looking for such particles.[1] It is one of those quantum enigmas the scientific community tries to ignore. They ignore it because of the awkward question it elicits: "How does the waveform know it is being looked at or is going to be looked at?" The answer is understood when we realize that there is only one consciousness. There isn't an "out there" or an "in here." There is only the consciousness we are aware of and the consciousness we are not yet aware of. And, as we have seen, the heart is the intermediary between our aware consciousness and our unaware consciousness. As with Christine's example, when we align our intention to a goal without the interference of self-sabotaging belief habits, we are able to bring about that reality, because the quantum field is at our disposal.

Gary Bobroff, author of *Crop Circles, Jung, and the Reemergence of the Archetypal Feminine,* said, "Ours is the era of the conscious realization of the unity of psyche and matter. With the reunion of body and mind in ourselves, comes the end of the illusion of separation from the world around us."[2] Spirit (Psyche) and matter (Eros) are one and the same. If we view Psyche as spirit or an inward flowing energy towards unity, then Matter is the outward flow. They come together to form spacetime in the same way as an ocean wave flows out to the end of the shore, pauses, then flows back to the ocean. That place where the wave pauses, the place of ocean foam on the beach, is where psyche and matter meet like an interference pattern. In this context, psyche acts like an attractor (Sheldrake) or an archetypal dynamism (Jung) that works through synchronicity, dreams, problems and pain, to impel us out of matter—to point us towards spirit or our higher, whole and unified Self (soul).

Rupert Sheldrake, in his book, *Science Set Free,* [3] describes the in and out flow of our Universe in terms of the force of gravity pulling everything together and the opposing force of dark energy that makes space expand. The force of dark energy is the expansive, outward force of Eros. Gravity is the inward force of Psyche, pulling everything back to unity. This is the idea behind the Chinese principles of Yin and Yang. Ultimately, they are different flows of the same energy—the Source. Both energies are vibrations or rhythm and connected to the same number rhythms. [4]

Marie-Louise von Franz described the collective unconscious as a field of psychic energy. The archetypes, she said, are excited points of energy within that field and that field has an order that is dominated by the number rhythms of the Self. [5] She explained that one aspect of this archetypal ordering is found in triads or triangles. Consulting *The I Ching* and using the process of Scalar Heart Connection are two methods for understanding the activation of archetypes and obtaining guidance on how to respond to our challenges. Using the process of Scalar Heart Connection, we can uncover the relationships between the activated archetypes and their motivations.

NOTES:

1. Fred Kuttner and Bruce Rosenblum, *Quantum Enigma: Physics Encounters Consciousness* (Cambridge: Oxford University Press, 2006), p. 12.
2. Gary Bobroff, *Crop Circles, Jung, and the Reemergence of the Archetypal Feminine,* (Berkeley, CA: North Atlantic Books, 2014).
3. Rupert Sheldrake, *Science Set Free,* (New York: Deepak Chopra Books, 2013).
4. Marie-Louise Von Franz, *On Divination and Synchronicity: The Psychology of Meaningful Chance,* (Toronto, ON: Inner City Books, 1980) p. 65.
5. Ibid.

CHAPTER 12

Ask Your Heart

If you're going through hell, keep going.
~ Winston Churchill

Picking numbers in the Scalar Heart Connection process is somewhat similar to using *The I Ching* or *Book of Changes*. Jung described the system of *The I Ching* as a method by which an inner state can be represented by an outer one.[1] In the method of Scalar Heart Connection, the inner state is represented by a number connected to a statement about our subconscious emotional state. Like *The I Ching*, the only criterion of validity of the method is the participant's opinion that the text of the statements chosen reflects a true rendering of their psychic/emotional condition.[2]

Picking a number is not different from picking a playing card out of a deck of cards. Most people experience an intuitive sense of what number is involved. Some people find that numbers come to them as mental pictures, like playing cards. At other times, they may visualize a row of numbers and wait to see if one stands out among the others. This is an individual process. The heart is imaginative and creative. How it communicates and tells us which number to pick is ever changing.

The process of Scalar Heart Connection operates in a matrix of numbers, meaning, and archetypal relationships. Through the process the participant can make contact with their unconscious. The wisdom of the heart will communicate to us if we approach the system with sincerity. We also need to have a specific question or problem. It is not the intention of Scalar Heart Connection to be an oracle for telling the future. It can, however, help create a positive future by clearing the negative influences of self-doubt that imprison us in limitation. In the experiments I conducted with audiences, approximately thirty percent got the wrong answer when asked to "feel" the nature of the next image that was about to be presented to them. Most of this thirty percent had never tapped into their heart. The idea of checking in with their own heart was unfamiliar and they weren't quite ready to accept the possibility.

Some of these people volunteered to do a session with me in front of the group. Before they told me their problem, I asked them to make figure-eight motions over their heart with their non-dominant hand. The motion was almost always difficult for them. The figure-eight went every which way except in the flow of a figure-eight. This told me that there was a lack of heart integration. After just a few minutes, they were able to find the flow. They usually let out a big sigh and then relaxed. Afterwards, they had no problem receiving a number from their heart and the session took them to some deep and life-changing places.

We now have all the ingredients necessary to create a matrix that our heart can utilize to communicate positive messages to us. The heart will guide us through the archetypal pattern leading us to the realization of what aspect of our socially conditioned mind is reacting to a particular issue in non-life-enhancing ways. The heart will also act as our faithful mentor and tell us what positive action or perspective we could adopt instead, leading to the outcome we really desire.

The twelve stages of the Hero's Journey, as outlined by Joseph Campbell, begin at the first stage with the Issue, which is the discomfort or problem we are facing in our Home in Society, our Ordinary World. The second step is the Call to Adventure, which is the emotion activated in response to not getting what we want. It is our feeling-level reaction causing us discomfort and hence the motivation to change. The third step is the Refusal of the Call, which we all experience because the mind, on some level, is comfortable and wants to remain that way. This tendency of our mind can and does work against us. The problem of global warming, for example, is of particular concern because the action we need to take goes against all the comforts of modern life that we have worked so hard to acquire. Our mind's belief or unproductive response is the Obstacle. When our problems are mostly invisible and their solutions require personal sacrifice, we tend to ignore them or justify our non-action. This is why the Hero often needs saving from his own slothful tendencies by the Mentor.

The Mentor is the quiet voice of heart-consciousness, of the higher-mind, innate wisdom. The message from the Heart Mentor is the Action. Once we have convinced ourselves that the problem or Obstacle is serious enough to act upon, we still have to overcome our self-sabotaging tendencies. In other words, we may outwardly agree and feign alignment with the required Action, but at some deeper level there is always a Mind Resistance. This is where the mind resists what the heart really wants. If we don't bring this resistance, which is our mind's fear of the unknown, to conscious awareness, we are only fooling ourselves that we will change our present course of behavior.

Ask Your Heart: the App Version

The Ask Your Heart App is a quick yet powerful version of the Scalar Heart Connection process. The App is available at the App Store and Google Play. You can also use the free web platform at AskYourHeartSession.com

Step A. Type in What is Troubling You (the Issue)

The first step in using the app is to type in the Issue you are experiencing at that moment. Then calm your mind with either the breathing or scalar figure-eight exercise described below:

Breathing

If a situation or upset makes us angry, anxious, or worried, it may be due to our mind being afraid. Our mind fears the unknown and becomes preoccupied with imagining all the worse scenarios. In this way, we invariably increase the impact of our problems by resisting what we don't have any control over. When the mind becomes agitated, the heart and the rest of the body also feel the tension.

One way to regain our equilibrium is through deep breathing while listening to the Quantum Healing Codes.

Deep breathing releases neuropeptides ("molecules of emotion") from the brain and sends them through the circulatory system and into the heart. If we focus on positive thoughts and have trust in the heart's innate knowing, the heart will send calming neuropeptides back through the circulation to our agitated brain. Deep breathing, at a rate of one complete inhale and exhale every four seconds, is harmonically related to the average heartbeat of seventy-two beats per minute in a musical ratio known as a minor third.

Scalar Figure-eights

One way to get back to a balanced and musically harmonious heart/mind rhythm is to use "scalar figure-eights." Simply pass one of your open palms from one side of your lower abdomen up through the heart and to the top of your head and then back down the other side in a large figure-eight pattern. Breathe in deeply as your hand moves up from your lower abdomen, picking up your positive, calm energy and feeling of trust from your heart and move them up to you brain. Then, as your hand moves back down to the center of your heart, breathe out all the negative mind-chatter, the worries, anger, and fears. Repeat this motion for a couple minutes or until you feel yourself back in synch with the natural flow of the heart and its connection with acceptance and trust, knowing that problems are only problems when we forget our connection to the Divine.

Step B. Find the Emotional/Feeling Center Holding the Discomfort

After you have calmed your mind and feel open and receptive to the messages of the heart, it is time to ask the heart to show you a number from 1 through 7, related to one of the seven chakra centers disrupted or out of balance in relationship to the Issue. The App will prompt you to select a number. The program will display the chakra along with the Quantum Healing Code Archetypal Pattern. It is not necessary to refer to the details of the pattern, but if you want more insight into the larger picture of your individual Issue, refer to the list of patterns beginning on page 143.

Step C. The Emotion/Feeling

The program will prompt you to ask your heart to show you a number related to the emotion or feeling that is activated around your problem (Issue). Once you have selected a number, the program will show you the emotion/feeling.

Step D. The Negative Mind-Brain Conditioned Response or Belief (the Obstacle)

Next, choose a number related to how your mind-brain conditioning is habituated to respond (react) to the situation. This will provide conscious insight into the subconscious pattern that you have been socially trained to tap into as an automatic response. This is generally the reaction that got you into the problem in the first place. It is how we react without thinking, which is why it is our Obstacle. More so, it is our non-heart-centered way of responding.

Step E. The Unmet Heart Need

The Unmet Heart Need informs you as to the heart's need that was not realized as a result of the activated emotion. The activated emotion has a chaotic energy pattern that displaces a positive resonance. Often the positive resonance was either not imprinted from birth or childhood, or it was lost from a trauma or negative experience. Unfortunately, this non-actualized need or vibration causes us to perpetuate the disharmonious resonance into adulthood situations and ways of being.

The Unmet Heart Need is the positive side of the emotion that came up in Step C. Switching from the negative emotion to the positive Unmet Heart Need is crucial for the Hero to overcome the Obstacle and move into resonance with the positive Action.

Step F. The Positive Heart Message (Action)

The program prompts you to choose a number related to the Positive Heart Message. This is the Action the Hero needs to take in order to overcome the Obstacle and slay the dragon (transform). It seems simple enough, but taking the right action is often the most difficult path. It is a way of being that is foreign to us. It is not in our nature nor have we seen it modeled in our family or friends. It is the energy of Uranus, motivating us to step out of our box, to break out of the limitations behind which we have imprisoned ourselves.

The twenty-four Archetypal Hero Patterns are not part of the App. However, if you are having difficulty putting the information your heart has given you into a logical story, ask your heart to show you a number from 1 thru 24, and then find the related pattern from the list beginning on page 145. The Archetypal Hero Pattern will give greater insight into messages and guidance being offered from your heart on the topic at hand.

Step G. Quantum Healing Codes

Because the Positive Action is so foreign to us, we may need the help of a modality to imbed this new vibration into our physical being. That is, we may need to shake up our cellular structures, both neuronal and genetic. One powerful modality is the Quantum Healing Codes. Step G prompts us to ask our heart to show us a number related to the code or note we need to play for our cells and molecules to realign with our positive Action.

Scalar Heart Connection for Practitioners

The Ask Your Heart App is a modified version of the full Scalar Heart Connection process. The expanded version, taught in workshops and online webinars, is perfect for practitioners who want a quick and powerful tool to access deeply rooted and subconscious emotional disruptions in their clients. However, many non-practitioners also learn the extended Practitioner Version for themselves and to benefit family members and other loved ones.

The Practitioner Version guides the client to ask the heart to identify the early experience or traumatic event that first created the mind's negative belief and hence established the behavior pattern that continues to be active in the present. The earlier experience could be something that happened while in the womb. If the heart points to the birth process, the client can also ask the heart what month in the womb the negative resonance pattern was encountered. It may have been the case that a traumatic event occurred with the mother while the participant was in the womb. When this comes up, the practitioner asks the client if they have any knowledge of what was happening with their mom during that particular month of gestation.

If our heart directs us to the category "Age," then we ask the client to also ask their heart for the number related to a specific age. Once the specific age is known, the client invariably remembers the exact incident and who was involved, as well as how the situation or the person made them feel about themselves.

If "Genetic/Ancestral" is chosen, then we know that an ancestor experienced a trauma that created a belief and associated behavioral pattern that have been passed down through the generations. Our negative mind-brain conditioning is often deeply rooted in ancestral patterns stemming from unresolved issues/traumas/beliefs from our parents' parents. If you believe in reincarnation, you can also look at this as resonant memory patterns carried over from a past life. There can also be members in your family tree who were traumatized, cast out of the family, or committed suicide. The memory resonance of these events can leave an energetic vacuum or, as current research is showing, epigenetic tags through a process called "epigenetic inheritance" (a parent's experiences can be passed down to future generations through modifications in gene expression). The good news is that the ancestral pattern can be reprogrammed.

If the client is directed by the heart to the Family Tree, it means that the session is no longer about the client. The session is transferred to the person in the family constellation. This will be an amazing experience, because the client is now channeling the memory matrix of their ancestor. The results are profound, because it shifts the genetic behavioral response for everyone in the family tree, including future generations.

The expanded Practitioner Version also asks the client to create a Positive Statement from the information gained from the heart. The client is also provided with both the Quantum Healing Code Archetypal Patterns and the Archetypal Hero Patterns. Together, these two patterns give 144 archetypal possibilities, which provides a highly personalized pattern.

Once our mind becomes consciously aware of our patterns and what is holding us back, we almost immediately begin to reconfigure our neuronal connections around the new possibilities. We literally make a shift in consciousness, in our perception of our imposed reality. We feel a sense of relief come over us or a wave of spontaneous joy ripple through our nervous system as we align to the expanded possibilities of our Positive Statement, which is part of the Practitioner program.

The expanded version includes information on the Mind's Resistance to our Positive Statement. This will be the statement that most closely relates to the resistance our mind has about what our heart truly wants. It comes down to the fear of the unknown. The mind will resist what it can't see in the future and when it has no guarantee that it will be safe. This is natural because it is a survival instinct. It is also a limited response in that we mostly imagine the worst-case scenario. This is because we have lost our trust and connection with our higher knowing—with the Divine; the Infinite Intelligence; God; Source; Truth.

There are 22 Quantum Healing Codes in the expanded version. This includes the six single note tracts plus fifteen interval combinations and the Open Heart Chord, whose vibrations produce a fourteen-node geometry when played through water:

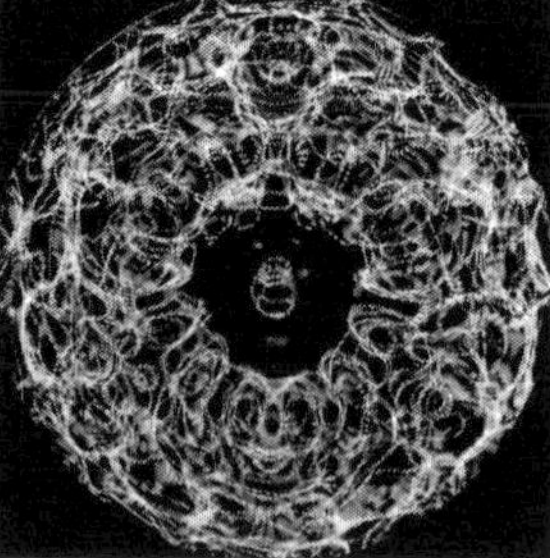

It is not the goal of the Scalar Heart Connection process to make life problem-free, but to give life the deeper meaning and value that comes with heartfulness. It is a method that helps us observe and respect what the heart presents. In this way, we go along with what is presented instead of resisting and struggling against our problems. Instead of focusing on the intention of healing per se, we accomplish more when we listen and observe what is revealed in the suffering.[3] When we stretch our heart wide enough, we embrace our problems and conflicts until there is nothing left to reject. The Quantum Healing Code Patterns and the Archetypal Hero Patterns offer tools to help put our issues into perspective. However, there is always the tendency to sweep what we don't want to see under the iceberg. For this reason, we offer workshops to teach people how to use the Practitioner Version. It can happen that mind-brain conditioning is so deeply rooted in ancestral patterns that we need to go deeper into the genetic influences. An alternative to taking the workshop is to have a session with a certified practitioner, who can help you embark on your own Hero Journey. More information on how to contact a practitioner is in the resource section at the end of this book.

Using the Scalar Heart Connection Cards

Some people prefer to use a deck of cards or may not always have access to a computer or cell signal. Sometimes you just want a quick reference to shed light on an emotion that comes up. Using the Scalar Heart Connection Cards you can pick a card from the Archetypal Hero Patterns. This will give you insight into what archetypal energies are being activated in your life at the moment.

Some mornings we just wake up in a funky mood. Maybe we had a bad dream. Maybe we have a task or some unpleasant chore we know we have to do later in the day. Whatever the issue, you can use the cards to quickly identify the Issue, Obstacle, Action, Unmet Heart Need, Positive Heart Message, and the Archetypal Hero Pattern that is activated.

Scalar Heart Connection Spread

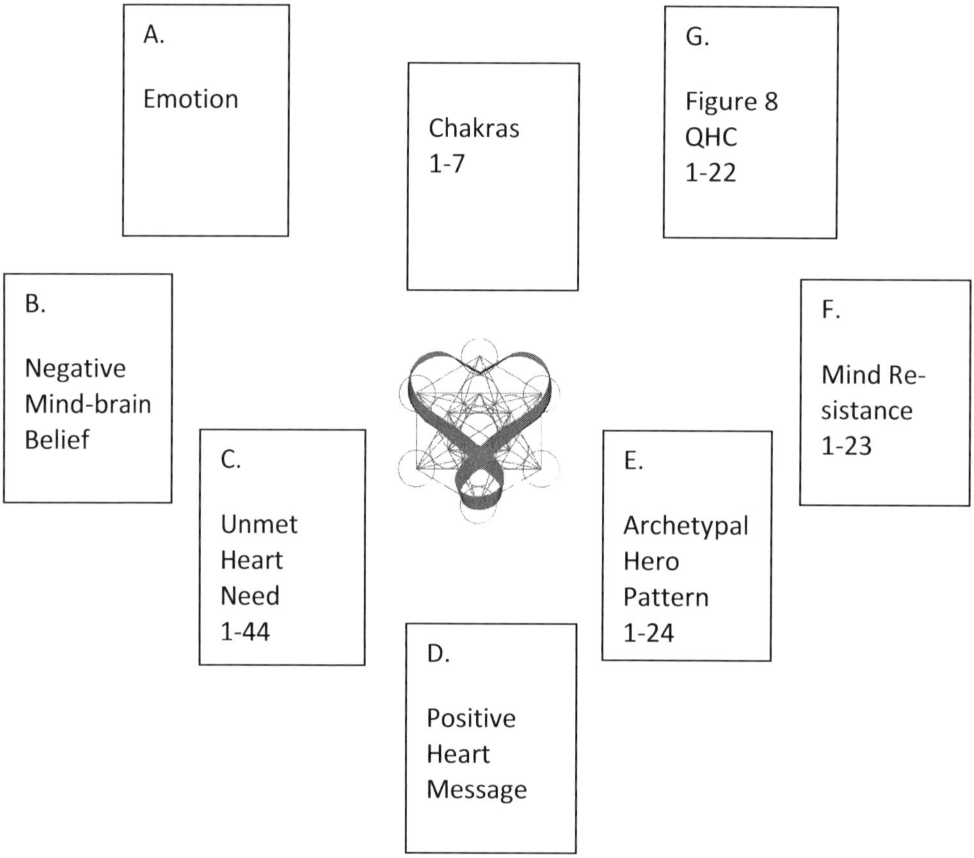

A.

Emotion

Chakras
1-7

G.

Figure 8
QHC
1-22

B.

Negative
Mind-brain
Belief

F.

Mind Re-
sistance
1-23

C.

Unmet
Heart
Need
1-44

E.

Archetypal
Hero
Pattern
1-24

D.

Positive
Heart
Message

Instructions

Hold the deck of cards close to your chest, over your heart, and feel the issue or what is making you feel uncomfortable. Take a moment to identify the **Issue** or problem about which you want to receive guidance from your heart. You may want to say what the **Issue** is out loud or write in down.

Place the cards face down in groups as labeled above. It is not necessary to place the cards in groups creating a heart, but it is a good reminder that the answers you are seeking are within your heart.

Pick up the group of cards labeled "Chakras." There are seven chakra cards. Ask your heart to pick one of the chakra cards by showing you a number 1 through 7. You can also fan out the seven cards and intuit which one is the one you need.

After you have chosen a chakra card, turn it over. You can discard the other six chakra cards.

On the face of the chosen chakra card, follow the steps listed A to G:

Step A. Find the **Emotion** by referring to the Emotion card that is connected to the chakra chosen above. The back of this card will display a set of numbers, like 1-4 or 1-5, etc. Ask your heart to show you the number you need from the numbers shown on the specific emotion card related to the chakra you drew at the beginning. Then turn the card over and read the statement corresponding to the number your heart guided you to choose. The Emotion is the Hero's **Call to Adventure**. The emotion causes us enough discomfort in our ordinary world that we decide to seek guidance from our heart.

Step B. Find the **Negative Mind-brain Conditioned Belief** card that is connected to the chakra you chose at the beginning. The back of this card will display a set of numbers. Ask your heart to show you the number you need from the numbers shown on the back. Then turn the card over and read the statement corresponding to the number your heart guided you to choose. The limiting or **Neg-**

ative **Mind-brain Belief** is the Hero stage of the **Refusal of the Call**. It is our conditioned beliefs that hold us in limitation. Our mind has been taught to judge and criticize, so much so that we may refuse to embark on a journey of expanded possibilities out of fear of what others will think of us.

Step C. Find the **Unmet Heart Need** card and ask your heart to show you a number 1 – 44. There is only one Unmet Heart Need card. After your heart shows you a number, turn the card over and read the statement corresponding to the number you choose. The Unmet Heart Need is the positive resonance that became displaced due to the disrupted vibration of the emotion. In effect, the Unmet Heart Need is the antidote to the Emotion. The Unmet Heart Need is part of the Hero stage of **The Road of Trials**. The Road of Trials is best represented by the Spiral of Life as a symbol for our journey through life's experiences, which brings us new lessons and truths.

Step D. Find the **Heart Message** card that is connected to the chakra you chose at the beginning. The back of this card will display a set of numbers. Ask your heart to show you the number you need from the numbers shown on the back. Then turn the card over and read the statement corresponding to the number your heart guided you to choose. The **Heart Message** is the **Action** we need to take in order shift out of our negative behavior pattern and into a new and positive way of being. This is the Hero stage of the **Mentor** where we accept the **Call to Adventure** due to the confidence instilled in us by the heart.

Step E. The face of the chakra card you chose at the beginning will list the number choices for the **Archetypal Hero Pattern**. Ask your heart to show you which number you need. Then find the related card that is connected to the pattern your heart helped you choose. Then refer to the specific details of that pattern found on the face of that card. Review the pattern and then go back through the previous steps to see if the messages from your heart now have a deeper significance.

Step F. Find the **Mind Resistance** card and ask your heart to show you a number 1 – 44. There is only one Mind Resistance card. After your heart shows you a number, turn the card over and read the statement corresponding to the number you chose. This is the mind's resistance to what the heart actually wants. It is the primary reason we hold onto the disharmonious resonance of the Issue. If we don't bring our mind's sub-conscious resistance to the forefront we take the risk that it (our mind) will sabotage the Heart Message. This is aptly referred to as the Hero stage of **The Supreme Ordeal**. It is here that the Hero wrestles with and conquers their conditioned limitations and worn-out belief systems.

If the Mind Resistance feels overwhelming to the point that it is standing in the way of bringing you into harmony with the Heart Message, then it is recommended that you do another spread using the Mind Resistance as the Issue. It may also be advisable to seek the help of a certified practitioner who can guide you through the expanded, full length version. In either case, you should complete the session as the Quantum Healing Code is often enough to shift any lingering resistance we may have about embracing the positive Heart Message.

Step G. Find the **Quantum Healing Codes** card. There is only one Quantum Healing Codes card. Ask your heart to show you a number 1 – 22. Then turn the card over to see which code you need to listen to. The codes are available on a CD inside the book titled *Quantum Healing Codes* (available on Amazon and ScalarHeartConnection.com).

Now listen to the code that your heart chose, and while listening repeat out loud three times the statement that came up in the **Heart Message** card (from step D). At the same time, use your non-dominant hand to make **figure-eight** motions over the front of your body from the root chakra up to the crown. Breathe in deeply as your hand comes up and exhale the negative mind-brain belief (card you chose in Step B) as your hand moves from the top of your head back down to the root chakra.

If your heart chose a **dissonant chord** (shown as an * after the track number on the face of the Quantum Healing Code card) then ask your heart to show you another number after listening to the dissonant. It is important to end the session on a **consonant chord**. You may need to listen to several dissonant chords before your heart chooses a consonant. These dissonant intervals help shatter old trauma patterns from the past and are necessary to complete before moving on to the new and harmonious patterns of the consonant interval.

If you don't have the Quantum Healing Codes, you can make the figure-eight motions while repeating the **Heart Message.**

This final step is the **Transformation** stage of the Hero. The new and positive resonance of the Heart Message is now imbedded and activated in your mind-body-spirit.

***

The final chapter of this book contains examples of other brave hearts who took up the Journey of the Heart of the Hero. Their Journey of Transformation will hopefully inspire you to embark on your own journey with the tools presented in this book and with the guidance of your heart.

NOTES:

1. Carl Jung, *Synchronicity: An Acausal Connecting Principle*, from Vol. 8. of the Collected Works of C. G. Jung, (Princeton NJ: Princeton University Press, 2010), par. 865, p. 36.
2. Carl Jung, foreword to *The I-Ching,* Trans. R. Wilhelm, Bollingen Series XIX, (Princeton, NJ: Princeton University Press, 1997), p. xxv.
3. Thomas Moore, *Care of the Soul,* (New York: Harper Collins Publishers, 1998), pp. 14-16.

CHAPTER 13

The Heart of the Hero in Action

Connie

At a public talk about Scalar Heart Connection, Connie volunteered to be the subject of a demonstration of the process. The shorter online version of the process was used to simplify the steps and to save time. Connie wanted to ask her heart about the chronic pain she was having in her lower back.

Connie's heart directed her to the Crown Chakra as the emotional center holding the **Issue** of discomfort in the lower back. The specific **Emotion** behind the disharmonious resonance in the Crown Chakra was the feeling of being "Out of Control." Connie was confused as to why her heart directed her to this feeling. She said she felt very much in control.

The next step in the process was to find the **Obstacle**, which is the **Negative Mind-brain Conditioned Response or Belief** that is involved in creating the **Issue**, which for Connie was the chronic pain in her lower back. Connie's heart showed her the number related to the statement, "I am trapped in tension unable to relax mentally or physically." Connie was confused by this statement as well because she felt relaxed and didn't particularly feel any tension.

Next, Connie asked her heart to show her a number related to the **Unmet Heart Need**. This is the vibratory quality that had become excluded from the body-mind system because of the chaotic energy pattern created by the **Emotion** "Out of Control." Connie's heart showed her the number related to "Limitlessness." Connie didn't have a clear picture of what the heart was trying to say about limitlessness and being out of control, therefore, we went directly to the **Positive Heart Message**. Connie's heart directed her to the statement "I am self-sufficient." Connie said she had always been self-sufficient.

At this point in the session, it was clear that the heart had a message that Connie's mind-consciousness hadn't yet been able to clarify. In other words, we hadn't connected the dots between what had come up in the session. This type of situation is behind the development of the **Archetypal Hero Patterns**. These patterns place the entire session into a deeper level of understanding in terms of the underlying dynamics that are at the foundation of our problems. The archetypal pattern reveals what our problems are trying to motivate us to grow towards.

Connie's heart chose the number related to the **Archetypal Hero Pattern** number 7-**3**-**1**. The 7th House in the 7-3-1 pattern is the **Issue**, which is the house of relationships. Connie immediately recognized that this pattern was speaking to a relationship problem she was having with her daughters. The **Emotion** "Out of Control" started to make more sense.

The 3rd House in the 7-**3**-1 pattern is the **Obstacle**, which is about the tendency to judge others or ourselves. Connie said her daughters judged her. She added, "I might be a bit judgmental, too." The earlier **Negative Mind-brain Conditioned Response**, "I am trapped in tension," made more sense when placed in context of the tension between herself and her daughters. The tension could now be seen, perhaps, as being held in the lower back. Issues with the lower back can also be about flexibility and how well we go with the flow—not needing to control.

The 1st House in the 7-3-**1** pattern is the **Action**, which is about learning to embrace the sense of identity in relationship to others without becoming controlling or dominating. The **Action** was related to the **Positive Heart Message** that had come up earlier, "I am self-sufficient." Connie realized that her heart acknowledged her sense of being self-sufficient, but it was about the "quality" of being self-sufficient. She said, "My daughters see me as self-sufficient, so they don't think I need them or need to have a relationship with them." It is actually working against me in terms of relationships. She realized that the action her heart was calling for was to relax or soften her unconscious need to be self-sufficient and judgmental in relation to her daughters so she could emanate a softer persona or vibration around them. In this way, her relationship with them would be "limitless."

From Connie's new perspective of the session, she created the **Positive Statement**, "I am soft in relationships—we are all One in our way of relationship."

Thanks to the Archetypal Hero Patterns, we went from a session that was not making any sense to one that was profound and life changing.

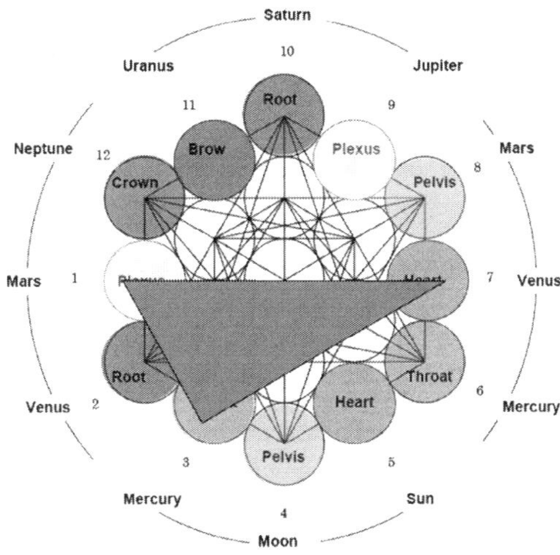

	The Archetypal Hero Pattern 7 – 3 – 1
Issue 7	An issue with relationships is also about how the Hero sees herself in relation to others. A lack of harmony and connection with others leads to isolation and loneliness or feelings of shame and guilt. These issues can also be a calling for relationship with the Hero's Higher Self and a re-connection with their authentic self. Before the Hero can continue his or her Journey, they learn to live harmoniously with others.

		Hero Stage: Accepting the Great Challenge—learning heart-centered compassion.
Obstacle 3		The challenge is their own mind-brain conditioning that judges others based on their differences. Their cultural prejudices can block their progress on the journey towards wholeness and attaining a state of unconditional love. Only by expanding the heart wide enough can the Hero encompass all illusions of differences. Hero Stage: Refusal of the Call—Relying on Mind-consciousness, which is generally driven by fear (fear of the unknown).
Action 1		The action necessary relates to learning to embrace the sense of identity in relationship to others without becoming controlling or dominating. It is still about desire, but how we go about getting what we want in a heartful and compassionate manner. Hero Stage: At Home in the Ordinary World, where we like things to stay just as they are or wanting control over our surroundings.

Melinda

Melinda felt disconnected from her infant daughter. She wanted to do a Scalar Heart Connection session around bonding with her child, but at the last minute she changed it to "bonding with my mother."

The emotional center holding this **Issue** was the Heart Chakra. The **Quantum Healing Code Archetypal Pattern** of the Heart Chakra is 5-2-8. The number 5 relates to the 5th House of Leo, the lion, the manifestation of personal power and creativity. The 2nd House is the house of personal resources and strengthening the sense of self-worth. The 8th House is the house of hidden, unresolved emotional issues from the past. The pattern is asking the Hero to regain their sense of self and realize their full potential in society. Their obstacle is the feelings of guilt and shame coming from unresolved issues of the past. The Hero is being asked to be reborn into a state of unselfish love and willingness to sacrifice their ego for the sake of others.

Melinda picked the number related to the emotional quality and received the **Emotion,** "Possessive." She recognized this as her possessiveness of her childhood trauma and not being able to let go of her history. The **Negative Mindbrain Conditioned Belief** was, "I feel trapped." Melinda said she was trapped in her possessiveness of her past. Her heart, on the other hand, gave her the statement, "I love myself and others unconditionally." She also received a **Positive Mentor Statement** from her lungs, "I am in synch with the natural rhythms of life." Melinda explained that although she was a professionally trained singer and knew how to breathe properly, she tended to be a shallow breather. She added that she often had pain in the area of her liver and felt tense in the area of her solar plexus. The heart and lungs are separated by the diaphragm, which she was trained to utilize when singing. However, when the heart center is constricted, the anxiety can become symptomatic in the area of the solar plexus or celiac ganglia. Perhaps her heart wanted her to release the emotional issues constricting her heart so her diaphragm would open.

Melinda then picked a number related to the **Level** of the mind-body-heart-spirit holding this unresolved issue. She chose the number corresponding to "Psychological." The Level statement under Psychological was "Depression." She said she had dealt with depression her whole life.

The **Earlier Experience** was "Genetic/Ancestral." She said, as far as she knew, her mom may have been depressed and was always looking for ways to run away—to avoid bonding with her. The **Unmet Heart Need** from this earlier experience was "Contentment." Melinda could relate to how her desire to bond with her mother had left her discontented since early childhood.

In the Practitioner Version of Scalar Heart Connection there is a section for **Triggers**. These are the places, people, things, etc., that trigger our cellular memory of past and unpleasant events. Often we may respond to triggers negatively without being aware of where the reaction came from. For Melinda, the **Trigger** was "Dreams." She clarified this and explained that she mostly daydreamed. By daydream she meant that it was easy for her to think about something and be able to see it clearly in her mind's eye. Mostly, she explained, she daydreamed bad stuff. "I ask myself why I spend my energy doing that."

When it came time to create her **Positive Statement**, she questioned whether she could give up the memory of her mother, as it was all she had left of her. "I will lose her if I don't have at least her memory," she said. She thought about honoring her mother's memory through her infant daughter, but said she didn't want her baby to see her shame and fear. "This is the reason I don't look at her in the eyes and why I can't bond. I don't want her to see that I am not whole and that I want to run away—like my mother."

She then had the thought that her grandmother was very critical. She started to think how that had affected her mother. I explained to her that the embryonic egg that would later become her was already in her mother's womb when her mother was in her grandmother's womb. Therefore, whatever energetic influence that was there for her mother was also there for her as well. This made her realize that her daughter was also present in her mother's womb along with her. The generational connection became more tangible.

The **Positive Statement** Melinda created was, "I have powerful visions and move from my heart in decisions about how to heal myself and others." This statement reflected her desire to learn various healing arts so she could help herself and others.

The **Mind Resistance** statement, which is the mind's resistance to what the heart really wants, was mostly about fear and the resistance to change. Melinda chose the statement, "I have to be better than I am to be loved." This meant that her mind-brain was driven to take classes, to learn new healing art modalities, out of a negative belief that she needed to be better than she was in order to be loved. This was the belief she had as a child: that if she were better in some way, her mother would love her and spend time with her, bond with her. On one hand, Melinda wanted to learn and become "better" so she would be loved, but on the other hand she didn't want to let go of the memory of her mother, no matter how painful. This helped her connect to why she had done so much "work" around this issue but always felt there was a piece missing—a piece of the puzzle that wouldn't let her resolve the issue. She suddenly got the insight that there was never anything wrong with her. "I am okay and loved just the way I am."

To fully entrain with this new and positive vibration of "I am okay and loved just the way I am," Melinda chose a number related to the **Quantum Healing Codes.** She chose the chords containing the frequencies 639 and 852. She needed to make scalar figure-eights from her pelvis to the top of her head while breathing in deeply, "I am okay and loved just the way I am." The code 639 is the frequency vibration of the archetypal pattern of the 6th House, the house of personal introspection and learning not to judge others. The code 852 is directly related to the 8th House where the Hero learns to overcome feelings of guilt or shame and blaming others.

For integration and closure, she needed "White Light of Unconditional Love." Using her talent for visualization, she could see this white light coming from her heart and connecting to the heart of her mother, and next to her grandmother, and finally to her daughter's heart. She said, "It looks like a polygon; it has geometric shapes." She said she felt a lot of love, unconditional love, buzzing in her head, heart, face, and arms. A few moments later, she said, "I am now quiet inside."

Several months later, Melinda shared that her relationship with her daughter had definitely changed since her Scalar Heart Connection session. She said it donned on her that her loyalty to her mother had prevented her from having a better relationship with her own daughter. "Most importantly," she explained, "I realized that my daughter doesn't know what perfect mothering is anyway. For that matter, neither do I. So we are both free to create whatever we like that is safe and playful for both of us. I now easily and joyfully look into her eyes and stay there without pulling away, without guilt, without fear, without depression, and that is a huge gain for me."

Mark

Mark wanted to ask his heart about his recent bout with a lung infection (bacterial pneumonia). He sensed that the infection may have related to a feeling that he was not as free and independent as he wanted to be. His heart picked the number for the Throat Chakra, which relates to the lungs. The **Emotion** activated in the lungs was "Sadness." Mark explained that he had recently lost a pet. He also shared that he felt sad about not feeling aligned with his purpose.

The Throat Chakra contains the **Archetypal Pattern** 6-3-9. The **Issue** in this pattern is about health (mental or physical) and the sense of well-being (lung infection). According to this archetypal pattern, the **Issue** motivates the Hero to analyze their behavior and actions with the purpose of leading to an awareness of their potential for perfection. Self-introspection helps the Hero grow beyond judgmental thinking and teaches them to become discerning and intuitive. This is a form of death of self, our ego-self. The **Action** in this pattern is to realize we don't have anything to prove, that we are connected to the Divine.

Next, Mark picked a number related to the **Emotion** activated around the **Issue**. He chose the number related to "Sadness." Mark already explained that his pet had recently died, but there was a sense that the issue of sadness went even deeper. To find the **Obstacle** Mark was facing, he picked a number for the **Negative Mind-brain Conditioned Response**, which was the perspective of, "I am a victim of circumstances." The **Positive Heart Message** the heart wanted to replace this with was, "I am a spiritual channel for creative expression." This was in line with the archetypal pattern of the Hero's need to re-connect to the Divine.

This was all making sense to Mark because he had dedicated many years of his life to the healing arts. Yet, there was something lingering in his subconscious that prevented him from fully expressing his creative energy. The heart told Mark that this **Issue** was on the **Mental Level**. More specifically, it was about "Money and Prosperity." His belief around money and prosperity came from family conditioning at an early age. His father was a successful businessman and his mother "came from money." However, when he was born there had been a financial strain on the household that prevented Mark from experiencing the vibration of "Harmony," which was what he chose from the list of **Unmet Heart Needs.**

The heart revealed that the **Memory Trigger** around his early experience was "Taste." Mark immediately recognized that the trigger was not about the sense of taste; rather it was his mother's taste for "fine things." In this regard, Mark said he had always been the black sheep of the family.

Mark's heart chose the **Archetypal Hero Pattern** 3-7-9. This pattern placed Mark's **Issue** in the 3rd House of Gemini and the mind. The 3rd House is the Hero's **Refusal of the Call.** The Hero in Gemini can get caught in the duality of good and evil and erect intellectual structures that turn into judgments and dogmas. These rigid mental classifications can block further progress on the Journey as we become fixed in our own paradigm and unwilling to see beyond the horizon. The judgmental Gemini mind, influenced by generational beliefs, becomes fearful—fearful for survival, fearful of not being recognized, fearful of not belonging, etc. Mark was caught in the mental level of feeling judged by his family for pursuing a career not driven by the acquisition of wealth. This caused him to react from fear: fear of survival, fear of not belonging (the black sheep). The Hero's mental rigidity and insecurity were preventing him from accepting the **Call to Adventure**.

The Hero's **Obstacle** in the 3-7-9 pattern is in the 7th House, the House of Libra, ruled by Venus. This is the house of connecting with others. Here, the Hero is challenged to find harmony in relationship with oneself and others. The Hero no longer relies on the outside world to define him, nor tries to fit in. This is also the stage where the Hero approaches the **Inmost Cave.** The Heart of the Hero is weighed against the weight of a feather and is tested for its purity. The Hero has to be ready before entering the Cave of the Dragon in the Eighth House. For Mark, the challenge was to move out of his **Negative Mind-brain Belief** that he was a helpless victim of outside circumstance. He was challenged to reconnect with his heart instead of looking for others to define him and his place in the world.

The **Action** required in the 3-7-9 pattern is found in the 9th House of Sagittarius, ruled by Jupiter. The action the heart was telling Mark to take was simply to realize that he didn't have anything to prove and to know he was loved at the deepest core, where he was connected to Divine energy. It is here that the Hero can then express their creative uniqueness and gifts in positive and life-enhancing ways. This is the stage where the Hero obtains the **Reward**.

When Mark was asked to put the story together about what his heart was telling him, he said, "I need to honor who I am versus what other people think I should be. I need to be free to be myself. It is only my mental state that creates the conflict I feel sad about in my lungs."

The lingering **Mind Resistance** was, "If I let go, it will happen again." His mind-resistance wanted to get the last word in and remind him that if he followed his own unique path he risked suffering financially. He was now facing his greatest fear.

His heart asked him to listen to Quantum Healing Code 852 while making scalar figure-eight hand motions over his heart and feeling the vibration of, "I trust my instincts instead of what others think." To integrate the session, his heart asked him to see himself surrounded by the "White Light of Unconditional Love" and to spend time in "Sunshine."

Sandra

Sandra wanted to do a Scalar Heart Connection session around her need to please others. The emotional center holding this energetic pattern was her Heart Chakra. The feeling in her heart was "Oppressed." The feeling of oppression was Sandra's **Call to Adventure**. The **Negative Mind-brain Conditioned Response** was, "Life is a constant struggle." This was her **Refusal of the Call**. Often our emotional discomforts motivate us to change, but subconsciously we hold on to conditioned beliefs that cause us to become frozen and static, accepting our fate.

Next, Sandra was asked to pick a number related to the **Positive Heart Message**. The number she chose related to the statement, "I am connected to the spirit of Nature, the planet, and its inhabitants." Another **Positive Mentor Statement** came from the lungs, "I am in synch with the natural rhythms of life."

Sandra was holding the vibration of this Issue on a **Psychological Level**, specifically a "Phobia." The specific phobia her heart chose was, "Being herself and public speaking." In reviewing her **Road of Trials**, Sandra said her father had made her feel held back. He gave her the ultimatum that he would pay for her college degree only if she studied the subject he chose for her. Sandra said this made her feel that she was not allowed to be herself. The **Unmet Heart Need** that arose from this infusion of perceived limiting energy from her father was "Contentment." And the **Trigger** for all of this was "People." She said she wanted to be free, finally, and courageous enough to step out into herself and shine in public. Thanks to the information she received from her heart, she could now see that she had taken on a negative belief about herself unnecessarily.

The **Archetypal Hero Pattern** Sandra's heart chose was 7-11-1. With this pattern, the **Issue** is more about harmony and connection with others, and less about feeling the need to please others. The **Obstacle** or challenge in the 11th House, the house of Aquarius, is about breaking out of old structures and awakening awareness. It is about transformation. The **Action** is in the 1st House, the house of Aries. Aries is about the sense of self-identity, which Sandra was lacking.

The 7-11-1 pattern allowed Sandra to change her story about herself. She said she wanted to flow like water and not be afraid of others' reactions when she was striving for personal growth. From this, she created her **Positive Statement**, "I am accomplishing my life's purpose with courage."

Next, Sandra needed to pick a number related to her **Mind Resistance** to her Positive Statement. The number she picked was the statement, "It is safer for me to stay small." To help shift this out-worn belief, Sandra listened to a specific Quantum Healing Code. Afterwards, her heart asked her to express a regret. Sandra said she regretted not being there for the ones she loved, because she erroneously believed that she had disappointed them.

The **Positive Action** her heart picked was "Sunshine." This made Sandra happy as she imagined herself basking in the light of confidence and self-fulfillment.

Suzanne

Suzanne had two large uterine fibroids. She wanted the Scalar Heart Connection process to help her hear what the fibroids needed to express in order for them to go away. She was aware that she always had difficulty accessing her feelings, particularly feelings of pain. She could relate to the idea that she was living in **the Hero's Ordinary World**, where everything was fine as long as things stayed the same. Using the process, she picked the number related to the Crown Chakra and the associated **Emotion** of "Lacking meaning and purpose." This was her **Call to Adventure**: the physical discomfort of the fibroids that were impinging on her Ordinary World, along with the emotional discomfort that she was not aligned to her life's purpose. The **Hero's Refusal of the Call** was the **Negative Mind-brain Response**, "I deny reality and conjure up my own world." This statement rang true with Suzanne, as she suspected the fibroids were trying to bring attention to something she was denying.

The **Mentor Statement** was the **Positive Message** from the heart, "Life is easy and I trust my inner voice." The Hero's **Acceptance of the Challenge** was related to Suzanne's recognition that she had been carrying this issue on the energetic level. The statement she received from the heart was, "Picking up energy from objects." Suzanne knew the objects were the fibroids themselves. With this piece of information, she felt confident to accept the challenge and move forward on her transformation journey.

The next stage of the Hero's Journey was the **Road of Trials**. Her heart picked the number corresponding to the "Genetic/Ancestral" pattern. She was not surprised, as her mother and grandmother both had surgery to remove uterine fibroids. The Hero's trials and tribulations also included the positive resonance of "Confidence," which she didn't experience when she was young as a result of her negative "Genetic/Ancestral" pattern around the belief that there was no cure for fibroids except for surgery. There was also a **Trigger** involved, which the heart revealed to be a scar. Suzanne connected this to the scar of having an abortion when she was nineteen. She said that when she was twenty-nine she became pregnant a second time because she thought a child would save her marriage. Her gynecologist mistakenly thought the egg was lodged in the fallopian tube. Consequently, the doctor gave her an injection that terminated the pregnancy but later discovered that the egg had been in the womb all along. Suzanne went into shock over the "accidental" abortion, and instead of allowing herself to access her anger over the mistake, she sought to console the doctor, who was also traumatized over the error. Suzanne was now aware that she had two scars—one for each abortion. She also had two fibroids.

The **Road of Trials** corresponds with the Sixth House of Virgo, ruled by Mercury. This is the house where we polish our life's experiences and any personality imperfections that would otherwise prevent us from reaching the treasure. Armed with a broader understanding of her earlier experiences, Suzanne proceeded to **the Hero's Approach to the Inmost Cave.** Here the Hero regroups and makes sure they have all the information and the heart-consciousness necessary before challenging the dragon that guards the treasure. This is also the House of Libra where the heart is placed on a scale with a feather on the other balance. The heart must be as light as the feather in order for the Hero to be ready and worthy of attempting the conquest and capture of the treasure. In the Scalar Heart Connection session, this was where Suzanne needed to create **The Story** of how her experiences had nudged her to a new level of awareness about herself.

The **Archetypal Hero Pattern** behind her experiences was the 12-4-6 tertiary pattern. This pattern is about the Hero needing to learn the lessons of the 12th House of Pisces, which teaches us not to become ensnared and sink into escapism and denials. This house often comes up when we feel stuck trying to conform to others' expectations.

Suzanne knew enough about her astrology chart to point out that she had the Moon in her 12th House, which related to accessing old memories. The **Obstacle** or challenge in the **Archetypal Hero Pattern** 12-4-6 is the 4th House, ruled by Cancer. Cancer is ruled by the Moon and is related to our emotions and issues with Mother. In Suzanne's case, it was about the emotions related to her mom, which she had suppressed. During her session she made the comment, "I tend to rationalize, deny my emotions, and move on. The abortions were horrendous so I covered them up; nobody knew. Afterwards, I couldn't have genuine relationships with my friends because of my lie. I just blocked the whole thing in order to disconnect from shame and guilt."

The **Action** Suzanne needed was in the 6th House, Virgo. We saw earlier how Virgo is related to the **Hero's Road of Trials**, where old personality behaviors are examined and polished. This related to Suzanne's **Positive Heart Message** to view life as being easy and to trust her inner voice. Suzanne didn't see anything "easy" about having two abortions, but because Virgo is about stepping into heart-consciousness, she was able to see how her fear of disappointing her parents made the situation more difficult in the long run. Suzanne emerged from the **Approach to the Inmost Cave** of the dragon who guards the treasure with a new positive resonance and belief— "I have complete access to my emotions and feelings of pain, and I release my guilt, shame, and grief now."

Supported with this new belief and awareness, Suzanne headed to the 8th House, the **Supreme Ordeal**. The 8th House is the house of Scorpio, ruled by Pluto. This is the house of the underworld, where all Heroes must descend in order to confront their biggest fears. Suzanne's heart was willing to battle the dragon in order to secure the treasure, but her mind resisted. Her **Mind Resistance** statement was, "I need to honor the memory." Suzanne recognized the statement as relating to the memory of the two lives that were lost. She realized that she had created two fibroids to serve as altars: one for "shame" and the other for "guilt." This shift in consciousness allowed her to be victorious over the dragon and she claimed her treasure—the gold in the shadow.

To help Suzanne make the journey back to her **Home** (a home now transformed), her heart asked her to breathe in the feeling of accessing her emotions and pain and to breathe out shame and guilt. While she was breathing, her throat became constricted with the feeling of grief. She began to tear-up, but continued to breathe until the feeling was released.

The final transformation around this issue came at the Hero's stage of **Transformation**, where her heart asked her to appreciate something. Suzanne said she appreciated the fibroids for the journey and the experiences they provided as opportunities for personal growth. She said she could now see how blind she had been to her own feelings and how she used the mechanism of denial to avoid feeling and pain. The final stage of the Hero's Journey is the **Return Home** with the Elixir (the treasure of transformation). To support this stage, she picked a number for a **Positive Action.** The number her heart picked was related to the statement "Other." Suzanne said she knew what that meant: that she needed to do a ceremony, a funeral for grieving. In this way, she could close the circle.

Terry

Terry wanted to do a Scalar Heart Connection session because she was having trouble sleeping and felt tired all the time.

Terry's heart directed her to the Throat Chakra as the center holding this **Issue.** The **Quantum Healing Code Archetypal Pattern** for the Throat Chakra is the 6-3-9 pattern. This pattern informed us that Terry's **Issue** of feeling tired was related to a lack of well-being arising from a **Negative Mind-brain Conditioned Response** that judges self and others. This pattern also indicated that Terry's solution was to realize that she didn't have anything to prove and that she was connected to the Divine.

Next, Terry's heart directed her to the over-activated **Emotion** in the Throat Chakra, "Grief." Terry recognized the emotion of grief and related it to her sister who died as a young child.

Terry's heart then showed her the **Negative Mind-brain Conditioned Response or Belief** around her Issue: "My creativity and self-expression are blocked." Next, her heart showed her the **Positive Heart Message**, "I deeply appreciate and accept myself." There was also an **Organ Mentor**, which was the lungs with the statement, "I am infinitely valuable." The **Level** of the unresolved **Issue** of being tired all the time was "Psychological." Specifically, it was a phobia of public speaking.

There was an Earlier Experience around the age of thirty-three that created the **Unmet Heart Need** of "Acknowledgment." The **Trigger** for this was a "Behavior." Terry recalled that at age thirty-three she was working at a job where she felt her skills and experience exceeded those of her boss. Therefore, she thought she needed to be careful not to offer too many suggestions that would make her boss look bad. She made herself small and subservient, and consequently believed she couldn't be acknowledged for her creativity and intelligence. Thirty years later, the thought of leading a group or sharing her knowledge with others drained her energy. When her energy was drained she was reminded of her father, who always seemed to her to be sad when she was growing up. She thought he was sad after her sister died, and always suspected that he carried grief from watching his buddies die and other episodes from the war that he never talked about. She valued her relationship with her father, who gave her support and acceptance. He died when she was eleven years old.

Terry's heart directed her to the **Archetypal Hero Pattern** 12-8-6. This pattern places the **Issue** in the 12th House, which is about dissolving old personality crystallizations. Here, the Hero can sink into escapism and denials. She may feel stuck trying to conform to other's expectations. This suggested that "feeling tired all the time" was a way of avoiding the challenge of facing life head-on. Terry lacked motivation because her earlier experience had taught her it was safer to hide her true essence and power. The **Obstacle** in the 12-8-6 Hero Pattern is in the 8th House, which is a challenge for the Hero to integrate deeply hidden memories and feelings. Here, the Hero learns to transform suppressed energies into desires for achieving group goals. The **Action** needed by the Hero is found in the 6th House. The 6th House reflects the potential for perfection. It is the Hero's stage of tests, **the Road of Trials**. The Hero is called to overcome the tendency to be overly critical of herself and others. They take action to grow beyond the preoccupation with their individual personality and learn to be of service to others. This was related to the **Positive Heart Message,** "I deeply appreciate and accept myself." From what Terry's heart revealed to her, she created the **Positive Statement**, "I am connected to my essence." Terry became conscious that she was not the subdued personality she assumed from her life's experiences. Instead, she was connected to the Divine and was infinitely valuable.

Terry embedded this new vibration into her body-mind-spirit with the Quantum Healing Code intervals 396 and 528, along with making figure-eight motions with her left hand over her heart.

Three weeks later, Terry reported that her chiropractor suggested trying a GABA precursor to help her sleep. After taking the supplement, she slept like a log but was still tired during the day. Terry realized that the solution was not directly related to a lack of sleep and wanted to do a follow-up Scalar Heart Connection session around the lack of energy and feeling tired.

The follow-up session revealed that the **Issue** of low energy and feeling tired was held in the Crown Chakra and related to "Meaning and Purpose." Terry's **Negative Mind-brain Conditioned Response or Belief** was, "I have to suffer." The **Positive Response** message from her heart was, "I am part of All That Is." The Cellular Memory **Trigger** was "Smells."

Terry said she had recently started smelling scents that reminded her of her trip to India. She described the smells as good smells. She was even noticing smells from India in her dreams. She had gone to a spiritual center in India and while there had suffered a seizure from heat exhaustion and was hospitalized. She said she was not ready to move into her life purpose at the time and went unconscious—literally. She felt her purpose was to share her light and wisdom with others. "I think I want it but I now see that subconsciously I hold myself back."

Terry was now ready to create the **Positive Statement**, "I trust the Divine." To embed this new vibration in relation to stepping into her life purpose, her heart directed her to listen to the Quantum Healing Code intervals 639 and 852, the tones for self-expression and connection to the Divine.

Terry realized how she had used being "tired all the time" as a mechanism for avoiding her calling. The second session took the **Issue** to the core of the subconscious behavior pattern that was sabotaging her desire to share her gifts with others. She slept soundly that night without the supplement and felt energized the next day.

Rebecca

Rebecca felt that her heart was closed. She recognized that she had not received a lot of motherly love. She also complained of pain in the left breast. She said she would feel better about herself and not so alone if she could connect with her spirit guides. She said, "I know they are there, but when I was seven years old, my father told me I could no longer talk to the invisible world. I shut it off and now I want it back."

Rebecca's heart guided her to the number of the Root Chakra and the **Emotion** of "Low self-esteem." Rebecca related that she felt her father's love was conditional, that she had to do well in school in order to please him. Her mother was busy raising foster babies. "I was the baby of the family and got picked on by my siblings."

The Quantum Healing Code pattern for the Root Chakra is 3-9-6. The **Issue** for Rebecca, according to this pattern, was in the 3rd House, the house of Gemini, the house of the lower mind. This indicated that she was caught in the snag of duality: right or wrong, good and bad. This is where the Hero may overthink or become judgmental. Their mental rigidity and insecurity prevent them from accepting the **Call to Adventure**. We saw this pattern activated in Rebecca's adherence for fifty years to her father's admonition not to talk to her spirit guides. The father's conditioning had dictated what was right and what was wrong. The **Obstacle** was in the 9th House, where the ultimate challenge for the Hero is a personal search for higher meaning and purpose. The Hero gains a broader view by moving beyond the limitations of others as well as a narcissistic self-image, the one that wants to be seen as good and proper. The Hero is challenged to travel, have new experiences, and/or attend schools of higher learning. The **Action** was found in the 6th House, which told us Rebecca's solution was in examining her behavior and tendency to be overly critical of herself. She was called to take action to grow beyond the preoccupation with her individual personality and to expand her horizon. Her heart was giving her permission to break free of the chains of the past and to soar to new heights.

Rebecca's heart directed her next to the **Negative Mind-brain Conditioned Response or Belief**, "I lack concentration and focus." She acknowledged that she could do fifty things at one time, but never finish any one thing because she lacked focus, adding, "But I could when I was a child."

The **Positive Heart Message** she chose was, "I do my best and my best is good enough, and I am good enough." There was also a Mentor Organ involved, which was the Large Intestines with the statement, "I release previous expectations and allow Source to support me."

The **Level** of the unresolved **Issue** was on the Psychological Level, specifically about "Over-guarding/protecting." Rebecca said, "Yes, it's the fear." The next step in the session was to find the Earlier Experience that set the **Issue** in motion. Rebecca's heart directed her to the number related to age forty-seven. We might have expected the earlier experience or trauma to be related to the age of seven, when she was told by her father not to talk to her spirit guides. However, her heart had something else it wanted to shed some light on. Rebecca explained that age forty-seven was the year that she ended her business relationship with her fishery and two other partners. She said it felt like a second divorce. "I had to prove myself. They got paid more than me because I am a woman. I was alone for a while after that. The break-up was a big one. I had a lot of fear around what they were going to do. They were jerks. It took the energy of the three of us to make the fishery successful, but they became greedy. I was afraid to go on my own. It was the self-esteem thing again."

The **Unmet Heart Need** that arose from this experience was "Sleep." This is the other side of the **Emotion,** "Low Self-esteem." At first glance, this appeared odd. However, the heart knows the true dynamics lying below the surface. Rebecca didn't need any time to think about the connection. She said, "You don't get much sleep as a fisherman. I felt like I wanted to be in an accident so I wouldn't have to show up and deal with it (the fishery). Low self-esteem—I always got my inspiration from dreams. Dream-time gave me direction or a connection to the other side. It gave me focus and a sense of self-worth because I know deep inside that I have lots of inner power. When I try to share my knowledge with others I forget all that I know because I am about feeling, and over-thinking gets in the way. Dad judged me based on my thinking. Now I want to be a feeler. Do I have permission to be a feeler and connect my inner power to others through what I feel in the moment?"

The next step in the Scalar Heart Connection process was to identify any **Cellular Memory Triggers.** Rebecca's heart directed her to the number associated with "colors." She responded, "I don't like red. . . my mother liked red." The color red is the color of the Root Chakra. It is also the frequency related to 396 Thz. The Root Chakra is about Gaia and our connection to the Earth. Rebecca considered herself to be a shaman, which was to be connected to the spirit of Earth. At the deepest level she was avoiding "mom issues," although her father kept coming up in the session. The pain she felt in the left breast was a clue to repressed mother issues (her mother had a tumor in the left breast). Rebecca said, "I had conditional love from my dad, but it is hard to really feel it because of the lack of connection with my mom. Mom is the feminine and that part I deny."

Rebecca's heart directed her to the **Archetypal Hero Pattern** 12-8-6. This pattern paraphrases the **Issue** from the 12th House, which is about dissolving old personality crystallizations. This is where the Hero loses her way and becomes ensnared into escapism and denials. She often feels stuck trying to conform to other's expectations. The **Obstacle** is in the 8th House and concerns the need for the Hero to integrate deeply hidden memories and feelings into their conscious sense of identity and personality. Social conditioning had taught Rebecca how to cope without getting in touch with her true feelings. The **Action** is in the 6th House, where the Hero is called to analyze her behavior and tendency to be overly self-critical. The Hero takes action to grow beyond the preoccupation with their individual personality and to learn to be of service to others. The Action in the 6th House from the Archetypal Hero Pattern was the same one that came up in the Quantum Healing Code Pattern. This was a fairly strong message to Rebecca that the Action she needed to resonate with was about breaking out of judgmental thinking and embracing the type of thinking that was more about discernment and unconditional love for herself and others.

Rebecca was now ready to create her **Positive Statement**. She created the statement, "I am enough; I am connected to a big love coming from the Earth, which I hold and share with others."

To complete the session, Rebecca needed to know if there was something still in her mind that would sabotage her new and positive outlook. This is the **Mind Resistance** to what the heart wants. Rebecca's heart directed her to the statement, "I need to honor the memory." Rebecca commented that she now realized that she had set up an altar to honor her anger towards her mother and her father's criticism. She was now willing and able to dismantle it.

Rebecca was now ready to listen to the Quantum Healing Codes. Her heart directed her to a dissonant interval. Two notes that are dissonant or discordant can act like homeopathic remedies where "like treats like." In a sense, it is similar to an opera singer who hits the precise frequency of a wine glass causing it to over-vibrate and shatter. In Rebecca's case, the dissonant chord helped diffuse the resonance of her unpleasant childhood memories from the cellular/energetic Level. Rebecca's heart chose four different dissonant chords, one after the other. Finally, Rebecca's heart was ready to imbed the positive vibration of, "I am enough, I am connected to a big love coming from the Earth, which I hold and share with others." For this, the heart chose the Quantum Healing Code interval 396 and 528. The frequency of 396 is the vibration of the Earth and 528 is the frequency of the heart. These two codes together helped Rebecca connect the Earth to her heart.

Rebecca's heart directed her next to the **Positive Action**. She picked the number related to "Walk on Grass." This was Rebecca's homework: a message from her heart for her to stay connected to her Source of shamanic inspiration—Mother Earth.

Valerie

Valerie felt that a past trauma was preventing her from moving forward in her life. She said she was almost terrified of the future. Her heart directed her to the Crown Chakra and the **Emotion** of feeling disconnected from meaning and purpose.

The Quantum Healing Code pattern for the Crown Chakra is 8-5-2. The **Issue** lies in the 8th House, which indicates that there are unresolved issues from the past. The 5th House, the **Obstacle**, is about self-identity and how we express our full creativity and self-confidence. It is also about learning to embrace our higher purpose. The **Action** is found in the 2nd House, which told us Valerie's solution involved releasing worries and anxieties about having enough money and personal resources. It was about strengthening her sense of self-worth and becoming mindful of the needs of others.

Valerie's heart directed her to the number related to the **Negative Mind-brain Conditioned Response** to her issue, which was the statement, "I am separate." Valerie said, "Yes, I am alone and separate."

Next, Valerie's heart gave her the number for the **Positive Heart Response**, "Life is an adventure—it is easy." She also received a message from a Meridian Mentor, "I accept and express my Divine right to personal power."

The next step in the Scalar Heart Connection process was to identify the mind-body-spirit **Level** of the unresolved issue. Valerie's heart directed her to the

Psychological Level, specifically a phobia of money. Valerie's response was, "That is amazing. Oh God, how money can take over people's lives or run them. I feel like the people I love the most are controlled by money and the pursuit of it. I don't have a balanced relationship with money. I feel ashamed to have it, sort of. The man that I am with now (for fifteen years) is always pursuing money, and not having good luck with it. It affects me. I am not connected with his business because there is a conflict around it. I have savings and he doesn't, so he feels like he has to work, work, work. We are not energetically aligned because of the money. With personal power I would make choices about how and where I want to live. I wouldn't be afraid of money that is available to me. I would allow the freedom to use the money that is available to me. I'm not necessarily afraid to work with it or to take ownership of the money as an adult, but I am afraid of bigger purchases."

We needed to know the origin of Valerie's fear of money. Her heart directed her to the number associated with "Genetic/Ancestral" (family conditioning). "Oh yes," she said. "Definitely my dad is very much Jewish about money. He is Jewish. He is also ill. He gets upset about spending anything even though he has so much saved. It's classic immigration stuff: not having anything and building from scratch. My mom loves flash, but my father is where I have my heart connection. He is my life-line. He is always kind and patient with me. I have some savings, but my dad has assets. If I needed money I would have to ask my dad and that is terrifying. My dad gave my husband and me enough money to buy a house. My husband died less than two months after we moved into the house and two weeks after my son was born. My current house is a kind of default house; it was supposed to be temporary—eighteen years later."

The session then directed Valerie to the **Unmet Heart Need**, the emotion or feeling that was displaced from the earlier experience. Valerie's heart chose the number related to "Gratitude." In Valerie's case, it was the resonance of gratitude and appreciation that she missed as a child due to the terror she felt asking her dad for money. Gratitude and appreciation were not available to her as a child because of the stress associated with asking for help. Whatever gratitude she may have felt from her father's financial support in buying her first house with her new husband was lost when her husband died two months later. Valerie realized that she had a subconscious belief around gratitude. She explained, "If I am grateful, it will be taken from me."

The next step in the session was to determine if there was a **Memory Trigger** that caused the unresolved **Issue** around gratitude to manifest in Valerie's life. Valerie's heart directed her to the number associated with "Scars." Valerie said she has a scar at the bottom of her spine. She explained that several years after her husband died, she saw a chiropractor who adjusted her coccyx because it was rigid from holding grief. The result was an outbreak of herpes-like welts at the base of her tailbone. The coccyx is about flexibility, particularly in relation to walking, or in Valerie's case, taking the next step in her life. She was emotionally frozen and it had manifested in her coccyx. One might speculate that the herpes virus had found the stagnated energy in her coccyx to be a good place to lie dormant. It was the chiropractic adjustment that stirred up the hornet's nest.

Valerie's heart showed her the number related to the **Archetypal Hero Pattern** 7-3-1. This pattern put Valerie's session in the perspective of the Hero's Journey. Her **Issue** of not being able to move forward in life could be seen as the Seventh Stage of the Hero's Journey, which is related to the **Approach to the Inmost Cave**. It is related to the 7th House of the zodiac, the house of harmony and connection with others. It is the stage where the Hero gathers the resources and strength needed to slay the dragon guarding the elixir. It is about issues with relationships. A lack of harmony and connection to others can lead to isolation and loneliness as well as feelings of shame and guilt. However, these issues can be a calling for the Hero to find a relationship with herself and a reconnection to the higher, authentic Self. Before the Hero can continue the Journey, they learn to live harmoniously with others and with their own self.

The **Obstacle** the Hero faces in the 7-3-1 pattern is in the Third Stage, the Hero's **Refusal of the Call to Adventure**. It requires the Hero to overcome cultural or ancestral prejudices so they can attain a state of unconditional love. The Obstacle is related to the **Negative Mind-brain Conditioned Response**, which for Valerie was the belief that she was separate and disconnected from meaning and purpose.

For Valerie, the other side of feeling separate from others was gratitude and appreciation, the **Unmet Heart Need**. Gratitude and appreciation lead to unconditional love. To make the shift from feeling separate to reconnecting to her higher, authentic Self required her to take **Action**. The action needed in the

7-3-1 pattern is in the 1st House, where the Hero becomes aware of their unique identity. The Action relates to learning to embrace a sense of identity in relation to others without becoming controlling or dominating. It is about getting what we want in a heartful and compassionate manner. The Action is related to the **Positive Heart Message**, which for Valerie was, "Life is an adventure—it is easy." And "I accept and express my Divine right to personal power."

Valerie suddenly saw how the pattern related to her experience. She explained that her first husband died on August 5th, the same date as her grandmother's death, although many years earlier. Her grandmother's father also shared the death anniversary date of August 5th. This synchronicity made her feel a strong connection to the ancestral issue of money and gratitude. She said, "My heart knows that life is a joyful adventure, it can be easy and light. My strength is my lifeline to Divinity as my primary Source. My mind stopped me because when I started to live and develop, everything shattered; so I went small, scared, and went back to familiar family patterns. I stayed loyal to my dad." From this insight, she created her **Positive Statement**, "I am alive and life is meant to be lived. I choose life."

Valerie then asked her heart to show her a number related to the **Mind Resistance** to her Positive Statement. Her heart showed her the number related to, "I need to be right or I will die." To this Valerie responded, "I need to NOT take risks in life or I will die. That was my old belief. Now I can see that it is better to live and die than not live at all."

The Quantum Healing Codes Valerie needed to help bring the new and positive vibration into every cell of her body were the chords 528 and 639. The frequency of 528 is related to the Heart Chakra and 639 is the Throat Chakra. She needed the vibration of heart-connection through self-expression. After listening to the codes, her heart directed her to surround herself with the "White Light of Unconditional Love."

Julie

Twenty-four-year-old Julie had become increasingly uncomfortable with her emotions. She was struggling not to get caught up in the drama they presented. She said her habit was to send all her emotions through her thinking filter, which she said was annoying because her thinking judges and criticizes. She wanted to do a Scalar Heart Connection session to see if she could gain insight from her heart on how to deal with her emotions.

Julie's heart informed her that that the emotional center holding her discomfort was the Crown Chakra. The **Quantum Healing Code Archetypal Pattern** for the Crown Chakra is the 8-5-2 pattern. This pattern informed us that Julie's **Issue** was related to depression arising from unresolved emotions from the past. The 8-5-2 pattern also informed us that Julie's **Obstacle** or challenge was to examine her heart's desire to control or satisfy her ego without consideration of others. The resolution or **Action** called for Julie to release her worries, strengthen her sense of self-worth, and trust in the wisdom of the heart and the Divine.

The **Emotion** activated in the Crown Chakra was "Meaning and Purpose." Julie's heart guided her to the **Negative Mind-brain Conditioned Response or Belief,** "Change is dangerous." To this, Julie responded, "I get stuck in these weird OCD loops. I'm afraid to let go of things from my past because there are also good parts of me there. I feel like there is a light in my past that is not reclaimed, so I'm afraid to throw my past away. This means I can't change because I can't let certain things in. My guard is up to anything that would bring me pain—emotions bring pain."

Next, Julie's heart directed her to the **Positive Heart Response**, "Life is an adventure—it is easy." The **Organ Mentor** was the Nervous System with the statement, "My life is perfect synchronicity and flow."

The **Level** of Julie's unresolved **Issue** was on the Emotional Level. Julie wasn't surprised since her emotions had driven her to want the session in the first place.

Julie's heart then directed her to the "Birth Process" as the place where the limiting belief first arose. Specifically, her heart directed her to the seventh month in the womb. Julie was born during the month of Leo. Counting backwards two months placed Julie under the influence of Gemini in the seventh month in the womb. This was when her parents split up. She still carried the belief that she was responsible for their divorce and more so that she wasn't wanted. Julie's Chiron was in Gemini. Chiron represents the early wound. She said, "I was the cause of my parent's breaking up. I was a bad mistake. I caused all this pain. I can't let go of this belief system because I might kill something good about myself if I do." Julie confided that in the past she suffered with suicidal thoughts and was prone to self-mutilation with razor blades. "I don't allow myself to feel love; it keeps me safe. I measure my self-worth by how I feel." According to Julie's birth chart, the Moon (emotions) was in her Second House, the house of what we value. The Chiron wound in the house of Gemini explained, in part, why she felt compelled to filter her emotions through the critical judgment of her mind instead of allowing her heart to be her guide.

Julie's early experience in the womb created a resonance pattern that blocked out the vibration of "Appreciation." Appreciation of self was her **Unmet Heart Need.**

Julie's heart then directed her to the 10-6-4 **Archetypal Hero Pattern.** The 10-6-4 pattern placed Julie's **Issue** in the 10th House, where depression and despair or obstacles and social structures/barriers can affect the Hero's sense of self-worth. The **Obstacle** in the 6th House challenges the Hero to rise above the lower mind's tendency to judge and criticize and embrace the high Virgo mind of discernment. This doesn't mean the traumatic events in the past should be forgotten, ignored, or suppressed, but rather, we acknowledge them as parts of ourselves that provide the wisdom and strength of character necessary to help others. The 6th House teaches us to expand our heart wide enough to fit our unpleasant past and still have room left over for other people's problems. The **Action** called for in the 4th House is the recognition that life's experiences and what we feel have a way of forcing the Hero into action. The Hero is called to re-examine their purpose and overcome their fears stemming from childhood memories and suppressed emotions.

Julie felt that her heart was telling her to connect with people from her heart—to see the adventure of life through the eyes of the heart. She realized that the light was always with her. The darkness from her early experience blocked out the light, but the light was who she was on the inside. She felt ready to let go of the rage she felt from the past, knowing that the good parts of her would always remain in her heart. She said, "I need to learn to live with compassion for myself and for others."

The insights from her heart helped Julie create her **Positive Statement**, "I live life with joy and ease and with compassion for myself and others." Next, Julie's heart directed her to the **Mind Resistance** to her Positive Statement. Her heart showed her the statement, "If I change, I will abandon those I love." To this, Julie said, "If I change I will abandon that critical, judging voice in myself. I am learning who I am not, and I am not my emotions."

Julie's heart then gave her the Quantum Healing Code 639, related to the Throat Chakra, which is about creative self-expression. Julie said she wanted to be a singer, and smiled.

Madeline

Madeline wanted to do a Scalar Heart Connection session around the issue of feeling like she was always competing with others. Madeline's heart guided her to the number related to the Throat Chakra. The **Quantum Healing Code Archetypal Pattern** for the Throat Chakra is 3-9-6. This pattern informed us that Madeline's **Issue** was about lacking a sense of well-being, a consequence of mind-brain conditioning that judges self and others. When this pattern is activated it is a call to realize that we don't have anything to prove and that we are connected to the Divine.

Next, Madeline's heart directed her to the number related to the **Emotion,** "Sadness." Madeline said she felt like she was never good enough and that she had a longing to be recognized. She suspected there was an issue of low self-worth stemming from the past.

Madeline's heart then showed her a number related to the **Negative Mind-brain Conditioned Response or Belief,** "I am silenced." Madeline said she was aware that the **Trigger** for her **Issue** was coming from a part she had auditioned for at school: a part that she won and then lost. The director loved her performance and offered her the part. Later, the director discovered that a well-known actress became available and decided to offer the part to her instead of Madeline. Losing the part made Madeline feel "silenced." It also triggered issues of low self-worth.

The next step in the process was to identify the **Positive Heart Message.** Madeline's heart showed her the number related to the Positive Heart Message, subconsciously "I speak and communicate my truth from my heart." Madeline responded to this message by saying, "I need to stay authentic to myself. Perhaps losing the part just gave someone else a chance to shine and I need to go and do my own thing—find out what works for me." The **Organ Mentor** for this session was the Lungs with the statement, "I am infinitely valuable."

The **Level** of this unresolved **Issue** was on the Energetic Level and the related statement was, "Connection to another person or group causing her the same problem." Madeline responded by saying that the whole theatrical group was always in a competitive mode whenever they were auditioning.

The Earlier Experience was in the "Birth Process," specifically the seventh month in the womb. Madeline said the seventh month was when her parents split up. She could still relate to the feeling of, "Hey, what about me?" She felt abandoned and a sense of competitiveness set in around having to be "special" enough for people to stay in her life.

The **Unmet Heart Need**, which is the positive resonance pattern that becomes displaced when the vibration of the negative belief creates an interfering and chaotic pattern, was "Respect." Madeline felt like she "got no respect." She said, "Otherwise, my parents would have stayed together. Respect is when people acknowledge me and my gifts and talents and boundaries—acknowledge how special I am and how valuable." Madeline then recalled the earlier **Mentor** statement, "I am infinitely valuable." This was the resonance pattern she needed to reconnect to in order to shift out of the limiting belief that she was always competing with someone else.

Madeline's heart directed her to the **Archetypal Hero Pattern** 11-3-5. This pattern is about breaking out of old structures (Aquarius ruled by Uranus). It is the Hero's stage of **Transformation**. The **Obstacle** or challenge the Hero must overcome is their own mind-brain conditioning that judges others based on their differences (Gemini ruled by Mercury). In this case the judgment arose on the basis of talent. The **Action** this pattern is requesting relates to gaining a sense of purpose. It is about what we create (Leo ruled by Sun). The Action is about reconnecting to our inner wisdom and creative spirit. It is the Hero's stage of crossing the threshold or accepting the challenge. It is also related to the **Positive Heart Message**, "I speak and communicate my truth from my heart." The story or message in the session from Madeline's heart was an encouragement for her to embrace being a lion and to break out of the habituated pattern of competing for her father's choice—his choice of leaving her and her mother. In this way, she could pursue her creative ambitions without the baggage of subconsciously feeling like she was performing for her father's attention and approval. She was now free to create for the joy of creating and expressing her authentic self.

Madeline created her new **Positive Statement**, "I am infinitely valuable." The **Mind Resistance** to the Positive Statement was, "I have to be in control." Madeline said, "I am in control of how I audition. Why can't 'they' see that?" The resistance of the mind was still trying to have the last word. The need to be in control was also an Aquarian attribute, albeit a negative one. Madeline heard her mind's objection and made the conscious decision to create a new and expanded resonance habit: to be infinitely valuable just as she was.

Madeline embedded the new and positive resonance into her field of consciousness with Quantum Healing Code 417. This code connects our childhood memories to our Crown Chakra, allowing their lessons to be integrated into higher levels of awareness.

Ginny: Part 1

Ginny had attempted suicide two months earlier. She was under the care of a psychiatrist. Her family urged her to have a Scalar Heart Connection session because she had grown despondent. She said she kept waking up in the morning with a lot of anguish and unbearable feelings of panic, fear, and pain. She felt abandoned, anxious, and had been carrying pain her whole life. She defined the word "pain" to mean the feeling of being alone, unloved, and carrying other people's issues (her children's and parent's).

Her Scalar Heart Connection session directed her to the Solar Plexus Chakra and the **Emotion** of "Integration" (not being able to digest or assimilate an emotional response to a trauma or situation). The **Quantum Healing Code Archetypal Pattern** was 4-2-6, which informed us that Ginny's **Issue** was related to the lower emotions of the 4th House. It also told us that her motivation for change, the **Obstacle**, was related to "lower identity" from the 2nd House. This pattern also informed us that the **Action** Ginny needed to take in order to change the habituated memory/behavioral pattern holding her in distress was related to the "higher mind" from the 6th House. This pattern essentially says that when we become entangled in childhood memories, we can lose sight of what is valuable and truly useful for our personal development. We may look for emotional security through mind-numbing substances and preoccupations. In the extreme, we may want to check out altogether. From this pattern we could see that the archetypes were calling Ginny to re-examine her worries and anxieties and release them into trusting that a greater power had her best interest at heart. In order to achieve this change in perspective and way of being, she needed to connect with her "higher mind," the one that is heart-centered and discerning, as opposed to the "lower mind" that tends to be overly critical of self and others.

The next step in the session was for Ginny to ask her heart to show her a number related to the **Negative Mind-brain Conditioned Response or Belief** surrounding her **Issue**. Ginny's heart showed her the number related to, "I am overly assertive, aggressive, and manipulating." Ginny said, "Yes, and angry. I'm sick of all of it."

Ginny's heart then showed her the number related to the **Positive Heart Message**, "I trust my heart's innate intelligence to nurture and take care of me." She also received a positive message from the Stomach Meridian, "I am comfortable with myself." Ginny's response was, "I am just now starting to take care of and love myself after all these years. I am a bubble in the ocean of God's smile."

Next, Ginny needed to know the **Level** her **Issue** was affecting. Her heart informed her it was on the Psychological Level, specifically about a phobia of food. Ginny said she had food issues her whole life. "When I was growing up, food had to be eaten in our house. We had to eat everything on our plate. Not eating was the only thing I could control in my life. Not eating made me feel powerful. As a result, I have not fed or nourished myself well. If I think of food as manna, food for the soul, then I don't feel worthy of it. It is hard to feel God's love for me."

Ginny needed to know the **Early Experience** that brought on her life-depleting belief. Her heart directed her to the "Birth Process," specifically the seventh month in the womb. Ginny said her mom got pregnant right after having her first child. It made her think she wasn't planned for or wanted. Her parents were stressed out. She also thought the seventh month could have been when her mom tripped over her first child and fell pretty hard. Ginny said, "I think it made me afraid."

The next step in the process was to identify the **Unmet Heart Need**, the positive resonance that was displaced by the chaotic vibration of not being able to digest or assimilate an emotion or feeling. The heart showed Ginny the number related to "Breath." Ginny said, "Yes. I am not breathing in life." Breath, then, was the opposite of not digesting her perceived feeling of not being wanted and life is not safe.

Ginny's heart then showed her the **Archetypal Hero Pattern** 7-3-1, her **Issue, Obstacle**, and **Action** as the stages of the Hero's Journey. The 7th stage is the Approach to the Inmost Cave, the stage where the Hero learns to be pure of heart. Only a pure heart is able to succeed against the dragon that guards the treasure. In terms of Ginny's **Issue** with overwhelm, feeling alone, unloved, and carrying the burden of other people's problems, it was a calling from the archetypes for her to connect to her Higher Self—her authentic Self. The **Obstacle** in the 7-3-1 pattern is the third stage, or the Hero's Refusal of the Call. This rephrased her **Negative Mind-brain Conditioned Response** of being assertive, aggressive, and manipulative as a challenge for her to step out of her habit of being judgmental and overly critical. She was being asked to take the Hero's journey towards connecting with herself, others, and the Divine. The **Action** in this pattern is related to the first stage of the Hero's Journey, which is **Home in the Ordinary World**. In Ginny's case, her Action related to learning to embrace a new sense of identity in relation to herself and others without wanting to control the outcome or others behavior. It was more about being comfortable with herself and trusting her heart's innate intelligence to nurture and take care of her.

From everything Ginny's heart told her, she created the **Positive Statement**, "I am the loving person God created me to be and that is all I need to be; I am able to receive God's love because I am God's love manifested." Ginny's beautiful **Positive Statement** didn't resonate well with her mind. Her heart directed her to the **Mind Resistance** statement, "If I am invisible, I am safer." Ginny said, "I just want to be invisible. I want to disappear and not be here anymore." When Ginny thought about her Mind Resistance in the context of what her heart was telling her, she realized that she had allowed her mind to adopt a belief and behavioral pattern that was just that—a limiting perspective.

Ginny's heart showed her the Quantum Healing Code 528 as the tone she needed to listen to in order to help imbed her new perspective into her body-mind-spirit. The note 528 cps is the frequency of the Heart Chakra.

To integrate and complete the session, Ginny needed to express a regret. She said, "I regret that I didn't know my children were being harmed by my husband and that I didn't protect them.

Because her regret brought her back into the past and to a place of undigested emotions/feelings, another session in a week was recommended, a session with the specific **Issue** related to trusting that her life experiences had meaning and were purposeful.

Ginny: Part 2

In Ginny's previous Scalar Heart Connection session, her heart directed her to the positive and powerful statement, "I am the loving person God created me to be and that is all I need to be." Her heart also showed her that her mind was still holding on to the belief that "If I am invisible, I am safer." Ginny's reaction to her mind's resistance was that she just wanted to disappear and not be here anymore. Her heart then directed her to express a regret to which she said, "I regret that I didn't know my children were being harmed by my husband and that I didn't protect them." Because her regret brought her back to the past and to a place of undigested emotions/feelings, it was recommended that she do a follow-up session in a week; a session with the specific Issue related to trusting that her life experiences have meaning and are purposeful.

For Ginny's follow-up session she said her **Issue** was about having a hard time letting go of her children and grandchildren and forgiving her ex-husband for hurting her children. She said she was feeling much better and more positive after her first session, but feeling tired.

Ginny's heart directed her to the Brow Chakra and to the **Quantum Healing Code Archetypal Pattern** 7-4-1. This pattern shows up when our Issue is about relationships and feeling isolated when we get bogged down with unresolved issues or suppressed feelings from the past. When this pattern comes up, we are being called to embrace a sense of identity in relation to others without feeling the need to control others or situations. The **Action** called for in this pattern is one of trusting the heart and our connection to the Divine.

The **Emotion** Ginny's heart directed her to was "Out of Control." Ginny said she tried to reach her grown sons, but they didn't answer or return her calls. She said, "They are still angry with me for attempting suicide, but I'm their mom and they should listen to me because I am their mom and I am in control. . . Oh!"

Next, Ginny's heart directed her to the **Negative Mind-brain Conditioned Response** behind the emotion of being "out of control": "I am trapped in tension, unable to relax mentally or physically." She said she had been feeling some anxiety, especially when she couldn't contact her children. She said she walked every day for about an hour, which helped her stay calm and get in touch with Nature. "I'm feeling much better, but I'm overly tired. It's hard to get up in the morning. I go to bed around 10:30 and get up between 1:00 and 2:00 the next afternoon."

Her heart led her to the number related to the statement, "I interact harmoniously with others." Ginny said, "Sometimes not talking to someone is the most harmonious thing to do." Ginny's heart then directed her to her **Mentor**— her Brain, and the statement, "Miracles are a natural part of my life." She said, "Yes, let and allow the miracles to happen without trying to force or control."

The **Level** on which her Issue was manifesting was "Psychological," with the statement, "Depression." Ginny said her doctor had been trying to get her depression under control but hadn't found the right dosage. "He also wants to give me something to help with my exhaustion issues, which come from the issues weighing on my heart and taking up all my energy."

The **Earlier Experience** that set her Issue in motion was something her heart told her happened at the age of thirty. Ginny said the age of thirty was just before she moved to Alaska. "It was when my boys were in the car when my ex got pulled over and taken to the police station. They were almost sent to child protective services. I had to go to work full-time because my ex lost his job. I tried to take the kids, but I needed to be the bread-winner and had to leave them home with my ex. It was a traumatic time. I didn't tell anyone. I didn't make enough money to pay all the bills. My ex kept drinking and fooling around. I finally left and he brought the kids to me later. The kids were angry with me for taking them away from their dad. I guess I am stuck in the past and my gown boys don't want anything to do with the past. I need to change and be in the present for them."

Ginny's heart then directed her to the **Unmet Heart Need**, "Stillness." Ginny said, "I stay in bed for fifteen hours a day to avoid the lack of stillness. I would sleep for twenty-four hours if I could. That way I could be invisible and just disappear."

The **Cellular Memory Trigger** for Ginny's Issue was: "People." She said she assumed by "people" her heart meant "family." "How do I make family and people not be a trigger? It's like I single out a few leaves on the tree of life and forget to love the whole."

Ginny's heart then directed her to the number related to the **Archetypal Hero Pattern** 5-9-11. This pattern puts Ginny's Issue in the context of the Hero's Journey and the Fifth Stage where the Hero Accepts the Challenge. This is where the Hero may hold themselves back from fully expressing their individuality, their power, and their full potential. When this happens, problems may manifest as problems with creativity, self-expression, self-confidence, and/or uncertainty around the sense of purpose. The Obstacle lies in the 9th House, which is about meaning and purpose. The ultimate challenge for the Hero is a personal search for higher meaning and purpose. The Hero gains a broader view by moving beyond the limitations of their ego-self. They are challenged to travel, have new experiences, and/or go back to school, study, learn new skills. The Action is in the 11th House, which is about breaking out of old structures and an awakening of awareness. Here, the Hero must break out of old and negative or limiting beliefs and overcome the emotional suppression of old wounds from their encounters with the world. They are called to share their wisdom and spiritual knowledge with the community and contribute to the outside world, knowing they belong to the whole.

It was now time for Ginny to create **The Story** of what it was her heart was trying to tell and show her. She said, "I have wanted to do creative things for years, but I am afraid to. I won't be good enough. After my last Scalar Heart Connection session I signed up for a painting class that starts in a couple weeks. I also signed up for a charity walk this weekend. If I can do these things, I feel like I will be honoring my sons and my grandchildren."

From The Story, Ginny created the **Positive Statement**, "I interact with others from a place of creativity, fun, and joy." Ginny then needed to hear from her **Mind's Resistance** to her beautiful Positive Statement. Her heart showed her the number related to the statement: "If I change, others will die." In her first session (Part One), Ginny was not able to fully re-program her mind's resistance to change around wanting to be safe by being invisible.

This led to this session (Part Two), where her heart provided deeper insight into where her Mind Resistance was coming from. Armed with this new information Ginny said, "I am willing to let the past go—maybe even my relationship with my sons and grandchildren for the time being." She realized that the heart didn't literally mean "others will die," but that she must be willing to change by letting the past die even if it meant blazing a new trail for herself. Perhaps her new trail would bring her closer to her children and grandchildren in the future and in perfect timing. She was now resonating with "interacting harmoniously with others and miracles are a natural part of her life."

To harmonize and reprogram her resonant memory field around her new way of being, she needed to listen to the Quantum Open Heart Chord. Ginny's heart directed her to the **Positive Action**, "Sunshine." Her homework was to get up early every morning and greet the Sun and to face it with her eyes closed for five to ten minutes. And to repeat this anytime she felt like she was slipping into an old thought pattern—to recondition and reroute her brain activity. To embody change, she agreed to "Get out in the world; Share; Teach; Be an example and support for other people's change. A few months later Ginny reported that she found a place to live and had a job being a nanny to a four-year-old boy and she loved it.

Karen

Karen wanted a Scalar Heart Connection session because she had been feeling an urge to cut herself. Self-mutilation was a pattern she stepped into when she felt isolated. She said she wanted to do a session around her attachment to pain and to ask her heart how she could learn to carry the sense of home and un-conditional love inside herself. Karen's heart directed her to the Crown Chakra and to the **Emotion**, lack of "Meaning/Purpose." The Emotion is the motivator of change. It was the uncomfortable sense of not being connected to a higher pur-pose that was causing Karen not to feel at home within herself.

The **Quantum Healing Code Archetypal Pattern** associated with the Crown Chakra is 8-5-2. This pattern informed us that Karen's **Issue,** in the 8th House, related to unresolved feelings from the past that can turn to anger and rage. When this archetype is activated we may seek power or control, as well as blame others for our problems. The **Obstacle**, in the 5th House, is about self-identity and how we express our full creativity. It is also about self-confidence and learning to embrace our higher purpose without getting lost in ego gratification or numbing ourselves to our feelings. The **Action,** in the 2nd House, showed us that Karen needed to release her worries and anxieties and strengthen her sense of self-worth, and become more mindful of the needs of others.

Karen's response to the archetypal pattern was a recognition that she was on the planet to learn how to love unconditionally and to flow in love. She said, "I need to see things from a place of understanding instead of passing judgment or placing things in good or bad categories. I get over stressed by trying to control things and people, and then I become destructive.

Karen's heart then guided her to the number related to her **Negative Mind-brain Conditioned Response or Belief** that "Money and material things are at the center of her existence." She said she tended to be a workaholic when things didn't go her way in relationships. "My projects give me a sense of self-worth, which is like money."

Karen's heart directed her to the **Positive Heart Message**, "I am part of All that Is." She also had a **Mentor** whose statement was, "I accept and express my Divine right to personal power." Karen realized that she made herself small so she could feel powerful through the sense of control she got from people paying attention to her during times of stress.

The **Level** on which this **Issue** was being held was the **Mental Level**. The specific statement was "Self-esteem." Karen said, "Yes, It's all about getting attention. When I am experiencing low self-esteem people pay attention to me, treat me special. It's why I don't let go of low self-esteem. It's a way to get a reward."

The **Earlier Experience** was "Collective Consciousness." This told us that Karen was experiencing an archetypal pattern that pertained to all of us on some level. In other words, the issue was not the result of a specific trauma or an-cestral belief, but rather a stage along the Journey that we all experience at one time or another.

The **Unmet Heart Need** was "Forgiveness." Karen was unable to assimi-late this vibration because of the dissonant resonance around a lack of meaning and purpose. Karen realized that by forgiving herself and others she could move into a new pattern of helping others. By moving out of low self-esteem and re-claiming a sense of purpose, meaning, and self-worth she could help others find purpose and meaning in their lives.

Next, Karen's heart guided her to the **Cellular Memory Trigger**, "Taste." Karen immediately thought of her taste for sugar. When blood sugar lev-els spike, an alarm response kicks in that adds to stress by the body's release of cortisol and adrenaline. To make herself feel better, she would eat more simple carbohydrates and the cycle repeated itself. She went from eating foods high in sugar to compensate for the feeling of low self-esteem, and then felt bad about herself when she crashed.

To put her session into the context of the Hero's Journey, Karen's heart directed her to a number associated with the **Archetypal Hero Pattern** 8-12-2. The **Issue** in the pattern, like the Quantum Healing Code pattern she received earlier, also in the 8th House, is about the way we respond to crisis. In this stage of the Hero's Journey the **Supreme Ordeal** occurs. This where the Hero encounters the dragon (their shadow)—their deepest fears, desires, and all the emotions they have buried deep in their subconscious. The **Obstacle** in this pattern is the 12th House, which is where the Hero dissolves old personality crystallizations and re-unites with their true Self by dissolving their sense of separateness and victimization. The Hero must disentangle from addictions and denial. The **Action** in the 2nd House is also the same as the one Karen received in the Quantum Healing Code Archetypal Pattern. This is the stage of the Hero's **Call to Adventure**. It is about gaining personal resources and strengthening the sense of self-worth.

Armed with these insights from her heart, Karen adopted the **Positive Statement** from her Mentor, "I accept and express my Divine right to personal power."

Karen then asked her heart to show her the **Mind Resistance** to her Positive Statement. Her heart directed her to the statement, "Taking risk leads to loss." Karen said she didn't like to feel out of control because it caused pain and pain sucks. "I control the pain by being self-destructive. Pain is unavoidable so I would rather take the risk and endure the pain from life's experiences, which is better than inflicting the pain on myself." She now realized that instead of stunting her own personal growth by avoiding pain, she could have faith that when unpleasant things happened it was ultimately for her evolution. In the process, she realized that it was only her mind that put her experiences in the categories of good or bad, pleasant or painful.

The Quantum Healing Code Karen's heart directed her to was the interval 528 and 852. The note 528 is the frequency of the Heart Chakra and 852 is that of the Crown. These two notes are in Golden Mean proportion and connect the heart with higher meaning and purpose.

The session then asked Karen to express an appreciation as part of her Integration. She said, "I appreciate all the hard work I put into learning to love myself." Karen's **Positive Action** was "Sunshine."

Charlene

Charlene wanted to have a Scalar Heart Connection session because she felt uninspired and disconnected from her passion and purpose. Charlene's heart directed her to the **Crown Chakra** and to the **Emotion**, "Meaning and Purpose."

The **Quantum Healing Code Archetypal Pattern** for the Crown Chakra is 8-5-2. This pattern informed us that Charlene's **Issue,** in the 8th House, was a calling to transform personal desire into desire for the common good of the group or global community. The **Obstacle**, in the 5th House, was about self-identity and how Charlene expressed her full creativity and self-confidence. The **Action,** in the 2nd House, called for in this pattern is to release worries and anxieties about having enough personal resources, both physically and energetically. As Charlene discovered in the session, she was being asked to strengthen her sense of self-worth and to reconnect to the world with a new sense of vitality and purpose.

Charlene's heart guided her to the number related to the **Negative Mind-brain Conditioned Response or Belief**, "I am disconnected from Source." The **Positive Heart Message** from Charlene's heart was, "Life inspires me." And the **Organ Mentor** statement was, "I accept and express my Divine right to personal power." Charlene's heart directed her to the **Psychological Level** and the statement, "Over Guarding/Over Protecting.

The next step was to find the **Earlier Experience** or trauma that created the disconnection from meaning and purpose that Charlene had been feeling. Her heart directed her to "Genetic/Ancestral" and specifically to "Dad." Charlene said her dad was depressed after his service in World War II. It all got too much for him after the war. He was on the front line for three years. War disconnected him from Source. Life was no longer inspiring. He was a family man. He enjoyed horses and his ranch and was involved in the community, but he just had too many wounds and pain."

Charlene realized that her discomfort in feeling uninspired and disconnected to her passion and purpose was coming from her father. She could feel her father's presence in the room. She could also feel his pain, isolation, and sadness. Charlene had earlier invited her friend, Maria, to sit in on the session. We asked Maria to be a proxy for Charlene's dad. Maria was inspired to say, "I am sorry

Charlene that I was not able to show you the life I imagined." Charlene responded, "You were such a wonderful father to me. I love you."

The **Unmet Heart Need** Charlene's heart chose for her was, "Peace." Charlene said her father never spoke a word about his experiences on the war front. She was grateful that her heart had led her to a session that would help her father find peace.

Charlene's heart guided her to the **Archetypal Hero Pattern** 10-2-4. The 10th House of this pattern represents a deeper level behind the **Issue**. Specifically, it tells us that depression and despair can affect our sense of self-worth and our ability to contribute to the global community. This made sense to Charlene when she put it in the context of her father's trauma. The 2nd House is the deeper aspect of the **Obstacle**. It is about discerning what is truly valuable and useful for our evolution/personal transformation. Here, we learn to release our worries and anxieties and become grateful for what we have and the opportunity to share our gifts and wisdom with others. Charlene was being asked to reconnect with Source and the Divine. In this way, she could reconnect with purpose from a place of inspiration. The **Action** called for in the 4th House is to re-examine our purpose and to overcome the fears and suppressed emotions stemming from past experiences.

Charlene's response to the session, **the Story**, was, "Wow!" She realized that she had been carrying a cellular memory/epigenetic pattern from her father's trauma from the war. "My dad was forced to kill when in his heart he was a peaceful man. He became disconnected from purpose and finding meaning in this messed up world. I am connected to my dad's depression and lack of motivation to get out in the world. Something in my dad gave up. I always felt like I carried his weight." At that moment a thunderstorm broke out over head and the house rattled. There was a huge shift in the air. We all laughed with relief.

The **Positive Statement** Charlene created was, "I am free now to live a life of inspiration, personal power, and passion." The **Mind Resistance** to Charlene's new intention was, "I have to be better than I am to be loved." Charlene realized that the session had been about her father. Therefore, the mind resistance was her father's resistance. She allowed her father's voice to speak through her: "I regret that I was not a better father. I didn't believe I was loved. Otherwise I would not have been put on the front line. I didn't give myself permission to be loved by God after all the horrible things I did in the war." Charlene realized that she had carried her father's belief of not feeling worthy of being powerful or inspired or connected to the Divine. Maria was inspired to speak as Charlene's dad: "I merged with the light when I died; all that doesn't hold anymore. I am at peace now."

The **Quantum Healing Code** Charlene's heart guided her to listen to was the Open Heart Chord. Charlene's **Positive Action** was to get a massage. She said, "Yes, I have been holding a lot of tension."

Relationship Session: Part 1

Elaine and John were having a conflict in their relationship. They wanted to do a Scalar Heart Connection session around the **Issue** of communication. We treated the *"Relationship"* as an entity of its own right, as opposed to being about two individuals. Elaine and John took turns asking their hearts to show them the numbers that were needed in the session.

The first step in the session was to find the Emotional Center that was in disharmony around the **Issue** of communication. The *Relationship* chose the number related to the Brow Chakra. The **Quantum Healing Code Archetypal Pattern** for the Brow Chakra is the pattern 7-4-1. This pattern provides insight into a deeper, more subconscious pattern that had become activated in the lives of Elaine and John. This pattern is concerned with relationships, the 7th House, and the feeling of isolation when we get bogged down with unresolved issues or suppressed feelings from the past, the 4th House. The pattern was calling for Elaine and John to embrace a new sense of identity in their connection to others and their relationship without feeling the need to control, related to the 1st House. It came down to a lesson in trusting the heart and a personal connection to the Divine.

The next step in the session was to find the distressed or over-activated **Emotion** in the Brow Chakra. The *Relationship* chose the number that contains the emotion of "Restlessness." Elaine said the restlessness was there because it felt like there was no resolution to the issue. The emotion is the Hero's **Call to Ad-**

venture. Restlessness was what motivated the *Relationship* to want to resolve the conflict in the way they communicate.

The *Relationship* then asked the heart for the number related to the **Negative Mind-brain Conditioned Response or Belief** around the unresolved emotion. The chosen number related to the statement, "I am out of control." Both Elaine and John agreed that on the thinking level the issue was "out of control." This is both the **Obstacle** and the stage where the Hero refuses the **Call to Adventure**, because the conditioned thinking response generally judges and criticizes and is afraid of what lies ahead in the unknown.

Next, we needed to know the **Positive Heart Message**. The *Relationship* chose the number related to the statement, "My inner voice communicates with me clearly and willingly." Elaine and John were enthusiastic about this possibility, but were apprehensive since they were both resonating with the mind belief that the situation was "out of control." This was the **Action** needed to resolve the obstacle of any habituated behavior pattern. It is also the Hero stage of encountering the **Mentor**. The Mentor is the innate knowing of the heart, which informs us of what is in our best interest. When the Hero trusts the Mentor the real journey begins.

The heart then directed the *Relationship* to the "Nervous System" as the **Organ Meridian** that was in disharmony around the **Issue** of communication. The Organ Meridian acts like an assistant mentor. The heart then directed the *Relationship* to the number related to the Organ Meridian statement, "I face the future confidently, knowing a benevolent universe supports me." The couple related this to a fight or flight response in the nervous system. Elaine said, "There is a wall of fear between us that comes up. John closes down when I try to communicate my feelings to him."

We asked the heart to show us the **Level** on which the issue of communication was being held, and we received the number related to "Energetic." The specific statement related to the energetic level was, "Picking up the energy from objects." The couple both agreed that the object was related to their work. They owned a family-operated photography business, which they started together when they got married. John had been thinking about retiring, but was unsure of how to pass the business on to their two sons. He was also worried about the financial needs of retirement. John was the photographer in the business and managed the finances. Elaine managed everything else: scheduling, manning the studio, all the work behind the scenes, and everything else that gets a portrait and wedding album out the door. When their two sons joined the business the dynamics changed and Elaine found she had less and less control. The struggle for control soon resolved itself by Elaine agreeing to leave the business. Unfortunately, this only exacerbated Elaine's feelings that she was not seen or heard. She now felt forcefully removed and outcast from the community of her family. She also related that John's purpose in life seemed to only be about working. Elaine became emotional and her voice louder as she said, "He works twenty-four hours a day. He comes home from the business and continues to work. It's like I don't exist." John remained silent, looked away from Elaine, and tried to fight off a yawn.

Once the Hero understands the dynamics of the **Level**, they have a better understanding of where they need to place their attention. From the standpoint of the Hero's Journey, this is the **Acceptance of the Challenge**. The heart of the *Relationship* had brought to the surface Elaine's feeling that she didn't exist because John seemed to be a workaholic in her eyes. John's conditioned pattern was to become defensive and shutdown as soon as Elaine became agitated. His yawn could be seen as a nervous system response serving to disengage himself from a perceived threat. The fight or flight response to a stressful or life-threatening situation is actually three-fold. We can stay and fight or we can run. The third option is to play dead and hope the danger will go away.

Now that we had brought to conscious awareness the essence of the problem behind Elaine's and John's communication Issue, we needed to pinpoint the original energetic disruption or **Early Experience**. The heart of the *Relationship* chose the number related to the "Birth Process," specifically the fourth month in the womb. We interpreted this to represent the fourth month of their courtship. Elaine and John shared that they had met at John's photography studio. After four months of dating, Elaine quit her job and started to work for John. The discovery of the background to the Issue is the Hero's stage of the **Road of Trials**. These are the earlier experiences that formed our behavioral responses in the present.

We now knew when the disrupted energy began in the relationship, but we still needed to know what energetic quality became disrupted when Elaine started working for John. This is the **Unmet Heart Need,** the positive life-enhancing quality that was displaced from the *Relationship* as a result of the early experience. The heart of the *Relationship* chose the number related to the Unmet Heart Need statement, "Peace." The couple volunteered that in working and living together all these years they slowly established a negative compensation pattern whenever a lack of peace presented itself. John said, "When Elaine becomes upset about something and expresses her feelings, I raise a barrier between us because I don't know how to handle her anger.

Elaine was not at peace because when the communication broke down she felt unseen and not heard. At this point, Elaine began to feel the pent-up frustration of not being seen or heard rising to the surface. She said, "Don't ever give up your life! I gave up my life and who I am. Now I feel stuck, blocked, and like I gave up my identity all over again." As the volume of her voice raised, John got quieter and quieter. Elaine became emotional and was encouraged to breathe deeply into the feeling. She recognized that she had problems with breathing fully and soon felt more relaxed. She also recognized that she hadn't ever fully expressed her deepest feelings around the issue. She now understood the Positive Heart Message that had come up earlier and the need to allow her inner voice to communicate with her clearly.

In order to obtain deeper insight into the unconscious patterns that were playing out, the *Relationship* chose a number for the **Archetypal Hero Pattern**. The number they received from their heart was the pattern 8-12-2.

The number 8 in the 8-12-2 pattern relates to the **Issue**, about communication, and the archetypal energies found in the 8th House of the zodiac. The 8th House is related to unresolved feelings from the past and how, when repressed, they can turn to anger and rage. When this house is activated, we might blame others or seek power and control. It is a calling for us to transform our desires for personal control over others into a desire for the common good of the group. From the perspective of the Hero's Journey, this is the stage where the Hero confronts their deepest, darkest fears. It is the **Supreme Ordeal**, where the Hero must wrestle with repressed emotions and desires.

The number 12 in the 8-12-2 pattern relates to the **Obstacle**, which is the **Negative Mind-brain Conditioned Belief** that came up earlier in the session ("I am out of control"). The 12th House is about dissolving old personality crystallizations. For Elaine and John it was a reminder that the dynamics of their relationship communication crystallized in the fourth month of their partnership. The challenge when the 12th House comes up is to re-unite with our authentic Self by dissolving our sense of separateness and victimization. This is the Hero's Stage of receiving the **Elixir**. This tells us that breaking free of who we think we "should" be is the great reward.

The number 2 in the 8-12-2 pattern relates to the **Action** we must take in order to shift the chaotic and negative energetic pattern found in the **Obstacle**. The **Action** ultimately shifts the **Issue** of communication but it does so by changing the negative belief pattern found in the **Obstacle**. The 2nd House is about what we own, what we value, possessions, our personal resources, and our home. The archetypal energies in the 2nd House challenge us to release our worries and anxieties about personal comfort, our resources for the future, and the need to control. The Hero strengthens their sense of self-worth and becomes mindful of the needs of others. This is the **Call to Adventure** stage of the Hero. The mind-brain generally resists the call because it is afraid of the unknown. John was worried about having enough resources for retirement. Recall that the Organ Meridian earlier in this session provided the *Relationship* with the statement, "I face the future confidently, knowing a benevolent Universe supports me." For Elaine, the Action in the 2nd House revealed the need to strengthen her sense of self-worth and to embody the resonance of belonging.

The next stage in the process was **The Story**. This is where the client (*Relationship*) described what they believed the heart was trying to tell them about the Issue. John said the take-away message for him was to relax about the business and start to do things he and Elaine enjoyed doing together, like travel. Elaine felt like she needed to learn to enjoy herself more and to re-establish her sense of identity. She found a hesitation around that idea because she felt a twinge of guilt that everyone else was working. Elaine agreed that she needed to support John in whatever and however he wanted to work. John agreed that he needed to support Elaine in her process of choosing something different for herself (to allow her a sense of freedom). They agreed to support each other in what they each loved. The Story and the **Positive Statement** (below) is the Hero's stage of **Approaching the Inmost Cave**. This is where the Hero becomes clear about the action needed in order to shift the energy of the issue.

Together, Elaine and John created the **Positive Statement**, "We are free to be ourselves and to communicate with ease and openness with full-hearted expression."

After creating the Positive Statement they needed to know if their mind-brain conditioning would go along with their new way of being. The *Relationship* asked the heart for a number and received the **Mind Resistance** statement, "We need to honor the memory." We discovered that on the thinking level the *Relationship* wanted to maintain what it had been doing for the previous thirty-eight years. Again, our mind-brain conditioning is afraid of change and the unknown. The question was whether or not Elaine and John would move forward in a different way. This is the Hero's stage of the **Supreme Ordeal**. The Supreme Ordeal is aptly named because it is where we must wrestle with the dragon (our shadow) and old way of being in order to be victorious and shift the old and negative behavioral pattern (neural network).

To complete the session the *Relationship* chose the number related to the **Quantum Healing Code** 396. This tone is related to the Root Chakra. The Root Chakra is about our connection to Earth and to community. It also relates to issues with survival. We recalled that John had issues with survival after retirement and Elaine felt disconnected from the group (the business and family). This is the stage where the Hero gets the **Reward**. The Hero listens to the Quantum Healing Code and every cell in their body resonates with the new and life-enhancing vibration of communicating with ease and having the freedom to be themselves.

The heart of the *Relationship* asked Elaine and John to breathe in the feeling of the Positive Statement while listening to the Quantum Healing Code. This supported Elaine's issue with deep breathing. This is the Hero's stage of the **Road Home**. The added action of breathing anchored the new resonance from the positive statement, making it more physically tangible.

The next step in the session was the **Transformation**—integration and closure. This is normally where the client may need to express a regret or say something to someone. In this case, the *Relationship* chose the number related to the statement that "nothing" was needed. This told us that a deep transformation had just occurred in the relationship. We only needed to see if there was something more needed after the session was complete.

The final step in the session was the **Positive Action**. For this, the *Relationship* chose the number related to a positive action they needed to do after the session. The number chosen related to "Breathing." This is the final Hero stage, **the Return with the Elixir**. This session brought up deep issues for both Elaine and John to examine and digest. They were both relaxed after the session and felt a sense of relief. However, the heart stirred up some past memories and buried feelings on both sides. They decided they wanted to take a few days to talk and integrate and then do individual sessions. The subsequent sessions Elaine and John did individually took them both to the core of some very old soul-level wounds.

Relationship Session: Part 2 John

John wanted to follow up on the relationship session he had with his wife Elaine. Specifically, he wanted to have a Scalar Heart Connection session around the **Issue** of being slow to change. He said he had just completed a session in which his grandmother had come up in the "Genetic/Ancestral" section. The **Negative Mind-brain Conditioned Response** at the end of that session concerning his grandmother was, "If I change I will die." John thought the aspect of his grandmother coming through in the session was interesting because he didn't know the identity of his real grandmother. Apparently, his grandfather drank a lot and somewhere in an alcoholic state got a woman pregnant. His grandfather's wife (he called her "fake" grandmother) put a pillow under her dress and pretended to be pregnant in order to protect the family honor. The emotion that came up in that session was "terror." John imagined that his "real" grandmother must have been terrorized by the thought of giving up her child. She may have also anguished over not being able to support herself and the baby. John's mother grew up with a disruption in the natural order or connection of love. As a result, John said, she was not big on change. "She mostly wanted to make everyone happy. She had her own business and worked all the time." John heard himself in the statement, "she worked all the time." This was one of the complaints brought up by his wife in the earlier relationship session. Both John and his mother identified themselves with their work. There was no separation between themselves and what they do.

To begin the new session, we first needed to know the chakra or emotional center holding the disharmony around change. John asked his heart to show him a number and he received the number related to the Pelvis Chakra. The Pelvis Chakra is energetically related to the bladder and kidneys. John said he was born with a horseshoe kidney. His kidneys never separated.

The **Quantum Healing Code Archetypal Pattern** for the Pelvis Chakra is the pattern 4-1-7. This pattern provided a deeper look into the subconscious nature of the session. It informed us that John's **Issue** around change was related to childhood memories and a subsequent sense of low self-worth, in the 4th House. The **Obstacle** in the 1st House is a call to be courageous, heartfelt, and purposeful in response to life's problems. The **Action** needed to rise above the wounds of the past lies in embracing heart-consciousness in relationship and community, related to the 7th House.

John asked his heart to show him the number related to the **Emotion** that was over-activated in the Pelvis Chakra. His heart showed him the number connected to the emotion "Desires." John said he wanted to spend more time with photography. "I like working."

The **Obstacle** or the **Negative Mind-brain Conditioned Response** John's heart showed him was connected to the statement, "I am weak." John felt this statement was connected to his weak will about change. He also connected this to his "real" grandmother's lack of power to change what happened to her.

Next, John's heart showed him the number related to the heart's **Positive Response**, "I am proud of who I am and my accomplishments." John said, "I am proud of my business. I know that neither my wife nor I get much credit for our accomplishments." The **Mentor Organ** that John's heart identified was the kidneys and the statement, "I am powerful and have control over my life."

The **Level** of the unresolved issue of not being able to change was identified by John's heart as being on the "Energetic" Level, with the specific statement, "Connection to another person or group causing you the same problem." John felt this was a direct connection with his mom and "real" grandmother.

The next section of the process was the **Earlier Experience**. John's heart led him to "Genetic/Ancestral," which we expected. However, the heart directed us to John's father, which was totally unexpected until we looked into it further. John's father was a photographer. He also worked a lot and was married to a woman John described as being much like his wife. John's father remarried sometime after John was born to a woman who was concerned about social status. She didn't approve of John's wife and didn't hide her feelings. At one point John told his dad that his step-mom needed to stop her negative talk towards Elaine or not talk to them at all. The result was that John's dad disinherited John and his wife.

John's heart then directed him to the **Unmet Heart Need** of "Understanding." John said his dad's wife was demanding. She didn't understand him and his needs. John felt a resonance with his dad on this level because Elaine didn't seem to understand that he needed to work because he was responsible for supporting three families (his and those of his two sons).

The **Cellular Memory Trigger** was "Sounds." John said when Elaine raised her voice it triggered a defense or a wall and he shuts down. He said his dad was different in that he would jump into an argument with his step-mom, but she would always win ("I am weak").

John felt the **Story** or message that his heart was telling him was that he was repeating old patterns from people before him. His dad was also a photographer and his wife also ran the business (money side). He realized that his sense of responsibility might be a trap. He said he wanted his sons to have a balanced life between work and spending time with their families—"at least more than I am having."

With the information and insights John received from his heart, he created the **Positive Statement**, "I embody change easily—I am ready and willing to step into a new pattern of spending more time in Hawaii with my wife, and doing what I love."

John's heart then directed him to the **Mind Resistance** statement, "It is safe for me to stay small." John said that his old belief, before this session, was" it is safe for me to work" (hiding my true self behind work).

John's heart chose the **Quantum Healing Code** 22, which is the Open Heart Chord. John's **Positive Action** was "Other." He said "My positive action is to go home right now and be present for my wife."

Relationship Session: Part 3 Elaine

Elaine wanted to follow up on the relationship session she had with her husband John. Specifically, she wanted to have a Scalar Heart Connection session around the **Issue** of creativity and self-expression, which she said were blocked. She said, "Out of fear of rejection I express to others an image of being small. I want to free myself."

Elaine's heart directed her to the **Brow Chakra** and the **Quantum Healing Code Archetypal Pattern** 7-4-1. The archetypal personality pattern in the 7th House relates to **Issues** with relationships and feelings of isolation that arise from unresolved issues or suppressed feeling from the past. The **Obstacle** in the pattern is in the 4th House, which calls us to look deeply into issues from childhood, where we are taught to suppress our feelings. We are called to re-connect to that small voice of heart-wisdom from within. The **Action** in the 1st House relates to learning to embrace a sense of identity in relationship to others without becoming controlling or dominating. It is about getting what we want in a heart-felt and compassionate manner.

The **Emotion** over-activated by the issue of creativity and self-expression was "Over-exhaustion." Elaine said she had been chronically ill for a long time. "I am just always exhausted."

The session then directed Elaine to ask her heart to show her a number related to the **Negative Mind-Brain Conditioned Response** surrounding the unresolved emotion of being over-exhausted. He heart showed her the statement, "I am disconnected from my heart's intuition and higher knowing." We found in her earlier relationship session that the **Positive Heart Message** was, "My inner voice communicates with me clearly and willingly." Elaine said, "Whenever I act from my knowing it looks like chaos and abandonment. So I don't always trust my inner guidance. I don't trust myself or Spirit."

Elaine's heart directed her to the **Positive Heart Message,** "I interact harmoniously with others." Elaine said that felt foreign to her. "I am always being judged for being me. I am the product of a failed abortion. My mother never connected with me. I feel isolated from others and aborted over and over again."

Elaine shared that she had skin cancer and that she viewed skin as representing separation and identity. For her, though, there was a certain resonance of mutilation involved. She was also extremely chemical sensitive. "I can't feel safe anywhere. I can't express myself. People misunderstand me and I feel isolated—aborted."

The **Organ meridian** involved was the "Nervous System," which made sense to Elaine because she had a constant headache since she was twenty-four years old (forty-one years).

The **Level** of the unresolved issue of creativity and self-expression was held on the "Energetic" level with the specific statement, "Sympathetic response causing you to suffer." Elaine said it was most likely a sympathetic response to the abortion attempt.

We next needed to identify the **Earlier Experience** that set off the trauma, upset, and limiting belief. Elaine's heart directed her to "Genetic/Ancestral." The ancestor involved was identified as her mother. Elaine said her mother was sixteen years old when she became pregnant. She said her mother was concerned about how others would judge her and thought this might have been the primary motivation for wanting an abortion. Her father married her mother five months into the pregnancy. She also realized that her mother didn't get to live the life she envisioned for herself. "I am the scapegoat for that."

Next, Elaine's heart directed her to **The Unmet Heart Need**, "Unity in Community." Elaine said, "Perfect! I never have unity in my family, not even in the womb. I started with enemies. I'm no longer connected to the business I helped run with my husband. I am an outsider with my two boys and the business. I don't feel seen or heard by my husband. I have only had one ally in my life, my dad's dad. Out of fifty-two grandchildren, I was his favorite. He protected me. He saw my parents were having a baby that wasn't wanted, so he stepped forward and took on the job of really loving me." Elaine then realized that her grandfather saw a situation and the situation was not about her personally.

The **Cellular Memory Trigger** was "Things." Elaine said, "It's just things. Not anything in particular. It is just things that set things off—one thing or another."

The **Archetypal Hero Pattern** that Elaine's heart chose was the pattern 12-4-6. Here, the 12th House is where we find the archetypal energies surrounding the **Issue**. Issues in the 12th House tend to be about dissolving old personality crystallizations or feeling stuck trying to conform to other's expectations. The 4th House is the **Obstacle**, where we are called to look deeply into unresolved issues from the past. This is the same house that came up in the Quantum Healing Codes Pattern at the beginning of this session. When we find the **Action** in the 6th House we know we are being asked to move away from judgmental thinking and towards discernment or keen insight. Discernment allows us to see through the eyes of the heart. This allows us to analyze our behavior, actions, health, and ways of being that are related to the community beyond our individual personality. This is a form of the death of self, of ego-self. The 6th House is the house of Virgo where we serve as an apprentice to learn to be of service to others.

Elaine was next asked to share the **Story** of what she understood her heart to be telling her. She said, "I get stuck. My survival pattern looks at what I think others want me to do or to be. I totally abandon myself and my creative expression in order to conform to others expectations so I won't be aborted. I need to wake up to my purpose and outgrow the abortion. My Divine spirit was wounded in the womb, but it is now time for me to get out of the emotional soup of feeling aborted all the time. Otherwise, I am short-changing myself and others by not stepping into who I really am. My mom is like an ostrich. She doesn't like to look at it (our lack of connection and what happened). She is now going blind and deaf. My mother was a twin and her mother almost gave her away during the depression. She was aborted in her own way. Ultimately she was kept, but she probably never felt a part of the family. I am repeating her experience."

Elaine then created her **Positive Statement**, "My Divine energy and spirit flow from my authentic self and I interact harmoniously with others (not from a place of survival, but as an expression of the Divine).

The **Mind Resistance** to Elaine's Positive Statement was, "I fear being nothing." Elaine said, "Because I have believed I am nothing. If I act harmoniously with others it might make me disappear. It is the only pattern I know. When I stir up the pot I force people to deal with me and their attempt to abort me. I am the Aborted One."

The **Quantum Healing Code** the heart chose for Elaine was the interval 417 and 852. The frequency of 417 cps is related to the Pelvis Chakra; the center connected to childhood memories and our deepest desires. The frequency of 852 cps is the vibration of the Crown Chakra and the connection to the Divine. Elaine's heart gave her the chord that transmutes the emotions of the past to a connection to our authentic self and the Divine.

In order to **Integrate** this session, Elaine's heart directed her to express a regret. Elaine said she regretted that she had abandoned herself.

Analysis of the Relationship Sessions for Elaine and John

Relationship Session

QHC Pattern: 7-4-1

Hero Pattern: 8-12-2

The session showed John that his need to work was taking time away from spending quality time with his wife. The issue behind his "need" to work was a feeling of uncertainty around the financial needs of retirement.

The session showed Elaine that there was a need to be seen and heard, which sometimes manifested as being controlling and then created tension in the community/relationship. She also realized that she was holding on to some resentment about not honoring her authentic self. She felt that she had given up a part of herself.

The Story: John said the take-away message for him was to relax about the business and start to do things he and Elaine enjoyed doing together, like travel.

Elaine felt like she needed to learn to enjoy herself more, but found a hesitation around that idea because she felt a twinge of guilt that everyone else was working. **Positive Statement**: "We are free to be ourselves and to communicate with ease and openness with full-hearted expression."

John's individual session

QHC Pattern: 4-1-7 (Note that John's Obstacle was Elaine's Action and Elaine's Obstacle was John's Issue. This suggested that their relationship was mutually beneficial for their individual growth.)

Hero Pattern: 6-10-12

The Story: John realized that his heart was telling him was that he was repeating old patterns from people before him. His biological grandmother gave up her child (John's mother). His mother felt abandoned and compensated by working hard to please others. His grandmother was also resistant to change out of her fear for survival. Like John and his wife Elaine, John's dad was also a photographer and his wife also ran the business (money side). He realized that his sense of responsibility might be a trap. He said he wanted his sons to have a balanced life between work and spending time with their families—"at least more than I am having."

Positive Statement: "I embody change easily—I am ready and willing to step into a new pattern of spending more time in Hawaii with my wife, and doing what I love."

Elaine's individual session

QHC Pattern: 7-4-1 (the same pattern that came up in the relationship session)

Hero Pattern: 12-4-6

The Story: Elaine believed her mother, as a sixteen-year-old single mother, tried to abort her. Consequently, Elaine resonated with being unwanted and an outcast. To compensate, her first consideration was to conform to others' expectations as a survival strategy. As a result, she abandoned herself and her creative expression. Like John, Elaine had an ancestral pattern of not being wanted. The difference was that John compensated by working hard for survival and acceptance. For Elaine, survival and acceptance meant fitting in to community. The friction in the relationship occurred because Elaine subconsciously knew she had given up a part of herself and wanted to be accepted for her authentic and creative self. Consequently, she sometimes came across as being controlling. The truth was that she challenged those around her because what she really wanted was genuine acceptance (she was testing them and herself). When she made a commotion John shut down because his ancestral pattern was to maintain the peace. The relationship could spiral upwards into greater harmony when both individuals forgive their past and integrate their experiences as lessons that taught them greater compassion for themselves and others.

Positive Statement: "My Divine energy and spirit flow from my authentic self and I interact harmoniously with others (not from a place of survival, but as an expression of the Divine).

Family Group Session

The grandmother at a family gathering invited everyone to come together for a group Scalar Heart Connection session to clear a possible ancestral trauma. She felt that a recent issue around communication, a sense of belonging, and tranquility may have been triggered by a suppressed trauma in the family tree. The group consisted of the grandmother, two of her sons and their wives, and one of her granddaughters.

The group went around the table anti-clockwise, like the movement of the zodiac, taking turns asking their hearts to show them a number in each of the steps of the process. The first number chosen was to find the chakra or emotional center holding the discomfort of the trauma. The number chosen was related to the Brow Chakra. The **Quantum Healing Code Archetypal Pattern** for the Brow Chakra is the pattern 7-4-1.

The 7-4-1 pattern informed the group that the **Issue**, in the 7th House, was related to feeling isolated, particularly when someone was bogged down with unresolved issues or suppressed feelings from the past. The **Obstacle**, in the 4th House, challenged them to look deeply into unresolved issues from the past, especially from childhood, where we are often taught to suppress our feelings. The group was called to re-examine their purpose and to wake up to that small voice of heart-wisdom from within. The **Action**, in the 1st House, related to embracing one's own identity in relationship to others without becoming controlling or dominating.

The next person chose the number related to the **Emotion** that was over-activated in the Brow Chakra and acting as the motivator for change. The **Emotion** that came up was "Over-exhaustion." Several family members commented that they felt exhausted with the struggle of life and were tired of dealing with the same old patterns.

The next step in the process was to find the **Negative Mind-brain Conditioned Response** to the emotion of being over-exhausted. The number chosen was related to the statement, "I am disconnected from my heart's intuition and higher knowing." The group recognized that when they struggled with life it was like falling off the magic carpet, where they lost a connection to a higher purpose and no longer felt that they were guided.

When we connect with our heart's innate knowing we are able to move out of our mind's conditioned and habituated reaction and move into a more positive and heart-conscious response, the **Positive Heart Message**. The number chosen for this was related to the statement, "I feel at ease and I feel joyful."

There was also an **Organ Meridian** involved. The number chosen informed the group that the meridian was the "Nervous System." The nervous system statement that the heart showed them was, "I am connected to Source, self and others."

The **Level** that was holding the unresolved trauma was "Energetic." The statement related to the Energetic Level was, "Picking up the energy of a traumatic event that happened." One of the family members got the insight that in some way the traumatic event from the past was related to men. This reminded grandma that her great grandfather, who fought for the South, had been killed at the end of the Civil War. She said his death was the reason her ancestors moved from Missouri to California.

The next step in the process was to identify the **Earlier Experience**. The earlier experience could be the original trauma or event that laid the foundation for the negative mind-brain reaction or inherited negative belief about the issue. The next person asked their heart to show them a number, and they received the number related to "Age." They were all certain that they would have received the number related to "Ancestral/Genetic."

They decided to trust the process and continue by asking the heart to show a number from one to eighty-one (grandma's age). The next person received the number related to the age of forty-nine. The astrologer in the family recognized the number 49 to be close to the 50-year orbit of Chiron. Chiron, in astrology, is symbolized by the "wounded healer." It represents our deepest wound, and our efforts to heal the wound. Grandma recognized the age of forty-nine to be the age of her great grandfather when he was killed in the Civil War. One of the daughters-in-law (Karen) said her grandfather also died at age forty-nine. His furniture factory burned down twice and after the second destruction of his factory he died of a heart attack. The other daughter-in-law (Mary) said forty-nine was the age of her mother when she died of cancer. She said she always believed that her mom felt stuck in a loveless marriage and cancer was her only way out. From that standpoint, she said she often felt that her mother's death was a kind of suicide. Her mother's name was Susan. Grandma said the wife of her great grandfather was also Susan. Grandma also said it was strange that suicide came up because her great grandfather died from a bullet wound that came from friendly fire. There are some who believe that some soldiers use friendly fire as a way to commit suicide. The thought of suicide reminded grandma that her sister committed suicide when her father was forty-nine. Her father never forgave himself for her suicide because he believed he could have prevented it in some way. Mary became agitated around the topic of suicide because she was taking care of her younger sister, who had attempted suicide twelve months earlier.

The next step in the process was to find the **Unmet Heart Need**, the positive attribute that is prevented from manifesting in our lives because the chaotic energy of the emotion blocks it out. In this case, the emotion was the feeling of "Over-exhaustion." The heart of the next family member provided the number related to the **Unmet Heart Need**, "Humor." This indicated that humor was the antidote to over-exhaustion. Karen said her father, the son of the furniture maker, didn't have a sense of humor. Susan said her mom was without humor. Grandma said her father suffered for the rest of his life after his daughter died. She also said she had letters her great grandfather wrote during the war to his wife and they showed a man with a broken heart. The group wondered how it was possible to find humor in the face of life's tragedies. We decided to hold off on that question until later in the session to see if the answer would appear.

The next person asked their heart to show them a number related to the **Cellular Memory Trigger**. This could be anything that in some way activates the negative aspect of the ancestral pattern. The number chosen related to the statement "Taste." It wasn't clear whether taste meant the sense of taste or an aesthetic taste. Karen said her grandfather had good aesthetic taste when it came to the fine furniture he made. Mary said her mom expressed her creativity through singing. Grandma's great grandfather was a poet and an artist.

The group wasn't certain, but generally felt the heart was referring to anything creative as acting like a trigger, holding them back from the joy of self-expression.

Next the group decided to ask the heart to show the **Archetypal Hero Pattern** in order to get a deeper insight into what had come up so far in the session. The pattern that was chosen was the **Archetypal Hero Pattern** 5-9-11. This pattern places the **Issue** (suppressed ancestral trauma) in the 5th House. The 5th House is the house of creativity and self-expression. It is about the sense of purpose and comes up when we hold ourselves back from fully expressing our individuality, our power, and full potential. The **Obstacle** in this pattern (disconnected from our heart's intuition and higher knowing) is in the 9th House. The 9th House is about meaning and purpose. The challenge is to gain a broader view by moving beyond our perceived limitations. We are challenged to travel, have new experiences, and connect with a higher purpose in our lives. The **Action** for achieving this expansive view of ourselves lies in the 11th House. This is the house of breaking out of old structures and behavior patterns. It requires that we break out of negative or limiting beliefs and overcome the emotional suppression of old wounds. It is about sharing our wisdom with the community and realizing that we belong to the whole. Earlier in the session, someone's heart gave the group the **Action** statement, "I am connected to Source, self and others."

The group thought about what the heart was telling them. Karen realized that her grandfather gave up after the second factory fire. Susan had given up. The Civil War soldier gave up. Everyone felt that none of these people had to die. They gave up the struggle. They were over-exhausted with life's struggles.

The family created the **Positive Statement**, "I meet life with courage, humor, creativity, joy knowing I am supported and belong, and I communicate my needs and ask for help." Someone said, "Life is art." Everyone started to feel that the struggles had been part of the process of creating a great masterpiece of art. If everything had been perfect right from the beginning, then what sense of accomplishment would we feel at the end? The joy of creating occurs when we can look back and know that we endured through the hardships. Some say art is more about the process than the final product. With that in mind, the group realized that the process was only worth engaging in if they did it with joy and humor. Perhaps our lives are not about accomplishing anything, but instead about enjoying or at least enduring every minute as it unfolds.

They now needed to ask their hearts if there was an aspect of the new Positive Statement that was not agreeable to their minds. This is the **Mind Resistance** to what the heart actually wants. The number that came up from the heart was related to the statement, "If I let go, It will happen again." This made grandma recall that her great grandfather's son committed suicide, as did one of his granddaughters. One of Susan's daughters attempted suicide. There were periods in Karen's life where she had contemplated giving up.

The group then asked someone's heart to show a number related to a **Quantum Healing Code**. They received the number related to the interval 417 and 639. The tone of 417 cps is related to the Pelvis Chakra, where we hold emotions and wounds from the past. The tone of 639 cps is related to the Throat Chakra, which is about personal expression and creativity. Everyone toned along with the chord as it played, and concentrated on bringing up the emotional wounds from the past and releasing it as they stepped into the higher and more positive vibration of the Throat Chakra and tapped into their personal power and creativity.

The **Positive Action** that came up was to say something to someone. Almost at the same time, everyone said they wanted to honor and acknowledge the lives of the people that were brought into the session and to thank them for the lessons they provided. "Your lives and hardships were not a waste."

The **Mind Resistance**, "If I let go, It will happen again," touched a deep chord in everyone. It felt like something was left unresolved. They decided to process the session for a day or so and then do another session specifically around the issue of suicides in the family.

Group Session with Earth

At the end of a recent workshop in Maui, we did a Scalar Heart Connection session for the Earth. The group consensus was to do the session around the **Issue** of the Earth's resilience and sustainability, particularly around her relationship with humans.

We let our heart guide us in determining who in the room would be the one to choose a number as proxy for Earth. The first number chosen was related to the Heart Chakra and the **Emotion**, "Selfish."

The next step in the process was to ask our heart to show us a number related to our **Negative Mind-brain Conditioned Response or Belief** surrounding the unresolved emotion of "Selfish." One of the participants chose the number related to the statement, "I am unlovable."

The group was overcome with the feeling of sadness with the thought that the Earth felt unlovable. The emotion of "selfish" started to feel like it was directed towards us humans.

Another participant then asked their heart, on behalf of the Earth, to show them a number related to the **Positive Heart Response** to the Issue. They chose a number related to the statement, "My heart is wide open to give and receive love easily." This felt like the natural state of the Earth and filled us with remorse.

The Heart Chakra is related to the Lung Meridian. One of the participants asked their heart to show them a number related to the **Positive Lung Meridian** statement. The number they chose was related to the statement, "I am worthy of living."

The next step in the process was to determine the **Level** upon which the Issue was held. The number one of the participants chose was related to the **Mental Level**. The Level statement that came up was "Self-esteem."

Someone in the group made the comment that our behavior toward Earth made her feel that we were impartial to Her existence—that we were only concerned with what we could take from Earth as opposed to being in relationship with Her. We then needed to know if there was an earlier experience of trauma involved that set this energetic pattern into motion. One of the participants was shown the number related to "Genetic/Ancestral." Another participant asked their heart to show them a number that would identify the particular individual in the family tree that first had this issue. The number their heart showed them identified the person as "Mom."

In Greek mythology, Gaia is one of the primordial deities born of Chaos (Void). As the primal Mother Goddess, she is the creator and giver of birth to the Earth and the entire Universe. In myth, Gaia was not without family conflict. She rebelled against her husband Uranus (Sky) for imprisoning her sons in her womb. Later, she was in conflict with her son Kronos, who defied her by imprisoning these same sons. She also came into conflict with her son Zeus when he imprisoned her Titan sons in the pit of Tartaros. So it seemed that family conflict, particularly with the patriarchal energies of control and exploitation, is prominent in Earth's family tree.

The session then took us to the **Unmet Heart Need**, which is the frequency of the positive resonance that was displaced by the vibration of the emotion "selfish." One of the participants asked their heart, in proxy for the Earth, to show them a number related to what the Earth's heart wanted but didn't receive. The number chosen was related to the statement, "Devotion."

The group realized from the session that the Earth feels sad and unloved and consequently developed a lack of self-esteem as a result of our (human) actions that are not in line with respecting Her, nor do we show any sense of devotion to Her.

On behalf of the Earth, we created the **Positive Statement**: "We are devoted to the Earth and to the energies of the Archetypal Feminine within."

We next needed to know if there was an unconscious **Negative Mind-brain Belief** lurking in the background waiting to sabotage our beautiful Positive Statement. One of the participants asked their heart to show them a number related to the statement we needed. They chose the number related to, "If I change, others will die."

To help shift the limiting vibration, we received the number related to the **Quantum Healing Codes** 417 and 528, which is a musical chord that combines the Water Chakra (417) with the Heart Chakra (528). This is a musical or sound connection between the womb and the heart—the womb of Earth and the hearts of Her children (us).

To fully integrate the positive resonance of devotion to the Earth and the Archetypal Feminine, the session led us to express an appreciation. Everyone took turns expressing their gratitude and appreciation for the Earth and for the life she provides.

Resources

Scalar Heart Connection Workshop

Join Stephen Linsteadt for two days of fun exploring the synchronicities found within our universe through conversations with your heart. Hear what your heart has to say about what is preventing you from living in rhythm with your highest potential——your true Self.

We will explore ancient patterns that all point to the heart as the interface between the seen and unseen world, and how this will keep you connected to your joy, inner connection, and harmony.

This workshop will provide a deeper understanding of the world around you, rooted in the rhythmic song of your heartbeat and the earth's heartbeat.

You will learn a tool that will not only empower you to be your own guide through your limiting beliefs, but it will provide you with the first steps to being the change we wish to see in the world (saving the planet begins within).

- Explore how synchronicity and the archetypes motivate us towards expanded consciousness.

- Discover the behavioral patterns from earlier experiences that condition our inhibitions and inner contradictions and cause us to lose our connection to our authentic Self.

- Learn how our negative mind-brain conditioning is often deeply rooted in ancestral inheritance patterns stemming from unresolved issues/traumas/beliefs from our parents' parents.

- Investigate how sacred geometry relates to quantum physics and provides a matrix for accessing negative emotions and stress triggers.

- Explore how archetypal patterns, the motivators of change, work together as Issue (problem), Obstacle (challenge), and Action (resolution/transformation).

- Find out how the heart is the gateway to the scalar field of unlimited potentiality and learn how to access the innate wisdom of your own heart.

- Examine the heart's ability to produce scalar waves through its built-in Möbius coil circulation system.

- Discover the "Quantum Healing Codes™" and how their vibrations come together to form Metatron's Cube (from the Flower of Life). From this pattern all else can be created. These codes support greater coherence within the resonance of what we want to create in our life.

- Learn and practice Scalar Heart Connection as a powerful healing modality that connects you with your heart's answers to what troubles you or holds you back from experiencing your inner power and connection to the heartbeat of the Universe.

To register or for more information: ScalarHeartConnection.com

What Others are Saying:

"As a practitioner of NLP and EFT, I found Scalar Heart Connection to be a process of freeing ourselves and others in limitless ways and solutions."
~ J. E.

"Amazing, interesting, NEW way of looking at things. I learned a lot and enjoyed it immensely."
~ Susan L.

"I was particularly impressed by the explanation of the Scalar Heart Connection® and the invitation to move the energy potential into action through our intention. I found this workshop to be informative and inspirational and I experienced it as supportive of life on all levels."
~ Jennifer J.

"This was a fascinating study of how universal archetypes and numbers can combine with intuition and sound vibration. I've always wondered how all of these elements come together. I loved the workshop. It was food for mind and soul and was emotionally satisfying. It gave me major insight into an emotional block."
~ Amber D.

"This is an amazing way of getting to the true me. It was hard for me to share in front of the group, but I am glad I did. This workshop helped me a lot."
~ Laura W.

"Wow, I had a real revelation connecting my birth to my issue."
~ Janice S.

"I do similar work to help folks identify negative core beliefs and then re-decide. It appears that this work can accomplish the same thing in a much simpler and faster way. I am truly optimistic!"
~ Tracy S.

"Stephen's presentation takes deeply profound material and presents it in a clean, calm, and simple way. This is the mark of mastery. His calm, peaceful presence and the presence of his beautiful family was deeply nourishing."
~ *Debra B.*

Other books by Stephen Linsteadt:

- Scalar Heart Connection
- Quantum Healing Codes book with audio CD
- Quantum Healing Codes audio tracks on iTunes
- The Heart of Health; the Principles of Physical Health and Vitality
- Scalar Heart Connection Self-guided Healing Meditation (audio CD)
- The Beauty of Curved Space (a collection of poetry)

Available at: ScalarHeartConnection.com

About the Author

Stephen Linsteadt is a traditional naturopath, painter, writer, poet, and a student of the heart. He is a certified nutritional consultant and a member of The American Association of Nutritional Consultants. He studied energy medicine and bioresonance in Germany based on the principles of Oriental Medicine. He was the co-founder of New Hope Clinic, an integrative center specializing in chronic illness, and has shared his experience in the book he co-authored: *The Heart of Health: the Principles of Physical Health and Vitality.*

Stephen is the founder of Scalar Heart Connection® and the author of the books *Quantum Healing Codes* and *Scalar Heart Connection*, a process designed to help people uncover negative emotional patterns behind ill-health and other challenges with well-being.

Stephen has a passion for sharing his knowledge about healthy life-style habits and has lectured extensively on the subject of the mind-body connection as well as created and conducted workshops internationally in the area of physical health and emotional well-being.

Stephen's poetry has been published in various anthologies. His latest poetry collection is titled *The Beauty of Curved Space* (Glass Lyre Press).

His paintings have appeared in various poetry journals and covers and were featured in the anthology *Woman in Metaphor* (WomanInMetaphor.com). His paintings can be seen at StephenLinsteadtStudio.com.